The Male Element

William F. Keefe

1

He locked the car and headed for the condo-ized building in which he lived with his "young bride," 42-year-old Jennifer. The earlier light rain had left puddles in the yellow-striped parking lot. Mercury-vapor light, generated from tall poles, bounced and floated beneath his feet. Holes of light in a black tapestry.

His feet wanted to run. He fought down the urge as you'd stifle an uncomplimentary remark at a social gathering.

James Bower Vandorn reflexively touched the surface of his jacket. The papers were there; they crinkled under his gentle pressure. They would go into his still-slim file on EMBRYOLOGY: BRAND. Ever the detail man, Vandorn figured he would need and use the papers when the scriptural moment came. . . Day of Judgment.

The phone was ringing as Vandorn, professor of Ethics at Franklin State University, let himself into the four-room deluxe unit. His hand shook slightly as he reached for the phone. That unusual reaction surprised him. More gruffly than he intended, he said hello. It was Jennifer.

"Thank God you're home," she said. "You had me worried."

"No need." He deliberately softened his voice. "It was a walk in the park."

"You know my overactive imagination."

"We didn't even hand-wrestle. And for weapons I would have insisted on epees." He was introducing a vague note of humor into his voice. "I'd feel completely at home with them."

"I thought it would be the mad ethicist against the mad embryologist. But enough of that. You're home and safe. And Lola says if you're hungry she's got a bowl of chili left."

"I accept sight unseen."

"I'll be home in twenty minutes."

Closing the conversation, he took off his jacket, removed the four sheets of paper from the inside breast pocket, and hung the jacket in the foyer closet. With the sheets in hand, he sat down in the stuffed chair next to the picture window in the living room. A standing lamp provided illumination.

He read the papers quickly. Three of them laid out schedules for operations and tests--on, apparently, baboons. The fourth sheet contained a summary of "results to date." The animals bore names, both male and female. There were Terry, rendered as Baboon Terry initially and simply as B-T subsequently; and Baboon Mavis, and Baboon Della. The fourth sheet contained a summary in narrative form with notes that specified what the project goals were.

He mused. Jennifer's twenty minutes would be thirty to forty minutes in actuality. She and Lola had long goodbyes.

In an ethics class he had been discussing private morality versus public and the ways in which society enforces its customs and culture-preserved lifeways. Typically, the means ranged from taboos to ritual or ceremony and on to public opinion and, finally, physical force.

Were there more? Threat? The word of authority? The *intervention* of authority?

Recalling the mild scenario at Brand's, he strode purposefully to the telephone. Dialing, he waited. No answer, not Malek Hart, his lawyer, not Malek's wife Hannah.. The message recorder came on: "You have reached. . ."

Vandorn left a message. "I'll call you tomorrow. . ."

He picked up a book, found that he couldn't concentrate, felt a niggling frustration. Where was Malek?

He drowsed, lost his place in the book, an old, comfortably worn exploration of the subject of ethics by John Dewey and James H. Tufts. Phrases formed and fled: the expansion of the individual, ignorance that equated with witchcraft and magic, advances in natural and social sciences. Inquiry without limits. Ah, there was the sticking point. Moral sensibility had to impose limits.

He heard Jennifer's key in the hall door. Placing a scrap of paper on the page he had been reading, he closed the book. At that moment the words "order and law" seemed to become enlarged, to lift off the page. He would study that page later.

Somewhere there had to be an answer to Brand. Aside from four pilfered pages.

2

Dr. John Schofield, University Hospital administrator, took a deep breath. He had turned to face the high windows at his left. Thoughtfully, almost coldly, he said:

"Let me get this straight. You are proposing that University Hospital give its sanction to the artificial embryonation of a woman who wants to carry and bear a child even though she has no uterus."

"That's right, John."

Looking out the windows that Dr. Schofield was facing, Dr. Emlyn Brand could see, across an expanse of dull-green lawn, the blocklike bulk of the Liberal Arts Building. Through the windows to his left Brand could study the much nearer presence of the Hillman Research Building. His own cubicle-sized office took up all of 110 square feet of Hillman's basement floor space. His inner sanctum. Four floors higher, somewhat to the south, his much larger embryology lab occupied a space more than triple that of the office.

I've been out of active practice for quite some time," Dr. Schofield was saying. "But if I recall correctly an abdominal pregnancy is extremely dangerous. Right?"

"That *was* right. We believe--."

"What we believe may have no bearing on the case at hand. In medical practice today, an abdominal pregnancy still carries serious hazards to the life of the mother."

"I brought an article for you to read." Brand took a folded clipping from his shirt pocket. "It says a live, normal, healthy child was delivered by Caesarean section at Post Memorial Hospital--from the mother's abdomen. The baby had gestated completely outside the woman's uterus."

Brand dropped the paper onto Dr. Schofield's desk. "The Post Memorial doctors describe some of the precautions they took to make sure the mother would be okay. They've had one other such case."

Dr. Schofield turned away from the window. He glanced briefly at the clipping, but did not pick it up.

"Do you want me to give you a guess regarding the odds against anyone else's repeating that performance?" he said. "Would you say a million to one? Two million to one after artificial embryonation?"

"Nowhere near that. Granted, the woman has to cooperate. She can't travel far--in case there's an emergency. Her doctor has to be on call. But with those and some other basic precautions, it can be done. In fact--"

"In fact no one can guarantee that you wouldn't be risking two lives--the mother's and unborn baby's--for what? So University Hospital can claim a little glory?"

"For what?" Brand felt a surge of impatience. You had to keep repeating every single syllable. You had to keep telling people that life--science--would pass you by unless you raced--unless you kept abreast of change. "Glory" was much less important than accomplishing the difficult or nearly impossible. "Not for glory, certainly," Brand said. Carefully, watching Dr. Schofield's shaggy, greying head, studying the impassive blue eyes, Brand added: "For both human and scientific reasons. Human, because the woman seems to have her heart set on carrying a baby to term and delivering it and mothering it. Scientific, because it can now be done according to a specific, detailed, stage-by-stage plan."

Dr. Schofield's eyebrows rose slightly. "Now? Not yesterday? Not the day before? Now? What do we have now that we didn't have in this hospital or that maternity clinic yesterday?"

"We have my work." He had spoken too quickly, Brand thought. In this company, in this corner office on the Admin floor of University Hospital, in this entire building, a great democratic leveling always took place. The staff of University Hospital, from the top surgeon to the lowest laundry worker, had to acknowledge Dr. Schofield's primacy, his authority, his leadership. The alternative might be termination, banishment. Witness Dr. Simondson's quiet but abrupt elimination a year and a half ago. No one had ever given a good reason for that--for "retiring" a nationally known internist at age 59.

Dr. Simondson, of course, had simply activated an alternative staff membership and moved over to Post Memorial. He was still practicing. But not everyone could stroll from one affiliation to another so effortlessly.

"*Mister* Brand," Dr. Schofield said. "I will call you *Mister* today, if you don't mind, because we medical doctors have not yet concluded that Ph.D.'s should hold the title of *Doctor*. Not in ordinary conversation, anyway. And this conversation has gotten very ordinary."

Dr. Schofield took a deep breath.

"I have to consider the good name of this hospital," he said, starting a series of remarks that Brand had heard in many staff meetings. "My responsibility reaches into every ward, every office, every laboratory, every single *room*. Every *closet*. The trustees have appointed me because, I believe, I have earned their confidence. They revere human life and want me to revere it. They do not want me to run a Nazi-style experimental clinic that sacrifices individuals to some ephemeral--and dangerous--dream."

"Dr. Schofield--" Brand began, impatience turning to creeping anger. His face was flushed; he could feel it.

"Let me finish, please. As I see my responsibility, it forbids me to grant you permission to use the facilities of this hospital for the kind of work you are proposing. I don't care whose egg or whose sperm you are going to use to engineer this--this embryo. I have no wish to go into this any more deeply than we already have. I have equally little desire to project human or scientific motivations on the parts of any principles. That includes you.

"I have to consider this hospital's basic mission and its essential thrust. We are here to heal sick people, not to risk human life. We have to think of our directors, the community, the churches; of possible repercussions from the traditionalists. They exist in our midst, as you know."

"You have other labs--."

"They have the purpose, primarily, of conducting tests. You know that as well as I do. And we do try to keep them busy, as you also know.

Your own testing and experimenting have helped us. But could I give you a word of advice?"

"Of course."

"Stick with animal experiments and lab tests--techniques for studying infertility--flushing the uterus--the genetics of normal reproduction--straightforward stuff that carries no hazards or human-heart problems."

"You are convinced that labs in general, and our labs in particular, should have no broader purpose than to conduct routine tests? Where would medicine--where would this or any other hospital be if everyone thought that way?"

Dr. Schofield's brows drew together, became knitted, as if someone were pulling on interior threads.

"I am convinced that our labs have one main job. That job is to serve our patients. And I haven't even touched on what I consider one of the key points here. You could not even perform this--this operation--."

"Office procedure. Embryonation takes--."

"I don't care what embryonation takes. The answer is no. We can't be assigning staff even to performance of an office procedure in a case like this. Am I clear? We will not countenance it."

Brand stood up. Picking up the article that still lay, half curled up, on Dr. Schofield's desk, Brand said, "Thanks for your time, Doctor." He was turning to leave when Dr. Schofield said:

"Listen to one other piece of advice. People around here are expected to be team players. No one likes it when individuals go off hunting their own glory. Will you remember that?"

"I'll remember it." Brand turned and left quickly. As he passed through the outer office he glanced at Susie Thatcher, blond, short, very efficient, Susie who knew everything and said nothing. While he watched, she screwed up her eyes in make-believe pain. Relaxing her face, she joined the thumb and forefinger of her right hand in a circle. It was like a silent cheer, a cry of "job-well-done."

He shook his head, raised his brows, and went on out. He was closing the door to the Administrator's office suite when he encountered resistance. It was Susie, coming out.

"Dr. Brand," she said hesitantly, making him pause, "I hope you're not going to let him stop you."

"Susie, I don't know that I have much choice."

"Dr. Schofield doesn't know what's going on," Susie said, almost whispering. "But--you know Laura's a friend of mine. I know how she feels. You may be her last hope."

"I'll keep it in mind, Susie."

"Oh, thanks." Impulsively she pressed his hand, turned quickly, and went back into the office.

Brand walked back to his office. *One more,* he thought. *One more time to ransack his office in search of those missing Goldmark report papers.*

3

He spent the rest of the day in a kind of nervous frenzy. Working in the fourth-floor lab, he broke a retort, something he had not done for years. He mislaid, then found, crucial notes on an entire series of tests. In conversation with Rod Fenton, supervisor of the University Hospital Animal Resources Department, commonly called "the zoo," Brand spoke more harshly than he wanted to.

"Keep your shirt on," Fenton said. "We'll have those baboons for you in short order."

"Thanks, Rod. I didn't mean to bite your head off. But those beasts are important."

Arriving home late, Brand put away the 1979 Datsun that he had bought "to beat the oil barons out of a few bucks." The days were getting longer, but with predictable perversity it had turned colder with the onset of spring. The tan raincoat that he wore seemed inadequate against the rising wind. He let himself in through the side door and immediately found himself in the midst of a domestic scene that carried him in several directions at once. Joanie, 4, pulled at his hand, while Micaela, 7, tried to relieve him of his briefcase. He was saying, "No, Moke, I'd better put that in the study. I've got some world-shaking papers in it," when Michelle came from the kitchen, smiling, wiping her hands. They kissed over the heads of the chattering children. He nodded when Michelle asked him if he would be ready to eat in 15 minutes, then was swept up in the child-spawned vortex.

In the girls' room he caught up on the day's events. Joanie showed him the Easter bunny she had painted in University Nursery School. "I did it all alone, Daddy," she crowed. Moke showed him an announcement for parents. It told of a field trip for the second-grade class at Glendon Elementary School. "Can I go, Daddy?"

"Did you ask your mother?"

"She said to ask you."

"Then the answer is yes."

He broke clear briefly and washed up. He had tossed his jacket and tie over the back of a living room chair. With the girls riding herd, he went down now to hang up the clothes and found that Michelle had already done so. In the kitchen Michelle shooed the girls out. "Back to your books," she commanded good-naturedly. "Your father needs a moment of peace."

They were alone. He could hear the girls racing upstairs. Michelle said, "You saw Schofield, didn't you? It bombed, didn't it?"

"It sucked." He sat down. They had bought this "small frame" five years ago, just before mortgage interest rates had gone out of sight. They considered themselves lucky to have seven rooms on two floors. It was a great place to launch a career from--for both of them. Michelle worked at the University as a research assistant and had aspirations in the direction of a Ph.D. in English Lit. The aspirations kept her taking evening--and sometimes day--classes with dogged persistence. She had a year to go.

They made their schedules mesh. He spent a lot of nights writing on fertility research, reproductive physiology, and related subjects. He had become what they called "a man with a growing reputation in his field."

"Yes, I will have a martini if you're pouring," Brand said. Michelle was already at the sideboard, anticipating him. He watched her, noted again the supple strength that seemed to flow through her slender, well-proportioned body. She had been a star swimmer in high school and, while deemphasizing that part of her life in college, had nonetheless continued to play tennis and other active games. She and Brand still played tennis and racquetball as time allowed. "Schofield did everything but threaten me with being canned," Brand continued, "if I don't get off this Laura Phillips kick."

"Oh, Em." She paused. He knew what she was thinking: that he *had* to do what he could for Laura Phillips. Michelle didn't want to intrude on his turf, he knew; but now she said without looking at him, "Well, you know what I think of that."

"Flocking easy to say." He had made that too strong. "Sorry," he said, "it's been a bitch."

"Apologies accepted. And do what you have to do. As you keep telling me, remember the monkeys." She had poured him a Gibson using ready-mixed martini, had added the onion, a small cube of ice. It occurred to Brand that they approached the evening drink with easy formality, as a small ritual; the same was true on a grander scale when they approached their love-making. No fancy shakers and crushed ice here; but, yes, they generally provided appropriate atmosphere, soft lights, classical music, and always gentle scents when they went to bed to love. "But I do have two strikes on me. I have to take a pretty long view of the whole thing. We're so close to the big one."

"I never advise, but I think you should stay with the big one, as you call it. I'll be seeing your name in lights one of these days." She was smiling. "EMBRYOLOGIST WORKS MIRACLE--IMPREGNATES HUMAN MALE!" You'll be doing the whole female population a great favor."

"I'll be climbing a mountain." He was feeling a soft, relaxed, pleasant numbness. "But if this meal isn't a rumor, we should sample it."

"The meal is NOT a rumor," Michelle said, standing. "And I think I'll join you."

As fallout from Brand's faceoff with Dr. Schofield, they discussed the future and what it might spin for them and their kids. She wanted to know the worst possible scenario.

"There's the one contingency that we haven't talked about," he said. "I could make it all work. I've got to turn Phillips over to someone, probably Dr. Madsen, and she carries a fetus to term and becomes ecstatically happy with her neonate. I do the male baboons test runs. They all chatter their ways through their pregnancies. We find a human male. . ."

"Maybe Arnold Schwarzenegger?" She was suppressing a smile. "Your favorite movie translated to real life."

He delivered a playful tap to the point of her strong jaw. "Do you want to hear the rest or not?" he said.

"Didn't mean to distract. Continue, please."

"Okay. I could then," he said melodramatically, "be run out of town on a rail."

"What are you talking about?" She was not challenging him but showing curiosity. She had a no-nonsense way of posing questions, of absorbing answers. Her honesty extended to all phases of life. He knew she had driven away two earlier suitors by insisting on a relationship before sex.

"A lot of people look with a jaundiced eye on genetic engineers," Brand said. "Those people might class me with the scientists who talk about cloning, or with the Nazis--do you know what Schofield said today?"

"Something about Nazis?"

"Yes. 'We don't want any Nazi-type experiments going on in University Hospital'--words to that effect. He wants us all to do the standard lab tests and experiments, no risks, be a team player, that shit. He even called me Mister Brand, as if a Ph.D. doesn't entitle you to be called Doctor."

"All this on the head of a maybe impossible embryonation project?

"Yes."

"As far as I'm concerned, you're onto the idea of a lifetime, or the opportunity of a lifetime. Picture where you could be in a year."

"It might take longer than a year." He was grinning.

"If you make it work, you'll have to have a lady obstetrician deliver the pregnant man."

4

Late in the morning Brand got through to Dr. Albert R. Madsen, obstetrician-gynecologist, and made an appointment for a professional consultation. Madsen had a gruff voice and a correspondingly gruff telephone manner, but in Brand's brief acquaintance had been extraordinarily accommodating. In any case he might be Brand's escape hatch, the way out of the Laura Phillips dilemma.

He called Laura, former Playboy bunny with the voluptuous contours who wanted motherhood more than anything in life. Brand would be listening for clues to her motivation, partly because he saw her project, if successful, as a stage toward his own scientific agenda.

"I've got some details to work out, but I think we can manage your case," he told the woman. "Could you and Tim stop over tonight, have a sip with us? I have to do this independently of the university."

"I can be there. I'm not sure about Tim. Any best time?"

"Say eightish?"

"Fine. One or both of us will be there. And Dr. Brand. . .?"

"Yes?"

"I appreciate what you're doing. Susie has told me what you're dealing with."

"I think maybe you should ask her not to talk with others about your case, just for safety. The heat's on, as they used to say in the movies."

"I'll make sure she gets the message. But I have confidence in her discretion."

"So do I. But you can't be too careful."

"I hear you. Could I ask one other question?"

"Of course."

"Does 'independently of the university' mean you won't be involved at all?"

"No. It means I'll be the background strategist, the unseen observer."

"I'm sighing with relief."

The courtesies completed, Brand hung up. Brand pictured Laura as he had first seen her: sitting in a chair in a waiting room down the hall, reading a copy of *Ms.* magazine. He could review what he now knew of her: uterus removed because it had become cancerous; prognosis unknown, or guarded, at least for another couple of years; in apparent love with her former-football-player husband in an admiring yet undemonstrative way; red-haired, determined beyond all measure; a career woman in interior design but capable of surrendering that for motherhood.

A bundle of contradictions, but genuine, believable.

Making his "rounds" in the zoo, Brand found that the baboons had fed. Now they sat regarding Brand silently, their eyes veiled. They might have been studying him, preparing some new gambit. They seemed to have immense reserves of untapped intelligence. They could reason with their fingers, their bodies--their minds? How far from man's lay their plane of reference?

Every few weeks an engineer had to modify the locks on their lower-level waste trays. The baboons then figured out the new combinations and "told" their neighbors. They all learned at the same time to pick the new locks and slide out the trays.

Mavis, two months abdominally pregnant with the embryo Brand had implanted in her stomach, showed no signs of discomfort. She had gained weight, visibly, but seemed alert. Somehow she had gotten hold of several of her squarish, light-brown stools and thrown them out on the smooth marble floor in front of her cage. They had good consistency. Going up to her cage, stepping carefully, Brand examined Mavis closely. With baboons, you knew instantly when a malaise or sickness of any kind was developing. Thespians by nature, they *acted* sick.

He went on to Della's cage. Ugly-tempered Della had glancingly bitten the finger of one of the new attendants. The man had run for help, howling. He had quit the job on the spot. He had been told on starting on the job that he should not attempt to pet the baboons; he had not listened.

Brand was visually examining Della, also pregnant, when Fenton came in. Like Brand, he had on a lab coat, the uniform required in the zoo. Somewhere the facility also had a rule requiring that masks be worn, but no one paid any attention to that unless a visitor came through. Each visitor received a cheap mask, held on with a rubber band stretched around the back of the head, to protect the animals from human contagions, particularly cold and other respiratory problems.

"Della looks great--to me," Fenton said. He approached the cage. "She looks as if she enjoys pregnancy, even artificially induced pregnancy."

"She does, doesn't she?" Brand wondered if Fenton would be quite so solicitous if he knew the fetus was nestled in Della's abdomen.

"I saw you come in," Fenton said. "I was going to walk down to your office, but this is better. Want to stop up and see my etchings when you're done here?"

It was Fenton's way of talking. Brand nodded. "Give me another few minutes. I'll stop by."

Fenton left. Brand finished with Della and went on to the other cages. Female baboons and two scrawny male macaque monkeys occupied most of them. A single male baboon sat quiescent in the cage farthest from the entrance. This was Terry, No. 1221. Brand would know in less than two weeks whether Terry was his first pregnant male baboon.

The other rooms held smaller cages that were occupied by mice, rats, guinea pigs. Brand had only experimental interest in them. Importantly, the "Operating Room" door was closed, locked. Finishing his tour, Brand went up to Fenton's first-floor office.

"Look at this," Fenton said, obviously pleased with himself. "It's the *Primate Newsletter*, March issue. They're offering 10 male olive baboons at $450 each. A steal."

Brand took the paper. Next to Fenton's pointing finger an ad had been circled. "Grab it if the budget will allow it," Brand said. "I'll be able to use all 10 over the next year or two."

"Males?"

"Yes. We're just about done with the females. The animals we have will cover my needs in that area." Brand read the classified advertisement. The ad had been placed by someone with a California address. "Incredible buy," he mused. "Aren't we paying about $600 per animal normally?"

"Yes. Up to $700." Fenton reached over and took back the copy of the newsletter. His hand shook a little as he held it up close to his face. His solemn eyes behind the black-rimmed glasses showed deep concentration. Brand saw him as a kind of human incarnation of his animal charges: ferretlike, jerky of movement, inquisitive. "I believe I could justify buying all 10 animals, especially at that price. But will you back me up on the need aspect?"

"Of course. I'll drop you a memo on it if you want."

"That would be perfect." Fenton seemed relieved. "Could you also put in a line or two about the types of experiments you'll be conducting? We're having to justify everything these days."

"To keep the record straight?"

"Yes."

"It will be a continuation and probably an extension of the Lambert Grant work. That means hormone changes, chemical balance, some embryonation, that kind of thing. Genetic stuff."

Fenton stood up. He was still wearing what he called his work clothes: the soiled white coat. He stuffed the *Primate Newsletter* into the gown's single pocket. "That's all right. I just want to be sure I have the file complete. Keep it on one page--two at the most."

"Will do."

"If you could give me that memo in the next day or two I should have the animals in the next week to 10 days."

5

During lunch at his desk--grilled chicken on rye--Brand finished the notes he was preparing for his conversations with Laura Phillips and Dr. Madsen. He had to explain logically, in some detail, to both persons. But Madsen would need chapter, verse, and punctuation; Laura's questions would very likely call for simple answers.

While writing, Brand recalled with a kind of unpleasant aftertaste Fenton's request for a memo. *I just want to be sure I have the file complete.* Had Schofield gotten to Fenton, asked him to make sure Brand had legitimate reasons for everything he did? Had the rest of the research unit staff been given the same kind of notice?

Something to ponder.

Brand finished his notes and his lunch. He had a feeling that some Schofield-devised aberration from the normal order was creeping up on him. He might be the last one to find out about it.

He smiled an interior smile. *The things you feared never materialized.*

Laura Phillips and her husband arrived a few minutes early. Brand brushed aside their apologies. "You did me a favor," he said. "I had no time to have dessert."

Before he could sit down with them he had to introduce the girls, who were lurking at the entrance to the kitchen when the doorbell rang. Joanie and Moke said their hellos quickly, in chorus, then left. Brand heard them half-whispering about "the pretty lady." He glanced at Laura; she was smiling. She had heard the offstage comments.

"Subtle, aren't they?" Brand said.

"Normal children."

Brand led the Phillips' to the room that he had turned into a study. It had just enough room for three chairs, Brand's bookcases and desk, and stacks of papers that lay on the floor along the outside wall. Brand had tried to tidy them up, then had given up. A sofa stood against an interior wall, filling it, end to end.

Michelle leaned in as they were sitting down. The four of them had met a month earlier at a cocktail party. At that time Laura, introduced to Brand, had half-jokingly asked him if he could help her. He had said he could, listened to the problem, mentioned the possibility of an abdominal pregnancy, and said she should call him if she wanted to pursue it.

"Anybody for a drink?" Michelle asked.

Both Laura and Tim specified white wine. Brand said he would hold off.

Tim started the conversation. A big man, he seemed to fill the room. But he moved with ease and grace. He had, Brand knew, a master's degree in Business Administration. He had a good job with a local electronics manufacturing firm--one of the few persons Brand and his wife knew who did not work for Franklin University or the hospital that was its pride.

"We've been doing some birddogging," Tim said, "about abdominal pregnancies. In fact, we saw a story in the local paper about one recently. Did you see that?"

"I have it here," Brand said. "I was going to show it to you."

"It caught our eye. The story makes the point that abdominal pregnancies are not only rare, they can be hazardous."

Brand nodded. "They can be; they *are*. But much of the risk can be eliminated if doctor and mother-to-be work closely together. In the case of naturally occurring abdominal pregnancies, of course, it's likely that neither the doctor nor the patient knows that it's an abdominal pregnancy. Much of the danger derives from that fact."

"And in Laura's case we'd know, obviously."

"Yes, if you decide to attempt this, we would know within 10 days to two weeks whether she was pregnant or not."

"And if not?" Laura asked.

"You could try again. And again. And again. We'd eventually accomplish it."

"It's not that routine a thing, then?" Laura showed curiosity unmixed with fear.

"It's not routine at all. You would, I believe, be a first. You might be famous. To the best of my knowledge, an abdominal pregnancy has never been planned, programmed, and successfully brought to term. There are test-tube babies, of course. The Brown baby in England is one. But that involved fertilization of the mother's egg outside her body, then embryonation. She carried the baby in her uterus."

"That's out for me, as you know," Laura said. She paused briefly. "Maybe that's what touched off my burst of motherly yearning. You suddenly realize that 30-something may not be as young as it once looked."

Listening, Brand felt reassured that she had the proper matter-of-fact approach. She could probably do it. And she was certainly strong. Her arms, covered only near the shoulders by her short-sleeved dress, were rounded and firm-looking. Her breasts projected spectacularly under the loose fabric.

"Actually, Laura's 37," Tim Phillips said. Michelle came in carrying a small tray and two glasses. Tim and Laura took the wine glasses, saying "Thank you" in tandem. Michelle left. In a businesslike way Tim added: "Could you outline for us what the possibilities are, the risks, the--." He searched for the appropriate words. "--The mechanics of planting a baby in a woman's abdomen?"

"I'll keep it as simple as possible. Assume that Laura is fertile--you have no evidence to the contrary, do you?"

"None at all, Dr. Brand," Laura said. "That's one reason why Dr. Leavitt left my ovaries in place. He said I might find some use for them even though he had to take out my uterus. What he didn't know--." She looked at her husband; he was nodding slowly, approving. "What Dr. Leavitt didn't know was that a disease may be running through my family. A disease we wouldn't want to pass on."

"Which disease?"

"Huntington's chorea. It's been diagnosed in my father in the past year or so."

Brand leaned back in his chair. He had seen advanced cases of Huntington's. He remembered the vacant stares, the shuffling, stumbling gait, the shaking hands. Many victims, he knew, degenerated into vegetable states from which there was no escape. Science had not yet found the way to help these sufferers. In succeeding generations, he had read, the disease might become more virulent. It passed in genes, usually to male offspring.

"That puts a different light on the situation," he said. "You would have had several alternatives if that weren't the case. We could have used your egg and Tim's sperm and fertilized in vitro--in a dish, the way Steptoe and Edwards did it in England. But your hesitation about passing on a disease like that is completely justified."

"There must be other options."

"Of course. You could use the egg of a fertile donor. Insemination with Tim's sperm could be an IVF, in vitro fertilization. Or it could be done by artificial insemination. Then we would simply flush out the embryo and transplant it into your abdomen."

"The baby would be Tim's."

"Yes. Half Tim's. There are other ways to go, of course. Surrogate motherhood has become relatively common, for example."

"No, I wouldn't want that. I've read about it. Sometimes the surrogate won't give up the baby."

"True. Beyond that, it could cost you up to ten, twenty thousand dollars."

"I'd rather try to carry it myself. That's what I really want. I want to take part in the process, *be* part of it." Laura lifted her wineglass, stared at it for a moment. "You know, Dr. Brand," she said, "ten years ago--five years ago--life was one long party. Or so it seemed. Now the problems and decisions come rushing at us. Life gets shorter by the minute. My cancer was cured by removal of my uterus, or so it appears. But now with my father--there's no way, they say, to cure or remove Huntington's chorea. I could come down with it one of these days." Her voice slowed, became more throaty. "Tim and I have to do what we want to do pretty quickly, it seems. One of the things I want to do is carry his baby. That would at least be a *good* problem. I don't really care how I do it. I would leave the recommending to you."

"There would be some problems--." Brand began. He was interrupted by Tim Phillips.

"We know there will be problems, Dr. Brand. But we're determined--both of us--to try to accomplish this. I have my own selfish interest, obviously. But we've done a lot of talking about it, especially in the past month. If you can help us, we want you to."

"I believe I can."

Tim was looking at his watch. He wore it on his right wrist. "Laura," he said, "I think we should give Dr. Brand the rest of the evening off. But let's see if we can talk again. We should organize our game plan."

Laura flashed that brilliant smile. "I agree," she said. "I have a million questions. And I'll have a million more. I'd be interested in having your opinions, Dr. Brand, on the psychological aspects of this kind of project. You know, bearing another woman's baby, that kind of thing."

"And on the legal and ethical aspects," Tim said. "The basics--how you find someone to contribute an egg, whether that gives the donor any right to the baby."

"I'll answer as best I can," Brand said. "But don't hesitate to get opinions from other people."

"Would you perform the--medical part?" Laura said. She was standing, preparing to leave. Tim was also standing, a lean giant with a boy's face and a crewcut.

"No. I'm not a medical doctor. I'm only a specialist in embryology, an experimenter, a clerk in a lab. We would have a medical doctor do the clinical work."

"Do you have someone in mind?"

"Not with his approval yet. But let's talk again in a few days. Since your minds are made up, I can go ahead. You will want to get the answers to your questions in any case."

"Tim," Laura said, "can we set another date now?"

"Pick one that's convenient to Dr. Brand. I'll make myself available. A weeknight might be best. We've got to resolve this or get off the pot." Tim paused. "How about your fees, Dr. Brand?"

"I have no fees. I'm an employee of University Hospital. Let's say this would be a labor of interest."

"No go. I'll ask you the same question next time we meet."

"I doubt that I'll have a better answer." He stood up. "If we're making medical history, it's enough to be a part of it."

He had relinquished part of himself. He felt that he was being drawn out of a life-context that had been relatively peaceful and ordered-- toward a target that approached too rapidly for clear identification. When Michelle said, "They didn't drink much wine, did they?" he came out of his deep reverie. He said:

"Didn't they? I didn't notice."

"Is she going through with it?"

"Yes. Both of them seem determined. I'll be talking to them again in a few days. But there are some complications." Feeling a sudden need for a change of pace, he said:

"You want to jog? I'm restless."

"You go ahead tonight, Dr. Fixx. I've got some work to do."

Going upstairs to change into his jogging gear, Brand found the girls still awake. He stopped in their shared room for a few minutes, kissed them goodnight, and went out.

Jogging helped to clear his mind. He stayed with it for half an hour, running against the cool night, trying to get the picture of Laura Phillips out of his mind. For once he didn't keep track of his time and distance.

6

Seated behind his cluttered desk, his shock of white hair silhouetted against the beige wall, Dr. Madsen looked biblically patriarchal. He also gave an impression of a self-assuredness that had unshakeable permanence and mountainous bulk. For Brand, he looked the part of a medical guru.

"Dr. Brand?" Madsen rose and stretched out his hand. The nameplate on his desk read, "ALFRED R. MADSEN, M.D." The office smelled of disinfectant, with the scent of a man's cologne subtly interblended. "Glad to make your acquaintance."

Brand took the hand. Dr. Madsen had to be a youthful and life-oriented 68 or 70. "It's mutual," Brand said. "Your reputation has preceded you."

"So has yours." Madsen waved toward a chair that faced the desk. "Have a seat. Give me a hint of what you're going to pick my brains about. That phrase was yours, as you will remember. Abdominal pregnancies aren't that common."

"I remember." Brand said, "I want only to talk a few minutes about that abdominal pregnancy." Now he added: "I may be faced with a similar case. Artificially induced."

Madsen raised his eyebrows. "Artificially induced?" If you're trying to pique my curiosity, you're on the right track."

"May I put it in a nutshell?"

"Of course."

"A local woman wants to have a baby. She has her ovaries, but no uterus. It was removed because it was cancerous. She can't or won't use her own eggs because of a disease in her family. But she knows that I have experimented with artificial embryonation in baboons. She wants to undergo the same kind of thing--while she can. Donor egg, her husband's sperm. She wants to carry."

"Stop--whoa!" Madsen raised his hands in mock impatience. "That's the biggest nutshell I've seen in some time."

"Sorry. But if I get into this new case, I'll be helping out on the same kind of problem you had--an abdominal pregnancy and delivery."

"Helping out?"

"A medical doctor--a gynie, probably--would be the primary consultant in the case. I'm a Ph.D."

"I see." Dr. Madsen steepled his fingers. "You're at University Hospital, aren't you, Dr. Brand?"

"Yes."

"Schofield's slammer. That's how we think of it since Simondson came over. Fine man, Simondson. Good friend of mine." Madsen paused, tapping his fingers together rhythmically, keeping them occupied. "Now: I could give you the book on the care of abdominal pregnancies, but you probably know it. It's mainly a matter of finding out early that you have such a pregnancy. Then you practically live with the patient, watching for emergencies. You know about the danger of peritonitis, of course."

"Yes."

"Okay, all that's largely rote and common sense. Some monitoring goes on, naturally. But--look, I'm much more interested in this artificial embryonation business. We old-timers don't get much chance to get into that kind of thing. Can you really do it? Is it legal?"

"I've had all that checked out. It's completely legal given the appropriate consents on the part of the patient and husband. All the parties in fact. We get them in writing, of course. And yes, I can really do it. I've done it--with animals. Baboons."

"Abdominal or uterine implantation?"

"Both."

"Carried to term? Normal?"

"Yes, in three cases of females in which the embryonation was successful."

"And this woman would be a human first?"

"Yes, as far as I know."

With an agility that surprised Brand, Madsen got to his feet and came around the desk. Brand saw that he limped slightly. "Feel like taking a bit of a walk?" Madsen said briskly. "The air's warmer today than it has been--thank God. And I swear that these walls have ears. You'd know about that, working at University Hospital."

He had not waited for Brand's agreement. Instead, as if the invitation were natural and irresistible, he stood aside so that Brand could precede him through the door. In a few moments they had passed under an EXIT sign and were outside on the Post Memorial Hospital "campus," nearly surrounded by buildings. The place had a cloistered feel to it. Tightly confined by its various impinging facades, the yard seemed dwarfed.

"I don't envy you, working at University Hospital," Madsen said as they walked. He might have been reading Brand's mind. "Too much restriction--and I'm not even referring to Schofield--even if it is partly state originated." He cleared his throat noisily. His spare, lean figure topped by the mane of hair had a slight stoop. But Madsen moved vigorously, limping along, towering over Brand by three or four inches. "But tell me about this plan of yours. Just how do you propose to go about inducing an abdominal pregnancy?"

Brand explained in detail. For a while he forgot where he was; the conversation absorbed him. The egg-and-sperm problem was relatively simple, Brand said. Since Laura feared--rightly--genetic transmission of Huntington's chorea, the procedure would need a donated egg. The donor should not be difficult to find. It might be a friend of Laura's. Fertilization would take place in vitro, using Tim's sperm. Implantation would then take place. The embryo would be implanted in Laura's omentum.

The method of implantation interested Madsen particularly. Give me *some* details, he said.

Brand described the process. In the normal case, the donor and recipient uteri would be synchronized. When they were functioning on the same ovulation cycle, give or take a day, the donor egg could be extracted in a relatively simple, if not unexceptionally successful, procedure.

Synchronization would be crucial to the normal program. The onset of menses in Laura or the donor would be delayed through the use of vaginal progesterone suppositories. The recommended dosage would probably be 50 mg once or twice daily. Treatment would start three days before any drop in basal body temperature. Menses would commence 24 to 36 hours after progesterone withdrawal. The ensuing cycle in test cases had appeared, very uniformly, to be normal.

The second step, retrieval of an egg from the donor, would be routine. *Back there in my briefcase, Brand said, I have a series of diagrams that will show the normal alternatives, including the one we--I--would probably recommend in Laura Phillips' case.* Remind me to show them to you. In one case you could transplant an egg from a fertile donor into the uterus of an infertile recipient. In a second case you could inseminate a fertile donor artificially, then flush out the embryo and transfer it to the uterus of an infertile recipient. In a third case--Laura's-- you would probably want to take the egg of a fertile donor, inseminate it in vitro, and implant in Laura's omentum. It would then develop its own placenta and come to term in nine months. Delivery would be by caesarian section.

"If Laura has no uterus, do you need to synchronize the women's menstrual cycles? To me, it wouldn't seem necessary."

"I think for safety's sake, I'd recommend it."

"Another question: you seem to favor the in vitro approach. Any reason?"

"The client may choose some other way. But it seems that we have greater control over the entire process if we inseminate in vitro. Then the recipient at a moment chosen by the attending physician undergoes the transplant procedure. That procedure is nonsurgical. No anesthetic is used. It is almost completely painless. The point of implantation can be selected precisely."

"Have you studied the possibility that this--Mrs. Phillips--might produce a defective offspring by this means?"

"That possibility exists, just as it does in natural insemination and childbirth," Brand said. "The risks seem comparable in both cases."

"On the basis of what evidence?"

"Well, at least four animal parallels have been documented. Embryo transplants have been successful in at least eleven species, including primates. No excessive number or ration of abnormalities has been observed. Some 10,000 healthy calves have been generated by this process. First and second generation cattle transplants have themselves produced healthy offspring.

"Very importantly, embryo recovery would be nonsurgical even if Mrs. Phillips decided that the egg donor should be artificially inseminated, with subsequent transplant to Mrs. Phillips. And of course embryo transfer would also be non-surgical."

"Have you the necessary tools for all this?" Madsen said.

"Can we go back to your office?" Brand came out of his "lecture mode." "I'd like to show you some designs."

"Certainly. I want to finish this short course and get my diploma."

They started back across the yard, following one of the cement walks. The air had turned cooler; Brand felt chilled. He could have used a cup of coffee. But that could wait. He sensed Madsen's deepening interest, and wanted to go as far as that interest would draw them.

In Madsen's office he removed from his briefcase the three designs he had created just for such situations as this. He spread them out on the desk. "They're numbered," he said. "They show just what they indicate. But remember, they illustrate a more typical case than Laura Phillips'. These drawings actually show how you'd go through a three-stage process--insemination, flush, and transplant--in inducing a uterine pregnancy in an infertile subject. The egg would be that of the fertile donor. The sperm would be that of the husband of the mother-to-be."

"Not exactly a Steptoe and Edwards process, but something like it."

"Yes. The deviations in Mrs. Phillips' case would be obvious--and controllable, I believe. Another woman's egg, same as here. Husband's semen, same as here."

"Where are you in your baboon work?"

"I'm about to embryonate another female artificially. Abdominal. Then--"

"Then what?"

"A male. I've done a couple of implants in male animals, but they haven't taken yet--as far as I know. Ask me in a few days."

"I'm interested in the Phillips case. I'm even more interested in the baboon implant process. What if I stand in as an observer when you do that?"

"You'll have a ringside seat."

"Before I sit down at ringside, may I ask a rather personal question?"

"Feel welcome."

"How did you get into this off-trail kind of project? It seems different from the usual lab-support role."

"It is. I'm actually hoping to find a feasible way for men to bear young. I'll be knocking on your door for help there too. I see that success in that will, to a small degree, equalize the disparity between the sexes. Maybe more than that--you read about Mrs. Jenkins' case?"

"The woman who died days before she was to give birth?"

"That one. I was called in to try to find a way to help her. Nothing worked. I can't get over it."

"As doctors we have unforgettable failures. My belated condolences."

7

Jim Vandorn didn't believe in coddling students. He rode them as he might have ridden, mounted, behind hounds. He could picture the teacher-student relationship in that way: keep them on the run.

He had taught himself fencing as he wanted to teach his students the subject of Ethics. Unshackle the bonds of memory; study just beyond the point where you normally dropped from fatigue.

This kid Blanton served as an excellent example. He thought he could fink his way through an Ethics course. He might as well have tried to pass for a gorilla, with that blond hair and those blue eyes.

Blanton was on his feet now, trying to make believe he had studied. He had studied in a pig's ear, Vandorn thought. To Blanton he said, "Push your principles aside now and do the right, intelligent thing. Tell me: Can we assume, with Fletcher, that man makes moral decisions in a history-free present--without reference to past or future?"

Blanton turned slowly away from the front of the room, thinking hard. Vandorn patrolled across the front of the room. "Think of it as a problem in identity," Vandorn said. "That might make it clearer."

Looking away, Blanton turned suddenly and faced Vandorn directly. "No, almost everyone making a moral decision does it while remembering the past and thinking of the future."

"You've got it," Vandorn said. "Congratulations. We could elaborate on that answer, naturally. But it'll do for today."

Vandorn went back to the teacher's desk. He felt frustrated. That little shit Margie Fiori had given Blanton the answer, he was sure. But he could prove nothing. "Let's carry on tomorrow," he said. "We're just about out of time."

They began to surge out like a movie crowd making for the exits. "You won't forget the study assignment?" he said loudly, catching at the last shred of their collective attention.

They chorused their negatives--"No, Dr. Vandorn," and "No, sir"-- and were gone. Rarely did any of them stay after class, and Vandorn knew why. They looked on the Ethics course as something that would round out a roster of valid credits. Three hours, snapperoony subject, just remember the Golden Rule, that kind of thing. In all his eleven years of teaching at the University, Vandorn hadn't been able to put to rest the ghost of that kind of talk.

The hell with them, he thought. He had a fencing class in an hour. In the meantime he had an appointment. A Laura Phillips had called. He walked over to his office in the Admin Building, that curiously shaped pile of concrete and steel that never ceased to repel Vandorn. It looked like something Frank Lloyd Wright and Mies van der Rohe had argued over, with its projecting upper floors and suspended wings.

His office appointment intrigued him. In eight years of teaching, Vandorn had responded to three requests for audiences--for advice on ethical matters. Each person had visited him only once. He had sent all three invoices "for services rendered." Two had paid. The two who had paid had known that he had once been a priest; they may have valued his counsel the more because of that.

"I have your name from a friend who works at University Hospital," Laura Phillips said. "She said you might be able to counsel me on a personal matter."

"What friend? I should thank him-her."

"Susie Thatcher."

"I'll thank her personally. But what brings you to the lair of one of the pariah--or less respected--subject areas of learning and knowledge?" Vandorn smiled vaguely and Laura reciprocated, equally vaguely.

"I believe it's a true ethical problem," Laura said. "But I should let you judge for yourself." As succinctly as she could, she described her situation.

"Let me get this straight," Vandorn said when she had finished. "You want to have a baby but you have no uterus. You don't want to have a carrier--a third party--gestate and deliver the fetus. You want to carry it yourself, in your abdomen. Your husband would supply the sperm. Fertilization would take place in the donor or in vitro. Then the embryo would be transplanted into your abdomen."

The woman sat across from him, breathtakingly beautiful, sumptuously endowed, her mouth open slightly, revealing perfect white teeth. She wore a simple grey pantsuit that could not hide those lunging breasts. "Yes, doctor," she said. "Like that. But we--my husband and I--want to touch all the ethical and psychological bases as well as the medical."

"I can see why." Vandorn put a foot on the wastebasket that he had crammed into the corner next to his desk. *Go slowly*, he said to himself. *You could be getting into uncharted waters.* "As far as the ethical aspects are concerned--may I ask whether you are religious, whether you profess any faith?"

"No. That is, not regularly. My husband is High Episcopalian. I was reared as a Roman Catholic. But we attend services only on special days. Like so many people nowadays, I guess."

"Yes, like so many people. That could affect the situation, you know. Leaving religious considerations aside for the moment, and I presume that you want to do so, I'd say you might be wise to think this over for a while at least."

"Do you mean forget it?"

"No. I mean give it deep consideration. You won't be getting into surrogate mothering. But you will, apparently, be using another woman's egg. You will be getting into parental adoption of a rather unique kind. The child would be one-half your husband's, one-half the donor's."

"I'm aware of that."

"Legally, you'd probably be on safe ground. The donor of the egg would carry the embryo only a few days--or not at all. You'd have signed papers."

"Yes."

"But you'd still be going outside the natural order, especially if you carry abdominally, which you'd have to. Is that procedure safe, by the way?"

"I'm told that it can be done."

"May I ask who said it can be?"

Laura paused. "That I'd better not say. Our arrangements are still so--tentative."

Vandorn tapped the pencil in his right hand with a thumbnail. *Goddam her!* Aloud, he said smugly, "It couldn't be more than one or two persons in this area. No matter, anyway. Of more direct concern for you is this whole web of decisions and events that could affect the rest of your life. Can you imagine an aborted pregnancy, a deformed neonate, maybe years of torture?"

She lowered her gaze. "I've thought of it all. And I'm still considering it."

"You have a choice now. You may not have one later."

"I know."

He had gained an advantage, perhaps frightened her.

Remembering a piece he had written for the *Ethical Record,* he said in a soft, mellow voice, "I had to do some research on this very subject. The authorities I quoted were very interesting. Want to hear a little?"

"I would," Laura said in a relaxed tone.

"The article covered artificial embryonation in general--of women or men. The main conclusion was that such embryonation means you are tinkering with the reproductive framework by which the race has been preserved and increased. You are violating the covenant that since the Creation men and women have been keeping with their God. Under that covenant, according to a promise as binding as any envisioned by Katkov in his *Untersuchungen,* humans procreate in a preordained way.

"People act on that principle as a given fact of life; they cannot depart from it, or violate it, or restructure it in any way without invading forbidden territory. Women bear children after insemination by men. It's that simple."

Laura seemed to be preparing to speak, but then remained silent.

"May I continue?" Vandorn said, and Laura nodded. "Okay, the ethics of a promise or covenant that places all humans in a mutually personal--even fiduciary--relationship with God have their echoes in the realm of genetics. Just as good should be rendered for good, evil may be rendered for evil. Invade the natural order and man may be compensated in kind. From in vitro creation of life man could inexorably move to experiments with all imaginable genetic factors, to competition with God, to Frankel's vision in eugenics, to taboos broken, to temples sharded, to entrance into forbidden regions.

"These are all theories, of course," Vandorn said. "I suppose the real question is this: Is principle to rule our lives, or are we to adjust our behavior to the case? Adjusting behavior to the case--situational morality--we can justify anything: mayhem, robbery, rape, name it."

She flared visibly. "What are you suggesting? That it would be a *crime* to bear a child that would not have my genes? I simply can't believe that."

Had he lost her? *Get it back on a lighter track.* Half-smiling, he said, "Even mother-love has to be tempered by wisdom and foresight. That's all I'm suggesting. We live in a world that has no mercy on the unwise, a world of rule and regulation."

"If the rule and regulation negate love, or human need, they may be misconceived."

"You only have to make certain that you aren't picking up that proverbial mackerel in the moonlight--the one that glitters but also smells."

"What does that mean?"

"Well, there are hazards that have to be faced, that's all. You know there could be legal complications. You should also think of the long-term aspects of all decisions that subvert the natural order. Take step 1 today and someone else may take step 2 tomorrow. On the third day we may be getting into mass production of clones. You may, in short, be an unwitting tool. Or stepping-stone."

"Oh, I'm sure Dr. Brand--." She stopped, embarrassed. "I'm sure there are no such possibilities here. I'm a--different case, in more ways than one."

She was gathering herself: preparing to leave. If she had had gloves, she would have been putting them on. He smiled.

"I don't know whether I hindered or helped," he said. "I only try to act as a sounding board in these cases. Do you--would you want to continue this?"

"No thank you. I really have to go. I'll call if we still have questions."

He held out his hand. When she took it, he held it gently, then let it go. "I do wish you all the luck in the world," he said. "And I'm sure you'll find it."

"I think you've pretty well settled my mind. You've certainly given me plenty to think about. I'll talk it over with my husband."

After she had gone he cleared off his desk. He put some manuscript pages into his briefcase. He threw some correspondence into the wastebasket, violently. Parts of it he had not even read. He felt reckless, iconoclastic-- as on that night when he and two other seminarians had gone into an unincorporated area at the far end of town and gotten smashed. They had found a broad, but she had wanted hard booze and the swizzle stick that came with each glass. They had played with her breasts, felt the beaver. She wore no pants. She went out to take a leak and came back complaining that she had splashed pee down her leg. She called them the last of the big cheapskates. While the three-piece band played "Alleycat," they guzzled down the last of their limited funds, investing in beer, and left. Dawn was roaring up the sky. He decided a month later that he had lost his priestly vocation, but never dropped his studies. Ordination gave him a sense of triumph, of topping his peers.

Mrs. Phillips had aroused him now, physically, mentally. But she would not be back, he knew.

He walked the two blocks to the gym and his fencing class. As he half-expected, he had a hard time focusing on the instruction. He could normally hold his own with the instructor, Herr Stromberg. But this day the foils seemed weighted with lead. At one point he left himself open for a riposte; Herr Stromberg stopped the exercise. "You're not concentrating," Stromberg said. "Let's try again when you're mind is empty of ethics." He was grinning his foxy Austrian grin.

It's not ethics I'm pondering, Vandorn thought. It's what I know about Dr. Brand and his unethics. He, Vandorn, had some bird-dogging to do. He might also look in on some primates.

He recalled a passage in the article he had discussed with Mrs. Phillips. The passage noted that 1990s ethicists were called on to adopt whatever viable strategy, within allowable limits, came to mind to combat offenses against the human entity of the future. He had wisely omitted mention of that call to arms.

8

"Have you ever seen anyone die of cystic fibrosis?" George Gustafson strode along next to Vandorn, step for step. Half a head taller than Vandorn, Gustafson looked the part of a bouncer in a nightclub. His full head of blond hair accentuated his height and contrasted almost comically with Vandorn's dark buzz-cut.

"No," Vandorn said, but I can imagine it. You run out of air, don't you?" Ahead, Vandorn could see a small sign projecting at a right angle from the wall. "Animal Resources Department," the sign read.

"You lose the capacity to breathe--slowly. You end up with lung failure. But before that, usually, just about anything and everything else has gone wrong.

"I don't see what that has to do with the Human Rights Amendment," Vandorn said. "But let's talk about it later. They should be expecting us here." He opened the heavy door. To the girl sitting at the grey metal desk inside, he said, "Is Mr. Fenton in? We have an appointment."

"In a moment Fenton came out, bustling. "Doctor Vandorn? Doctor Gustafson? We don't often have visitors from the Philosophy Department. I hope you don't mind, but visitors are supposed to wear gowns and masks." He opened a metal cabinet. "Strange germs, you know."

A dozen flimsy gowns hung in a row inside the cabinet. On the shelf above lay a disordered pile of gauze masks.

"Rules are rules," Vandorn said. Selecting a large gown, he pulled it on over his suitcoat. Gustafson did the same. Each took a mask and put it on. The masks covered their noses and mouths down to their chins.

"This is a stickup," Gustafson said, gesturing with his right index finger.

"If you shoot me, I'll sue," Vandorn replied.

"This way, gentlemen, if you're ready." Fenton became pleasantly officious. He led the way down the hall to a door identified only by an "EXIT" sign. Their footsteps echoed as they went down the two flights of stairs to the Zoo. Here a heavy door stood open. A button on the wall next to it had a tiny sign beneath it: "Please Ring."

"Looks like you've got tight security," Vandorn said.

"We have to. One, these animals cost money and could be stolen. Two, you can't have people wandering through here unescorted, maybe spreading germs. Three, some of the animals, like the baboons, are dangerous if you get careless."

"They bite?" Gustafson said. They were inside the Zoo now, and the smell assailed them, raw, earthy, almost a taste in the mouth.

"The baboons do--in a spirit of fun, of course. They are very sensitive animals. For safety reasons we keep them locked up from 5 p.m. until 8 a.m. During the day there's some traffic here, so we feel safe in leaving the door open."

"How many animals are in here?" Vandorn said as they walked along a row of large cages.

"About 200 of all sizes, shapes, and species."

"And baboons?"

"Eleven right now. All females but one. We're ordering some more--males."

"Males?" Gustafson said. "For experiments?"

"Yes, we use both sexes. More females for a while, more males for a while. Dr. Brand needs the males for his genetic work." Fenton paused; a man in a white gown was coming toward them.

"Mr. Fenton--." The man seemed agitated. "Could you come with me for a minute? It's the white mice."

"Yes, of course." To Gustafson and Vandorn Fenton said, "Could you excuse me, gentlemen?"

"Take your time," Vandorn said.

"Just stand back from the cages."

"We shall."

Left alone, Gustafson and Vandorn began to examine the caged animals. Three baboons lay in the backs of their cages, oblivious to what was going on in the room. The others sat or lay along the front bars, gimlet eyes flicking intelligently, curiously, missing nothing.

"If you worked here you'd get to smelling like this," Vandorn said.

Whispering, Gustafson said, "I think your Mr. Fenton does."

They walked slowly, stopping in front of the separate cages. Many were empty. "Human Life Amendment," Gustafson said, picking up. "It has everything to do with cystic fibrosis. If the Amendment passes, you shut down all possibility that CF could be identified in the early stages of pregnancy and terminated."

"By abortion?"

"Of course. It's legal, Jim. I know you're against it--a born-again right-to-lifer. But think of this: you could literally rid the world of CF. You just put the prospective mother through some tests, including amniocentesis. You find out whether the fetus has CF or any of a dozen other incurable diseases. If it has, you abort."

"You talk like some of the people who work in this Zoo. It's utterly contrary to everything I teach and believe."

"You should look at this more closely. We spend millions annually supporting CF kids--and CF adults up to 20 or 30--and then watch them die uselessly, purposelessly. Why not rid them of their misery before they're born?"

"You sound utilitarian to the point of ignoring natural law. Diseases like that are nature's way of reminding us that we're human. They keep things in balance. Remember? We wouldn't know good unless we also had contact with evil?"

"There ought to be better ways where diseases are concerned."

Fenton reappeared, walking briskly. "Minor problem that has to do with feeding schedules. We lost two mice. Shall we continue our tour, gentlemen? You haven't seen the small-animal cages."

They walked on. Back in his office later, Vandorn made some notes. *Safety door to Zoo open from 8:00 a.m. to 5:00 p.m. Place lightly guarded. Help substandard. Baboons in first room to right as you enter. Food the size of an orange would not fall through the floor perforations. Animals eat vegetables, whole fruit. Hall leads underground to Hillman Research.*

After a thoughtful pause, Vandorn called Gustafson. "Hello, newest member of the Philosophy Department," he said. "You liked your promotion from those stinking test-tubes in Chemistry?"

"I'll stay where I am, thank you. Have you decided yet about an arsenic sandwich for a baboon?"

"Not yet. I have to verify what Brand is doing. Soon as I do that, I'll have some work for one of your goons. In this case you're right about preventive euthanasia. I'm convinced Brand--well, you know my suspicions. I will be in contact."

9

"You've set your sights pretty far down the road, haven't you?" Madsen was saying.

"I guess you could say that. I'm convinced that we can't know too much about these things. As someone said, we're creating knowledge."

"I agree."

"I've developed these new types of uterine catheters for use in the flush-and-transfer process," Brand said. He held up a rough sketch. "That's what you see in diagram 2. They have a bullet nose, no sharp edges, and yet they retain adequate rigidity for penetration. They're flexible enough to conform to the uterus when a uterine transplant is called for. They are, of course, transparent."

Working quickly, he prepared two syringes, drawing 2 cc. of lidocaine into each tube. Two cc. would be enough for a 40 pound baboon. It would keep baboon Meg asleep and in peace for an hour or more. Or it should. If she returned to consciousness, he would use the second syringe.

As he worked, he explained each step to Madsen.

This would be the night. He would find Meg pregnant and recover the embryo. He would successfully implant Matilda. Madsen's participation had given him a psychological lift, a kind of high that would not go away.

The squeeze cage in which he kept Meg was working perfectly: a welcome switch. All too often it refused to operate at all. It would groan, resist. If you encountered major resistance when cranking, you told Elward, Fenton's assistant. In God's and Elward's good time it got fixed--oiled or rejiggered or whatever was required. Then it would work smoothly for another few weeks.

Meg seemed content but brooding. Her doglike face peered solemnly at him through the bars of the cage. He tossed her a piece of raw carrot and, languidly, as if she had more time than anything else in life, she reached out and picked it up. She began to chew on it.

"At this time of evening these primates are usually quiescent," Brand said. "They've adapted to our human 9 to 5 schedule." He smiled. He had never worked 9 to 5 and probably never would.

"I know what you're thinking. I'm in the same syndrome."

The squeeze cage closed on Meg slowly. This time it caught her in the perfect position. She looked insulted as Brand reached in through the bars and sank the needle into her arm. Almost at once her face became completely tranquil. She was asleep, eyes open, wizened face relaxed.

Brand wheeled a gurney up to Meg's cage and opened the barred door. Widening the space she occupied by retracting the movable walls of the cage, he moved her gently to the gurney. She felt heavy. Her canine teeth showed in a curious kind of soulless smile. The wise researcher learned early to stay out of range of those teeth.

From cage to "operating room." Baboon onto the operating table. Tie her down, all four limbs. For comfort--hers--make sure her spine lies in the ridge that runs down the middle of the table. Spread her legs. Brand had done the routine so often that it came automatically. He could do this in his sleep. Feet into stirrups.

Now the delicate, sensitive part. If Meg was carrying an embryo, he wanted to retrieve it without damaging it. At this stage, when it consisted of no more, at the outside, than 200 or 300 cells, it would show up under his microscope, but just barely. Ideally, it had reached the 100 cell stage.

Brand inserted the flushing instrument into Meg's vagina. He knew when the flexible needlelike tube passed the baboon's cervix: he could feel a slight, momentary resistance. Now, he thought, we will be inside the uterus. Slowly, carefully, he flushed again, and did so a third time. If an embryo existed there, he would now have it captive in the medium inside the little tank that caught the flush fluid.

Withdrawing the tube, he went to the microscope. He was examining the flush liquid with its base of calf's blood when he felt--heard a stirring. Meg was waking up. A bother. He left the microscope and took the second syringe from Madsen, who was holding it ready. This time he sank the needle into Meg's buttock, on the left side. The baboon ceased to stir.

Seconds later, peering into the eyepiece of the microscope, he felt unreasoning elation washing over him. He had found it, he was sure: the infinitesimally tiny embryo swam there, a baboon in microcosm but no more recognizable as such than if it had been a mote of dust.

Now to prep Matilda. The recipient. First setting out his instruments, including the laparoscope, he made sure he had everything he would need. Two more syringes, one for the initial knockout, one for any subsequent emergencies. Why had Meg begun to awaken? He couldn't say. Sometimes it worked that way. It depended on the primate's mood, perhaps. These animals had minds and personalities; they reacted differently from one situation to another. They improvised furiously, now play-acting, now sulking, always responding to some secret, unexplainable, primordial urge to survive.

Had man come from these animals? You could almost believe it when you examined their bodies, or those of chimpanzees, and found them nearly perfect facsimiles of the human body. Think of the millennia during which they might have established a unique place in the world's ancient ecological hierarchies. Find a single unique source of food and drink, face up to the problems that protection of that source engendered, and you could see man emerging. Picture primate-man driving a mammoth over a cliff. Food for a month. Time to think. This man would enter history hairy and inarticulate, perhaps, but he would make some kind of entrance.

"Take a look?" Brand said. "That speck may be our embryo."

Madsen leaned over the mike. "I think you're making history," he said. Still peering into the eyepiece, he said, "I'm not deep into microscopy, but I think you've got it."

"I think so. But now we come to the hard part. The transplant." He got the gurney from the hall. Untying the straps that held Meg down, he rolled the baboon onto the wheeled table. He transferred her back into her cage and locked the door. Matilda lay on her side, unconscious.

A lump of fur. She had gone under more slowly than Meg. That, Brand thought, probably meant she would feel the anesthetic longer.

Madsen was watching him. "You could keep in condition moving these animals around," Brand said. Back in the operating room, he strapped Matilda down in the exact place where Meg had been. He put a finger on her belly. "Right there, that's where we implant." Madsen stood close, watching.

"The omentum."

"Yes."

Gently Brand scraped the slide that had been in the microscope. From a small cup that he had already sterilized he sucked the fluid with its living embryo into the specially designed laparoscope. "This instrument you'll remember from my diagram," he said. "A special-use laparoscope."

"Ingenious," Madsen said. "There should be other uses for it."

10

First, Brand injected CO_2 to inflate Matilda's stomach. He talked as he worked.

The laparoscope has an obvious advantage. You can search out the exact spot where you want to deposit the embryo, as I'm doing now. There, Doctor. Want to have a look?

Madsen looked, nodded.

That's the kind of fleshy spot we need. You'll note that we're no more than a quarter or a half-inch under the skin. It would be about the same in a human. Brand felt the simian flesh quivering slightly, like a hide shaking off flies. A drop of sweat was running down the back of his neck, under his collar, to the edge of his T-shirt. *Now the needle. It makes the hole we need for planting. Look again?*

Madsen did.

You've been through this a thousand times under other circumstances, where you have to keep the instrument absolutely motionless. Here it may be more important than ever because of the relative size of the patient. We can complete the implant now. Brand pushed the plunger-like handle of the laparoscope. The tiny pocket of fluid moved down through the transparent tube, disappeared where the instrument pierced the baboon's skin. *Implant complete, we hope.*

Matilda was stirring. Strapped to the table, she could not really move. But she heaved slightly.

This is hardly a pinprick for this young lady. She's not reacting to the incision, only about being tied down. Well, she's done now. I'll take her back in a couple of minutes. Do you see anything in this procedure, Doctor, that would present any difficulties?

They talked about it.

Madsen said, "What do you figure are the odds against succeeding in one of these transplants--implants--the first time out?"

"Large. This is my first try with Matilda. I've tried three times with another animal. I'm not even sure that practice makes perfect."

"So we'd face the same kinds of odds with a human patient." Madsen stated it as a fact, not a question.

"I'd say so."

Brand rolled Meg out, made her comfortable in her cage. He had opened it to its full width of about four feet. "As a precaution I check the laparoscope after I'm done to make sure whatever was in there was ejected." Locking Meg's cage, he went back into the operating room. The laparoscope appeared to be completely empty. Brand looked at it under the stereo lens; it contained only the residue of the medium in which the embryo had floated. "I do believe we cleared it out," Brand said. "I see nothing here."

"That means you'll know about Matilda in eight or 10 days? Almost like a human?"

"Yes. Same tests as the ones you'd use to check for pregnancy, only here we will be looking for Bcg, not Hcg. Baboon chorionic gonadotropin, not the human kind." Brand looked at his watch. Madsen was hanging up his lab coat, changing into his street coat.

Now? Brand thought. *Test the water now? Why not?*

"Like a cup of coffee, Dr. Madsen?" Brand asked. "The bucket of blood down the block is open 24 hours."

"I'd like it. I'm fascinated."

The "bucket of blood" had a steam-table and a substantial list of cheap specials. Brand ordered coffee, Madsen hot chocolate. "I've had to avoid that stuff for years," Madsen said, nodding toward Brand's coffee. "Too much stimulation."

"It doesn't bother me." Brand almost said *yet*, but held it back. "Dr. Madsen," he said, "can you extrapolate with me from these experiments I've been undertaking?"

"To what?"

"To providing a service for women who want to have kids but can't have them for one reason or another. Congested tubes. Some other physical problem. Or--more importantly--some genetic problem. You know. Like Mrs. Phillips'."

"I run into that all the time, in simpler terms. 'Will my baby have--' whatever. But you were talking about extrapolating. To what else?"

"To males," he said. "Baboon and human."

Dr. Madsen sat quietly for a long time. His head rocked gently, as if he were pondering some great problem of universal significance, one that required his attention to an ultimate degree. His hot chocolate was cooling; its surface rippled almost imperceptibly.

"Male baboons?" Madsen said at last.

"Them first. Human males second." Brand took another sip of coffee. He felt conspiratorial, elated. "But male animal first, of course. No shots in the dark. If we can do it with an animal, we could certainly do it with a human. As always, I want no accusations that I'm doing what the Nazis did--original experimentation on humans." He pictured Schofield, fleetingly. "Even though our subject would have to be a volunteer."

"That could really be interesting," Madsen said. He drained the last of his hot chocolate. "Historic first. Can we talk about it again later?"

"Of course."

"Where do we stand with Phillips?"

"I'll be seeing her this week. Then we'll know where we stand. In the meantime I'm looking for her donor--of an egg and embryo."

11

"They're beauties," Fenton said into the phone. He was twirling the cord like a jumprope. "At least this first batch is. Why don't you come down and look at 'em?"

"Can you give me 15 minutes to finish up some work?"

"Certainly."

Brand went back to work. He had taken Fenton's call on the lab phone. In testing an ovum of a University Hospital patient, he had found what he believed were clues to a cure for the woman's infertility: abnormalities that could have made fertilization impossible. He had been preparing his notes on the findings when Fenton called.

He finished the case update. His part-time assistant, Durward Allen, was engaged in microscope work on the far side of the lab. Brand told him where he was going and left. He stopped at Fenton's office and together they went down the iron stairs to the Zoo. Fenton had already had the four newly arrived male baboons assigned to cages, two to a cage.

They *were* beautiful animals. Brand had to admit it. "I think I should follow the *Primate Newsletter* more closely," he said.

"We both should." Fenton was smiling, happy that he had scored one that would help Brand, his most active client. Living alone, he had in a sense made the Zoo his life and the Zoo residents his children. You need that kind of dedication, Brand believed, even if the dedication masked a life-vacuum. He took Fenton seriously, something that could not be said of many others on the University Hospital staff. Schofield, for example, thought Fenton slightly unbalanced, if effective in his job.

"When will you be starting to work with these guys?" Fenton asked.

"In a couple of weeks at the longest. I've got to finish some work with the females first."

"You know how to get in and out by now, I guess."

"No problem. I can handle the whole thing. I can find help in moving the animals if that becomes necessary."

"You know, I got some questions on your memo. But then it got a quick okay upstairs--or nearly half an okay."

"What were the questions? What's half an okay?"

"They were questioning the need for 10 males. Wanted to know whether the research was changing direction, whether something new was going on, or what. I said all I knew was what you had written. This would be an extension of the Lambert Grant work."

Brand felt it again: resentment mixed with suspicion and a dash of anger. They had a million and a half dollars for the grant work and now they're pinching pennies? "Does this mean that four will be the whole shipment--this is all we'll get?"

"They never confide those things to me," Fenton said in his sometimes prissy way. "I guess time will tell--unless you want to resubmit a requisition for six more primates."

"Let's leave it, see what happens." Had they forgotten that Troy Lambert was one of the hospital's most generous supporters? Anyway, Fenton was right. Time would tell.

12

The way Michelle prepared for a party gave Brand laughing fits. Even these reserved faculty-staff affairs gave her a kick. She would make sure days in advance that she had an outfit ready. She might lay out multiple outfits just to have options for any weather. The day of the event she might try on each of her evening's choices.

Invariably, she would ask Brand whether her final choice "filled the bill."

"With all those outfits to choose from, your taste has to be flawless," came the usual answer. And she would smile.

"I have to wear dowdy stuff to class or get a lot of cold shoulders. Now I can dress up."

"Can't have cold shoulders."

Walking to the Quadrangle where the regular late-spring bash was taking place, Brand and Michelle caught up to Dr. Abel Gorowski and his wife. The four entered the building together. A psychiatrist, Dr. Gorowski had a penchant for talking shop under any and all circumstances. His wife did the same--but "shop" for her was the kids and their sicknesses, their school problems, their TV habits.

Once inside, with the growing crowd sorting itself out, Gorowski became declamatory. "Great to see you Brands in this sinkhole of conservatism," he said.

Greetings were going around; the women began to talk of domestic things while Gorowski started to relate the case of a woman patient who had tried to commit suicide. A long-timer on the hospital's medical staff, Gorowski never mentioned names but did go into such detail that Brand could easily have established the identities of the subjects. Fixed by Gorowski's gaze, Brand felt embarrassed, as usual; Gorowski was being indiscreet again. To forestall further confidences, Brand said:

"We should be heading for the bar, Dr. Gorowski. Join me while we fetch the ladies a drink?"

"Sure." Undeterred, Gorowski continued his story as they moved to the bar. Brand nodded as if he were listening; he actually concentrated on his order. At the bar he asked for a vodka martini for himself and a Bloody Mary for Michelle. Gorowski also ordered; talk flowed in the pattern set earlier: two separate and divergent conversations. Brand was looking for an opening that would make possible an escape when Vandorn joined them.

"We need more research into the genetic roots of mental disease," Gorowski was saying. "We know only that people with any kind of problem, long-term or short-term, will pass on a tendency to the disease in a given percentage of cases."

"Why bother with more research when we already know the percentages?" Vandorn said. Brand, watching him, measuring the roundish head under his dark crewcut, remembered an earlier occasion. That time, Vandorn had challenged Brand for publishing an article outlining the possible effects of genetic screening. Now, Brand sensed, it would come up again. Something would. Vandorn had had at least a couple of drinks. His dark eyes that seemed perpetually shadowed had an unnatural sheen.

"Why, everything we do is research," Gorowski was saying. "We have to do research--lab and office research--in a more formal way so as to advance knowledge, save lives, plow new fields, correlate sickroom findings--."

"But under careful controls," Vandorn said. "I'm sure even Dr. Brand understands that science needs direction. Letting it run amok could destroy the meaning of every earlier discovery."

"Tens of thousands of species disappear every century," Brand said mildly. "Maybe man will be one of those that disappear this century or next. But I've got to deliver this drink."

"Same here," Gorowski said.

They began to walk, Vandorn accompanying, tenaciously pursuing the conversation. Brand and Gorowski gave their wives their drinks.

"We can prevent human extirpation by maintaining the moral framework," Vandorn said.

Gorowski was shaking his glass irritably. The ice tinkled against the glass. "Who's going to impose the framework--or set the limits?" the psychiatrist said. "Once you start establishing frameworks you need a central authority, an Office of Ethical Guidance or some such thing. Are you volunteering?"

Vandorn shook his head: No. Brand spoke then before Vandorn could. "Do you deny the ability of the marketplace to do its own regulating?" Brand said. "Look at sex-change operations. They were supposed to be the total answer for men who had feminine urges and characteristics. But how many have there been in the past few years? The studies show that the operations don't change things much for the subjects--and so very few persons undergo them any more."

"You can't seriously maintain that that would happen in every case," Vandorn said. He stared at Brand; some new tension had changed his face, given it a strained aspect.

"It would happen in one degree or another. Under any circumstances you can't set up a committee or agency even for science--as Dr. Gorowski says, you'd be playing God with every single research situation, trying to determine in advance whether it would be worth it or not, terminating some very promising projects--."

"Such as your own?" Vandorn's voice had a new timbre. "Such as the test-tube bastard projects, the sickle-cell anemia work, the embryo transplants?" Vandorn's voice rose, attracting the attention of others. The wives had stopped talking. Gorowski was backing away, slowly, thoughtfully, as if he might run for cover. He had been emphatic but good natured, verbose but jocund. Vandorn said: "Such as Laura Phillips, Dr. Brand?"

"I don't see that that's any of your business." Brand felt Michelle's hand on his sleeve, pulling gently. He stayed rooted firmly. "We were talking about the validity of research, the need for a free climate for research--."

"And about genetic screening, the murders of unborn persons, the incubation of human babies in carriers."

Vandorn was declaiming now, carried away by his own rhetoric. Tightly, reining his emotions carefully, Brand said, "This isn't the time or the place for this. If you want to argue it in detail, let me know." He took a sip of his martini, and half-turned. Michelle continued to tug at him.

"Argue-debate! That's the answer! But let's make it public."

"Wherever you want, whenever you want. Now if you'll excuse me--."

"No, don't go! Let's settle it. When? Where?" Vandorn grinned humorlessly at the people who had gathered and were now observing from a respectful distance. "On TV? Want to go public with this? I'd certainly like to."

Provoked, Brand said, "I said wherever, whenever you want. Set it up. Spell out the question or questions. Let me know. But let me go."

He turned and started to walk away. Michelle followed. A woman was saying, "That's one I'd want to watch." Vandorn had begun to talk to the people around him. "The real question is whether we can stick our noses into God's affairs," he said. The group began to drift away.

Groups of guests eddied, moved away. Others including both hospital staff members and university faculty members stood around talking about *the confrontation*. Brand heard parts of it; what he heard made him wonder whether these affairs really did need some injections of adrenalin. Any kind would do.

Two things happened: he was drawn into conversations wherever he went and he could not really mesh with all the small talk. It left him, without his willing it, feeling remote, inaccessible.

At one point Marina Montoya, wife of a Spanish-born professor of philosophy, asked him whether he was really working toward the development of a master race.

"No," Brand said. "But some people are moving in that direction." He hoped Marina understood English well enough to catch his point. "We have test-tube babies growing in bottles in labs. Some of them we place in continually twisting, turning Ferris-wheel kinds of things-- miniature, of course. These embryos and fetuses learn to withstand the pitch, yaw, and roll of motions that they'll have to withstand when they become astronauts."

She was smiling.

"Some others we subject to continuously extreme heat levels. These will be hot-weather people. They won't even want to return to more temperate climates once they've found their niches as--oh--anthropologists or jungle guides, or perhaps beachcombers on Ipanima."

"Go away." She was smiling. "You've been reading *Brave New World*."

"Well, maybe." Now Marina's husband, Joe, spoke up. "If you're experimenting with human life, you really are on shaky ground, you know." Joe's softly featured face had a kind of frightened look. "What can you really say in your defense? A lot of people still remember the Holocaust, the experiments on living persons, even our own CIA's ventures into prohibited areas."

Michelle stood at Brand's elbow. He sensed discomfort in her, a withdrawal. For the first time she was seeing the face of the enemy, he thought. An unnerving experience? "You philosophers should be more pragmatic," he said. "You take life so seriously that you invite heart attacks." He was smiling.

"I'm not defending--our friend." Joe's eyes rolled significantly toward the spot where Vandorn had created his minor scene. "But in today's context more and more people are questioning the whole principle of total allegiance to science."

Four men and two women were in the group. They nodded their heads in agreement with Montoya. "Science and some politicians are moving us toward nuclear war," one woman said.

"In embryology, in genetics," Brand said, "we would be absolutely in the dark ages if we had hurled all man's earlier findings into the nearest sump. Don't you realize that we almost have to move ahead in these fields?" He smiled palliatively. "Besides, you women will be glad when we invent the first pregnant man. Won't that be equalizing the burdens between the sexes?"

"You'd probably make a mint on the serial rights alone," one of the men said. "Maybe two mints." He paused thoughtfully. "But not for me. I'll leave that department to the ladies."

"See, you're being sexist," Brand said, "not to say disgustingly conservative."

"Are you really going to debate?" Marina Montoya said.

"Why not--if my superiors don't object?"

"And if they do? What then?"

"I really doubt that they'd care, Marina, if you want the truth. It will remain theoretical. The university and the hospital will gain some publicity. 'Nuff said?"

Brand guided Michelle out of the assembly hall a while later. "I've never been so glad to leave a party," Michelle said. They were exiting into the cool spring air. Just a couple of blocks away, the lake thumped restlessly under a northerly breeze. The research center lunged skyward no more than a half-block from where they were walking. Some of the windows on the upper floors glowed brightly.

"Same here," Brand said. "Vandorn got under your skin, didn't he?"

"I guess so. I just wish you weren't really going to debate. It seems so--so public. Did you see Dr. Schofield watching you?"

"Yes. But he's a weasel in public. In private, or in staff meetings, he's a wildass man-eating monster. Besides, Vandorn will forget all this bullshit."

"You hope."

13

Glorious in the simplicity of a soberly pleated dress, Laura visited Brand in his office. "We want to go ahead as soon as possible," she said.

He had been updating notes on two experiments. "I can start planning it if you're sure of that."

"I'm sure."

"Do you mind if I try to outline what you face?" She sat across from him, cool, composed, decorous, a sentient, sensitive woman who wanted the immortality that came with motherhood. Watching her, Brand felt stirrings of--what? Desire? Why had she wanted to come to his office?

Brand stood up. "I can give you a sketchy outline right now." He picked up the pencil he had been using. Taking a sheet of yellow paper, he leaned on the side of the desk. She had stood up and moved close to him. He could smell her scent: a distilled essence that carried in its bouquet a hint of hyacinth and forest glades. At the top of the sheet Brand wrote:

"PROBABLE CYCLE, ARTIFICIAL EMBRYONATION." Underneath that he began to make notes rapidly, writing large. Their shoulders touched. "I'll make a copy of this when I'm done," he said. "Then we'll both have one." He was printing so that she could read:

"-- Interview/counseling/informed consent (signature)

"-- Medical evaluation and workup as required

"-- Husband's semen, freeze in small aliquots

"-- Donor research, screen, match

"-- Monitor donor/recipient's menstrual cycles

"-- Synchronize cycles of donor/recipient

"-- AI donor (if time correct)

"-- Monitor donor for embryo entry date (uterus)

"-- Uterine flush, repeated as required

"-- Anti-pregnancy procedure

"-- Monitor donor for multiple ovulations, etc.

"-- Scan, isolate, clean culture of embryo

"-- Non-surgical transfer of embryo to recipient

"-- Hormone supplementation as required

"-- Pg determination

"-- Evaluate, monitor pregnancy; ultrasound, amniocentesis."

Brand set the pencil down. "That should cover it." He was scanning the sheet. "Want to give me one minute?" he said. "The Xerox station is down the hall."

"Of course, Dr. Brand." She sat down as he left, and was still sitting, composed, when he returned a minute later. Now that fugitive scent pervaded his office, crowding out the usual chemical smells. Brand handed her the original sheet of notes. "You'll undoubtedly have questions," he said.

She ran her eyes down the list. "What's the medical evaluation and workup?" she asked.

"You would go through a series of tests to make sure there are no unexpected abnormalities. A routine. It wouldn't be done here--more likely with your family doctor or gynecologist, or Dr. Madsen. Your husband would want to have similar tests, to make sure his semen is healthy, for example."

"I have no gynecologist," she said. "Only the man who took out my uterus. I've already asked him whether he would take part in an artificial embryonation. He said it's impossible. He doesn't know about your method."

"This would be your choice. I'm sure you could have the tests done by Dr. Madsen. He's going to do the office procedure in any case if you and your husband agree."

"Dr. Alfred Madsen? The gynecologist?"

"Yes."

She was looking at the sheet of notes again. "AI is artificial insemination?" She glanced at Brand and he nodded. "How many times might you have to flush the donor to obtain an embryo?"

"Maybe two. Maybe 20. We have no way to tell."

"So it could take a while."

"Yes. If you go the petri dish route, we could probably shorten the time substantially."

She read farther, then paused and said: "How do you synchronize ovulation times?"

"We would use progesterone. Dr. Madsen would prescribe it and specify dosages."

She was folding the paper he had given her. "You would be supervising this entire procedure?"

"Yes, in effect. There are things I can't do, as I probably told you. But I'd be keeping a log on the whole set of procedures. Madsen would too. We'd really be double-checking each other. He would be almost totally in charge after we achieve embryonation, of course. At that point it becomes a medical responsibility."

She stood up. "I'm grateful for your time, Dr. Brand. Will you have word on a donor soon?"

"I hope to. I'm running an ad in the Gazette."

"How about Susie? The woman who spoke to you in Dr. Schofield's office?"

"She might be ideal. Will you check with her?"

"I will. I'll let you know."

"Do you know Susie well?"

"Yes, I think so. Is there a question about her?"

"No, not at all. I'm just thinking that you are taking a big step when you accept her for an egg. It would be normal to measure her against some standards."

"What kinds of standards?"

"What you'd expect. I'll do some more sketching out if you want. If you'll give me a ring tomorrow, I'll give them to you. They're not complicated."

"I'll call in the morning. You're going to get sick of hearing from me."

"Never." He smiled, softening what was to come. "But one thing--
we should meet off campus, probably. Not here in my office. As I must
have told you, the walls have ears around here."

"I'll remember."

God, how she hated to visit her parents these days. If only, Laura
thought, she could reestablish some of the old parent-child spirit, fan
it back to life. But she couldn't. Each time she went to visit she did
the same things--carped at her mother to have her father thoroughly
tested, medically; asked her brother, now 36, if he had found work yet;
helped clean the place up. . . Always the same. Couldn't her mother see
that Joseph Romano Sr. needed help, that his condition was getting
worse?

Tim would no longer go inside with her. On these mandatory
visiting occasions he always had work at the office. He dropped her
and picked her up two hours later. This had been going on for more
than six months.

Climbing the steps, she tried to devise a new tack, a different
approach. But nothing occurred to her. She rang the bell. Her mother
opened the door. Though grossly overweight, Mrs. Romano could still
flash a beautiful smile. "Come on in, Laur," she said loudly. She might
have been alerting someone in the background to the fact that they had
a visitor.

Inside, Laura saw her father sitting--slouched--in the ancient easy
chair with the flowered cover. She had left him in exactly that position
a week ago. Had the power of locomotion left him? she thought with
an access of mixed hope and fear.

She went through the usual greetings. She kissed her father,
thinking: *two hours until Tim comes to pick me up.* She noted her father's
trembling hands, the increasingly vacant stare.

"Did I tell you that Mabel Rohr died?" her mother said. In almost
the same breath she added: "Will you have a glass of something cold?
Your father's going to need one--if he doesn't spill it." She threw a good-
natured, sidelong glance at her husband. His head, by way of answer,
rolled in his wife's direction.

"A soft drink please," Laura said. "Low sodium." She was watching
her weight. In some shallow recess of her mind, she wanted to remain

attractive. Would Tim some day be able to slough her off as he had obviously sloughed off her parents? "I'm joining the war on flab," she added, "like everyone else."

"You!" Her mother spat out the word, but not resentfully. Proudly she ran her eyes up and down her daughter. "You watching your weight. You could use 20 pounds."

"I'd look like a beachball."

"With grapefruits attached."

Laura laughed. Her mother's earthiness never ceased to amuse and amaze her. As her mother left now, Laura turned to her father. "All okay, Dad?" She was beginning to talk to him in monosyllables, in short sentences. She could remember back no more than six or eight years, before he had retired from the Police Force, when he had loomed in her eyes and imagination as the symbol of power and authority. Now she had to watch his deterioration as it progressed by perceptible stages.

Her mother might not notice; Laura certainly did. She thought her brother might be entering the incipient stages of the same curse. He seemed languid, mentally scattered.

Her father was nodding, trying to talk. She leaned closer to him. Some spittle leaked from the corner of his mouth. She got up and wiped it off. He smiled vaguely, sensing tenderness, and tried to say something. It came out as a series of grunts.

"You don't have to talk," Laura said. "Do you want the TV on?"

He shook his head No.

"Anything else you need?"

Again No.

She began to tell him about the vacation she and Tim were planning for the summer. Then she realized that he was not listening. She also realized that she might not be taking a vacation trip this summer. *You'd have to stay in close touch with me and your doctor*, Brand had said. Motherhood started with successful embryonation. Or before it.

14

"Dr. Schofield, I feel strongly about this. I realize you may not want to make a big issue about it, but ethically it's completely out of bounds." Vandorn sat forward on his chair, his eyes fixed on Schofield's face, probing, measuring. *How much cooperation could he expect from this quarter, if any?*

Schofield said: "I understand completely. I feel the same way, but in a more direct way. I'll take whatever action is necessary. I've already made that clear to Dr. Brand."

"Do you think that's enough?"

"I think so. At least for now. He does do a great job for us in the area of embryo research. We've even developed a--a sort of reputation because of his work. You know, writeups in the technical press, that kind of thing."

"But don't you have to keep your eye on the main chance? Don't you have to keep in mind that he may make negative headlines one of these days? You know he's going ahead with that Laura Phillips embryonation."

"I haven't heard that. I do know I spoke to him about it--about not doing it on the hospital premises, not using our personnel or facilities in any way. I did make it quite strong, Dr. Vandorn."

The administrator's voice told Vandorn that Schofield was becoming nettled. Could the case be put on a less personal, more scientific plane?

"For me the question goes back to the whole problem of test-tube babies, cloning, artificial insemination--the whole bit. You're dealing with a human being when you're experimenting with embryos. You put yourself in the role of Magister Ludi when you start moving embryos from one woman to another, or when you create one in a laboratory dish and then implant it in a woman for gestation. You come back to the key question: When does life begin? Pope Pius XII said it all, I suppose. The family and the people in it cannot become parts of laboratory experiments."

"You are very persuasive." Schofield still seemed irritated; he sounded as if he felt he was being lectured. "But you don't have to persuade me. I'm doing what I can short of--anything extreme."

"You know he and I are going to debate some of the issues involved in reproductive experimentation?"

"I had heard that. In fact I heard it at the staff-faculty get-together."

"That's where we decided on it. I'm hopeful that will end it, but I don't know. It may take action of other kinds."

"Are you making this into a personal, one-man crusade?"

"No; I'd like to mobilize some feeling about it in the community, though. If a lot of people were to express their opposition, Brand might have second or third thoughts."

"Possibly." Schofield left off; a silence fell, effectively terminating the interview. Vandorn stood up. He wanted some kind of commitment from Dr. Schofield, yet he had to extract it gently.

"We have the same basic interests, Dr. Schofield," Vandorn said. "You are thinking of the hospital and its reputation, of course. And I'm thinking of ethical or bioethical aspects, the community aspects. But our interests do coincide."

"I'd agree with that."

"I may need your help at some time in the future. Or your advice. It would be good to know we could talk again."

"We can, of course."

Vandorn left. He could read Schofield now; the administration would protect its own neck in its own way. At least Vandorn had done what he saw as necessary. No one would launch any Brave New Worlds in this area, not while Schofield had breath left in him. But he, Vandorn, could not rest. On the steps outside he recalled what else he had to do; he reversed direction and went back into the lobby and to a telephone.

He dialed the Admin Building number, knowing a phone would be ringing at a switchboard that could not be more than a few yards away, hidden in some glass-enclosed cubicle. When the operator came on, he asked for Mr. Fenton.

"I will ring him," the operator said.

He heard a buzzing. It seemed to grow louder as the girl let it ring three, four, five times. "They must be out," she said. "May I take a message?"

"No, thank you. I'll try him again later."

Vandorn checked his watch. A few minutes before noon. He walked down the hall to the Animal Resources Department, tried the door, and, when it opened, entered. No one home. Quickly he opened the metal cupboard and took out a gown and mask. He put the mask on first, then the gown. From the empty office he went to the stairs leading down to the Zoo. The reinforced safety doors stood open.

Vandorn went straight to the baboon cages. The smell assaulted him; he ignored it. More cages were occupied now, but the females were still where they had been. Vandorn went close to the two middle cages and looked in. No doubt about it: these animals were pregnant. One lay on her back on the perforated floor, gazing up at him curiously, her belly distended.

It took him only seconds to return to the office, hang up the gown, replace the mask, and leave. His watch told him the whole maneuver had taken five and one-half minutes. Back in his office, he called Gustafson.

15

Anyone watching would have said the tall, swarthy young man had visited Animal Resources on a regular basis. Baseball-style cap worn backward, he went straight to the door that opened on the stairs to the lower regions where the animals were. Negotiating the steps with a kind of skipping gait, holding his book bag with one meaty hand to keep it from jouncing, he reached the lower floor in seconds.

Without hesitation he walked into the right-side room that housed the baboons. At once two or three of them began to chatter. Some of the sounds they made resembled barks. Listening, the young man reached into the book bag and pulled out a thick volume. He checked the book carefully, as if he were seeing it for the first time.

Satisfied, he opened the book and appeared to study a page. As he read, he moved along in front of the cages, walking very slowly. At the third cage he stopped, whereupon the rather plump primate inside the cage threw a piece of reddish material at him. It missed him and fell to the floor. It might have been a lump of chewed orange.

As if making it a game, the young man first looked around, listened, and then tossed four uncut, unchewed pieces of food into the cage. He drew each piece from the book bag. Standing close to the cage, he made sure that each piece went through the bars and landed near the baboon occupant. The animal began at once to suck on the newly arrived treats.

Still holding the book, the young man headed deliberately toward the door. In the hallway he put the book into the bag and went up the iron stairs.

He was gone less than a minute later. He had seen no one.

16

The days grew longer. Brand found his work expanding to fill every empty niche of time. He saw less of the girls--and of Michelle. He ate more snacks at the bucket of blood. Weekends gave him some respite, but not much. At least he had opportunities to squire the girls around, buy them lunch, and search out entertainment with Michelle. On his jaunts with the girls he always had a notebook handy; in it he could catch ideas, make notations.

At a Sunday afternoon chamber music concert, listening to some of his favorite music, a sonata by Pergolesi, he fell asleep. Awakening, he knew his head had drooped. Michelle gently roused him. For a minute or so he was the focus of attention. The incident embarrassed him.

He couldn't help himself. Tyrant time pursued him. He was bringing Laura's project along, collecting donor applications, instructing her, sealing the three-way working relationship with Madsen. Brand was also pushing ahead with the baboon experiments. He succeeded in embryonating Matilda on the fifth attempt, and suddenly had three abdominal pregnancies to attend to. He tried to plant an embryo in Baboon Terry twice more, without success. He worked out a schedule for additional attempts.

The notebook became journal, thesaurus of ideas for immediate or future application, philosophical resume. It served the latter purpose because Brand understood at the back of his mind that he would need something on paper--a synopsis, a summary, *something*--when he faced off with Vandorn.

They had given him a TV date a month after the faculty-staff fiasco. Brand would collide with Vandorn at the end of July. When the day came he planned to be ready. In his notes he deep-sensed in global terms at times, knowing he might not use the observations but needing to establish a foundation for other ideas. . .

There are, really, few first-principle laws in science, no immutable relationships, nothing fixed and formal and unchanging. Nothing means anything except as a launch-point for research, discovery, exploration. Man himself is a collection of chemicals and a subject for analysis and improvement. You can manipulate man as you manipulate other objects of research--if you observe protocols, cause no permanent harm, have a chance of advancing science. The eternal conundrum: How to protect and preserve life while also analyzing and dissecting it?

What is here today, what is true today, will not be here or true tomorrow. If one line of inquiry doesn't effect improvement, you abandon it, move to something else. If you discover something better, you do it again, and try to learn still more that will bring about improvement. You can't stop. Scientific research is no more stoppable than an express train. If you don't do it, someone else will. Discovery may be the real law of life.

His mind overflowed with details. He drew up lists of things to do. He lost some, X'ed out most of the items on others. He almost never X'ed out all the items on any given list.

Laura was leaving to Brand the task of choosing an egg donor. Susie Thatcher became an applicant. At 3:00 one morning Brand put together some notes and spelled out the considerations that would guide him as he selected the woman who would provide the egg or eggs. He wrote it as a letter.

Dear Tim and Laura,

We haven't had much opportunity to explore what we should be looking for in the donor of the egg(s) that we will be using. But this is important. I'm passing on a few thoughts that I've collected in note form over the past few years.

First, there are five aspects of genetics that should concern us-- characteristics that are inheritable. The five are mental health, physical health, longevity, personal appearance, and intellectual capacity.

Second, of these five I believe we should be concerned primarily with physical health and longevity as demonstrated by family history. Mental health characteristics would come next, followed by intelligence. Personal appearance factors like hair color and skin pigmentation would come last.

They are far less important than any other factors. Some people would rate mental health first, and in my view that would present a problem.

In a nutshell, we can only do our best to weight mental health as a qualifying factor. The reason is that nearly everyone has a mental health skeleton in his or her hope chest. If we eliminate everyone who has a problem of this kind, we will be eliminating nearly all our applicants. I'm talking about the direct bloodline--parents, grandparents, and so on, not Uncle Eddie or Auntie Jo.

Third, we should not be trying to create a Superman, the progenitor of a Super Race. We might be accused of that; but it's nonsense. We would be trying to find the genetic background for a normal, well adjusted, healthy person who could survive in life without abnormal aid or support.

The Superman or Super Race concept is so fraught with emotion that it acts like a catalyzing agent: people who may be otherwise rational become enraged. They can't think about it dispassionately. They never stop to think that all people who mate feel that they can and will produce a superior human being. The result, of course, falls generally short of expectations; the new addition turns out to look like pa or ma, or grandpa or grandma, and may have--like great-grandpa--a wart on a kneecap and a permanent case of the sniffles.

If you run into someone who taxes you with trying to launch a Super race, you may want to have some simple answers ready. The fact is, we can't really control much in this business. We can only play percentages. But some people will interpret this whole effort as evil--as genetic engineering--as playing God. These people may align themselves on the side of what they see as God.

Here Brand paused. Another sentence along the lines of what he was writing could inspire fright. He could say, for example, *For these people, standing on the side of God opens the way to any kind of extreme action or behavior--violent, aberrant action in some cases. You'd be wise to give a wide berth to the Godly fanatic.*

He let his senses probe the false dawn. The window stood open slightly, and he could hear birds chattering outside. An owl hooted. A car passed noisily, its muffler rumbling, on the street in front of the house. A tomcat shrieked from the next block.

Frighten her? Tell the truth. He wrote the sentence into the letter and went on.

Fourth, I will follow your wishes regarding Susie. If you have a preference, I will make her the No. 1 candidate. But I would prefer not to do that. My feeling is that we would be better advised to consider all our candidates--and we have a number in response to our ads--on the basis of the factors I've outlined above. We might want to register all the candidates. Susie can, of course, be No. 1.

If you have questions on this, I'll be available to answer them as needed. Incidentally, Dr. Madsen concurs in these basic views.

We are probably a month to two months from an initial effort to start your embryonation procedures. I'll call you later, touch base.

Brand mailed the letter on the way to the lab in the morning. That afternoon he had a call from Fenton. One of the pregnant baboons was seriously sick. There was a suspicion that poisoned food had been tossed into the baboon's--Mavis's--cage. Fenton had already called the hospital vet. But would Brand want to come over?

Brand would. He had already begun to prepare his garage to serve as a mini-zoo. As a temporary home for Baboon Terry, perhaps one other animal. Would he have to move Terry now? Prematurely? When he might be delicately pregnant?

If you didn't have one problem, you had two others.

17

The questions lay like a scratchy blanket over Brand's mind as he watched the vet trying to flush out Mavis's stomach. The procedure succeeded even though Mavis had vomited violently earlier. But through no fault of his own the vet had come too late. Mavis died two hours after Brand arrived.

Mavis's number on her cage and in the official records was 3685. Her death would go into the official records of the Zoo with the identifying number and no name. While Fenton made notes on a clipboard, recording everything precisely, Brand talked to the vet. They would do an autopsy, yes. They would check for chemical substances, yes.

"It would be standard procedure in a case like this," the vet said. "Unnatural death, I'd say. We'll send the liver out for check too. That means we'll have a report in three to seven days."

"We don't know for sure yet that Mavis was poisoned," Fenton was saying. The clipboard lay in front of him on his desk. He had pulled a report form from a drawer of the desk and was contemplating it. "But Mavis was one of the healthiest of our baboons."

"I'd guess it was done deliberately. Someone knows your routine," Brand said.

"We haven't had any new faces--wait. We had a couple of faculty types come through here, oh, maybe four, six weeks ago."

"Names?"

Always the bureaucrat, Fenton opened a file drawer, yanked a folder, opened it. "One was Dr. Vandorn," he said. "One was Dr. Gustafson."

"You've told me all I need to know. And I'm worried. About security here, in the labs, in my office, everywhere."

"You could keep one animal upstairs in the lab, you know." Fenton sounded mildly offended.

"I may do that," Brand said, adding soothingly: "But I doubt that we could do better there than you do here. We would probably do worse. Too much traffic. Light nighttime security."

The vet's report came in: strychine was the cause of Mavis's death. It had been injected into a tangerine. Or more than one.

In imagination Brand began to see Vandorn moving around him, circling, moving in concentric circles. The core and center was the Zoo. It didn't help when Schofield called him in to talk about the report of Mavis's death. When Brand got there, Fenton was already in the administrator's office. Surprisingly, Schofield had himself under control.

"Who would want to kill one of our experimentals?" He always shortened "experimental animals" to "experimentals."

Brand shrugged. *Tread lightly.* "It's hard to say. There are animal-hating nuts everywhere, Dr. Schofield. We've had some mysterious deaths among the smaller animals before."

Fenton concurred, conditionally. "But not poisoning, not for a long time. With some of them, of course, we can't always tell whether the cause of death is poison or a virus or what."

"Also," Schofield said, "I can't remember a baboon attracting this kind of lethal attention--at least not in my time."

"There may have been a case or two some years ago," Fenton said. "But not recently, no."

Schofield was reading Fenton's report. "It's certainly not the most serious problem we'll have this year. But you--." He was looking at Fenton; "--may want to tie up your security arrangements a little more tightly."

"Will do. For one thing, my secretary and I are now going to lunch at different times. That gives us a little better handle on it."

"And you," Schofield said, looking at Brand, "may want to steer clear of 'those animal-hating nuts.' This animal was pregnant, this report says. Some of those nuts may resent experiments involving animals, or reproductive research, for whatever purpose."

"Will do. I'm committed to one or two things, one a TV debate with Dr. Vandorn. But after that I'll--."

"You know the one I'd worry about," Schofield said. He leaned back, signaling that the conversation was over. As Fenton got up to leave, Schofield motioned to Brand to remain seated, then he said a brief goodbye to Fenton and, when the Zookeeper had left, placed his elbows on his desk, arms stretched forward. "You know what you're up against now, I guess."

"Yes. A raving fanatic."

"You understate it. I've got to say, Brand, that you're taking a huge personal risk. That means your life or limbs may be on the line--not just your job."

"I realize."

"Be forewarned. And, again, keep University Hospital out of it. I can't make this too strong: our interests do not run parallel where experiments on people are concerned. Animals, possibly." He paused, then added: "And please keep your debate theoretical."

Brand went back to work. He had finally done it with Baboon Terry, or he thought he had. Terry, if Brand was right, would be the first male baboon to be embryonated--and, hopefully, to carry and deliver.

Baboon murders could destroy him. He spent hours on each embryonation. Loss of one pregnant animal could set him back months. Rummaging in the lab building's basement, Brand found two unused aluminum baboon cages, complete to waste drawers. He also found a dust covered, wheeled stainless steel table. He signed for one cage and the table.

Back in the zoo, he observed Terry carefully. If the animal was abdominally pregnant, a historic experiment was under way.

Terry would be the Great Paradigm. After Terry, embryonation of other male animals would either remain experimental or become a routine procedure. After Terry, embryonation of human males would be the logical next phase.

He talked with Madsen about it. They were going back to the Zoo to do a final test on Terry. This test would indicate whether Terry had a live embryo in his belly--or nothing. With Madsen, he explored the different male and female symptoms.

"The female example, human or animal, only shows that the progesterone level keeps rising during pregnancy," Brand said.

"Up to about the sixth month. Then it remains steady or drops off." Madsen carried a cane this evening, his obeisance to a damp day in May. "At least that's the case with human females."

"This is what puzzles me: If Terry is pregnant, can we stop injecting hormones--progesterone? Stop all artificial procedures? Let the placenta do all the manufacturing?"

"Good questions." The night watchman had them sign in, then let them into the Admin Building. Their footsteps echoed on the marble floor. "And you're shooting in the dark with No. 1. Wouldn't you be well advised to embryonate two, three--up to four males? Then if one or two die or naturally abort you'll have others to observe and work with."

"That's my plan. We have four new animals. I'll use all or most of them."

Terry sat in his cage, chewing on a piece of carrot. "Placid looking devil, isn't he?" Madsen said. "Little does he know that he may be the first male of any species to bear offspring."

"That thought would drive some people around here up a wall. I don't even dare think it."

"How about producing humans in a bottle?"

"Even worse." Brand had moved the squeeze cage up to Terry's cage. Terry jumped eagerly into the new home. He began to chew noisily on the carrot Brand had brought him. Brand began to turn the crank that reduced the size of the cage. The back wall began to collapse on the baboon. At once, violently, Terry threw the remains of his carrot through the bars of the cage. His barked complaints echoed, arousing the other animals. They began to bark too.

Over the din Brand said, "I'm going to knock Terry out. Then maybe we'll be able to draw some blood in peace."

The back wall had now trapped Terry against the front bars. His furious barking continued as Brand readied the lidocaine. The noise ceased almost at once when Brand jabbed the needle-end into Terry's arm.

"It's been over two weeks--actually 18 days--since I implanted this guy," Brand said. He went into the closet-like operating room, returning with another syringe. "I figure that should be enough. Something should show."

Terry lay in his induced sleep. From time to time he twitched. Moving close, Brand gripped the animal's upper left arm and squeezed. The arm lay an inch or two away from Terry's body, pushed upward by the pressure of the back wall. Brand handed the syringe to Madsen, then dropped a rubber tube between the arm and the body. Quickly he retrieved the lower end and tied off the free ends of the tube.

"All set," he said. Madsen handed him the syringe. Injecting the needle into Terry's arm, he pulled back on the plunger. The syringe filled half-way up with blood. "That should be enough," Brand said. He straightened up, removed the rubber tube, and began to twist the crank again.

"Feel like coming up to the lab?" he said to Madsen. "I can run this test in an hour." Terry now lay relaxed on the floor of his cage.

"I'm with you all the way."

"We could go down that hall and get into the lab building that way, underground. But it's too spooky at this time of night. Let's take the aboveground route."

18

He let the blood clot, then spun it in the centrifuge. Now he had serum. He put a portion of the serum into a prepared chemical mixture. He had half an hour to wait.

They stood at a window of the fourth-floor lab. Parallel, wide hallways ran along two outer walls of this wing. Between the hallways, which looked out south and north on the grounds of the hospital complex, half a dozen laboratories stretched from side to side. Both ends of the laboratories opened, doorless, on the hallways. From each laboratory you could look through huge plate glass windows toward south and north. Stepping close to the windows on either side, you could look west toward the lake.

The labs on this side included histology, embryology, anatomy, others.

Brand was wiping his hands on a paper towel. A sense of expectation, of elation, gripped him. He could not quell it. When he went to check the results of the test, it was as if he knew beforehand that it had worked. Terry was pregnant; the serum in the chemicals had precipitated to the bottom of the test tube.

"Let's go have a drink," Brand said. "The animal's making history."

"I don't drink," Madsen said, "but I'll watch."

They bypassed the bucket of blood and stopped at a "real" restaurant.

When Brand got home, it was 12:50 a.m. and Michelle was asleep. Brand slept on the couch in the living room, using a blanket that he kept in a downstairs closet for emergencies.

His head was spinning. The wine had given him a eureka feeling. He kept thinking, "I did it. Now we have to go on. I'm going to find out everything there is to be learned." Thinking of that sentence, he wanted to laugh out loud. Once, half asleep, he did laugh. The back of his neck itched; he ignored it.

In the morning Michelle avoided his eyes. She avoided *him* after preparing breakfast, going upstairs to straighten up rather than have coffee with him. The girls asked him when the monkey would move into the garage. "Soon," he said.

On his desk when he went to check yesterday's mail lay three "While You Were Out" notes. Laura Phillips had called. So had a TV station. So had the editor of *Gay Community*, a newspaper for homosexuals. The paper, Brand hoped, would help in the search for the first pregnant human male. The TV people wanted the debate *soonest.*

He saw the girls off to their respective schools. A few minutes later he heard Michelle leaving. She had not said goodbye. She had not asked for a ride to the University complex. Brand had no defense against this phenomenon; it puzzled and irritated him. He had, after all, been with Madsen.

"Baboons are bulky, ground-dwelling monkeys in the order *Primate*, family *Cercopithecidae*. They are classed into two genera." Reading on, Michelle found another sentence that caught her eye: "The canine teeth are long, the jaws powerful, and the limbs extremely powerful, making the baboon a formidable fighter."

Her hand shook slightly as she put the book back in the space reserved for Volume 2.

She was researching the subject of sexual dysfunction in human females. She had long since grown accustomed to the sometimes exotic, sometimes pedestrian subjects that professors chose for elucidation in one form or another. So sexual dysfunction seemed routine--and easy. Writers like Powell and Associates, Shusterman, Masters and Johnson, LoPiccolo, Duddle, Sadack, and Spitz had been making their contributions to the literature for an astounding number of years. Her glance into an encyclopedia represented a momentary detour.

Her work was going well. She couldn't, however, get her mind straight on what was happening at home. Em goes out to celebrate a pregnant male baboon and forgets to call her. Half their garage is rearranged, preempted.

The neighbors would see all this. They would be watching the Brand house like buzzards tracking surface animals.

Worst of all, their home life had evaporated. *Home life* included *sex life*. Em had time only for his work--and that didn't seem fair to the girls. On second thought, Michelle included herself as one of those to whom it didn't seem fair. She could not feel sorry for herself. But they had established something personal, familial, and it was evanescing like morning mist. It seemed like a useless sacrifice.

He would now come home, go to bed early, dead tired, and awaken before dawn--to work. Em had never smoked. But now she smelled cigarette smoke and ash in his study. She believed he was on tranquilizers, another first. A medicine bottle had appeared in the kitchen trashcan without explanation. She had noticed it, feeling guilty, while emptying garbage after dinner.

She had encouraged him to pursue his star. If she had known . . . this would invade, twist her life.

Now the baboon in the garage. Or almost in the garage. She, Michelle Brand, was about to take a role in a--to her--frightening scenario: a garage as monkeyhouse, laboratory, delivery room, simian crematorium?

Was she making a mountain out of a molehill? Who could detach his or her mind in such a case? When and how were absolutely impartial judgments possible? The monkey could be the backbreaking last straw. Most frightening, she saw danger for her babies. That had to be her primary concern. Something terrible, ominous was moving into her life, her soul.

19

Baboon Terry wouldn't cooperate. He kept wheeling away from the front of the cage, avoiding Brand, staying out of his reach. Then when the back wall of the squeeze cage had closed on him, forcing him toward the front bars, he went into a frenzy. He jumped and barked and hurled himself at the bars. Finally Brand had him pinned firmly, and could give him a shot.

With the two maintenance men standing by, Brand worked quickly. He hauled the gurney over to the cage and pulled Terry gently onto it. For safety, he wound lengths of clothesline around Terry's forelegs and hindlegs. As the men stepped forward to help, Brand followed them. Imitating him, they gently rolled the gurney out of the research facility and through the door that led out to the loading dock. A freight elevator took them down to the street level, and in seconds, guided by Brand, they had moved baboon Terry into a waiting cage and deposited the cage in the back end of an ambulance-like van.

Driving his own car, Brand led the van with its valued load to the rear of his own garage. In seconds more, the men had transferred the cage, with Terry in it, to the table in the garage.

Situation normal. Terry still asleep. Fenton had given him permission to take Terry to his home laboratory for a period of "intensive observation." While Terry was at the Brands', he would have the same food and, approximately, the same care that he would have had at the research facility. Fenton's aid, young Phil Tyler, would help tend the animal.

Time. Time and energy. Brand didn't mind. He had to do this, had to protect the first pregnant male baboon.

The two cages sat on wooden frames over large trays. The removable trays would enable him to clean out the waste materials that fell through the perforated floor. Because the cages were light, weighing no more than 20 or 25 pounds, Brand had collected some bricks--weights that he could place on each cage to anchor it. Without the weights, Terry might overturn his cage and hurtle around the garage, ramming cabinets and lab equipment, a projectile powered by immense strength.

He pulled into the garage. All quiet. Terry was invisible, anesthetized, silent, in the trunk. But Brand didn't want to meet any inquisitive neighbors.

He closed the garage door and inspected his equipment. While he was checking, Michelle appeared.

"The girls were asking where you went," she said. "I told them you had to go back to the hospital."

"How right that answer was." He kissed her lightly. "A beauty, isn't he?" He pointed to the back end of the car. "Take a look."

Wrapped in a housecoat, she shook her head. She shivered. "I can't look," she said. "I think you should take him back."

"Take him back? My God! I just got him here."

They stared at each other.

"Em," she said. "It's too dangerous. That animal could kill someone. One of the girls. A neighbor child. Then you--we--will be responsible."

"I'm keeping him locked up. He'll never leave that cage." He went to the back of the car, opened the trunk. The cage door stood open. He was about to lift Terry out when Michelle said:

"He's going to drive us apart. I'm telling you tonight: This goes beyond the call of duty, of everything. For both you and me."

"Why are you worrying? I've got it under control." He heard the tension in his own voice. Lifting Terry, Brand laid the animal in the open cage. The wiry fur brushed his hands, his wrists. *An animal shall lead us.* "This cage will be permanently locked," he said, "and weighted." He turned; Michelle had left.

Closing and locking the door of the cage, Brand tested the brick weights, placing them carefully on the cage roof, centered, so that their weight would have the greatest effect. In the morning he introduced the girls to Terry. Their eyes opened wide. "A monkey," Joanie said.

"A baboon," Brand corrected. "A kind of monkey, yes."

"Will it live here?"

"Yes, but just for a while." He knelt down next to his daughters.

"He's our houseguest for a few days, Joanie, Moke," he said. "You may have to help me to take care of him. But only when I'm here."

"Yes, Daddy." Joanie was staring in fascination. Her curiosity might have been mixed with awe--or fear.

"He won't be able to have visitors," Brand said. "He likes to live alone. A man is going to help me feed him and keep his house clean." Brand was watching his daughters. Joanie seemed apprehensive.

"Can't Katie come and see him?" Moke said.

"Well, we might be able to arrange that." Brand considered. "Sometime. But let's talk about it later. I'm going to be working with him some evenings anyway. If we can get Katie in to see him, we will. But not yet."

The girl seemed satisfied. She touched the bar of the cage. Baboon Terry watched her silently, fully awake, and Joanie drew back. "Not like that," Brand said. "You have to stay away from him." He stood up. "Time to go," he said. "By the way, his name is Terry. Baboon Terry."

They went out, cage locked, garage door locked. A night-light on in the garage, permanently.

"It's all over the neighborhood once Joanie knows," Michelle said in the kitchen. "Old blabbermouth. What do you do when the neighbors start beating our doors down?"

The new Michelle was speaking. Defiant Michelle. Unreachable Michelle. At least she was talking.

20

The garage had just space for the two stalls. The one on the south side had once been the repository of diverse Lares and Penates: storage for ice skates, unused furniture, some clothes for rough wear, extra tubular aluminum chairs, tools, a lawn mower, other things. Now, cleared to accommodate the cage, table, cabinet, makeshift sink, and elementary lab equipment, the south stall had the look of a primitive laboratory.

Terry completed the picture. Brand had had the two south side windows covered by plywood squares, so that Terry lived in a perpetual dusk. *As in the Zoo,* Brand thought. *We have to hide these animals, but why? To keep people from thinking of what we do with them?* That was a consideration worthy of Vandorn.

Whatever the time of day or night, Terry always seemed alert, wakeful. Brand went to see him evenings and mornings. The eyes never failed to glow in that half-light that contrasted so starkly with the brightness of the north side.

At least Brand had help. Tyler, Fenton's helper, came over daily to clean up, leave food. Each time, finishing his work, he left with a plastic bag of waste materials: scraps of food, body waste, dirt swept off the floor. The minizoo remained clean, but the smell of baboon pervaded the entire garage. Paraphrasing his father, now deceased, who had described offensive smells with the phrase, sweet essence of cesspool, Brand thought of the minizoo odor as *sweet essence of baboon.*

The girls remained curious, Michelle difficult to reach. A few days passed, and she seemed to relax somewhat. She had been talking to her mother, Brand knew. But what they discussed he could only guess at.

He combed his mind for ways to bring her back into his orbit, largely because he needed and loved her; also, he hated close-range strife or disagreement. It ruffled the waters. But the path back to her love and their old intimacies seemed overgrown. You couldn't hack your way through the jungle growths.

They spoke mostly in monosyllables. They spoke when the girls were present. Most nights, pressed by work, Brand slept on the couch in the living room. Their common bed had grown cold, unwelcoming.

He let slide many things that once occupied moments of his life. The softball team with which he had played for six summers wanted him to come out for practice. He apologized and said, "Not this year. No time." Two articles that he had been working on sat unfinished in a drawer in his study. He gave up on a book discussion group-- "Temporarily."

He felt himself turning somehow grey, like a frog kept in the dark, away from sunlight.

He had a date for the TV debate with Vandorn: June 28. Always, whatever occupied his surface attention, he planned for that day, tried to devise answers, approaches. He had decided to keep his side of the debate light, humorous where possible. He would be addressing Dr. Schofield as much as professor Vandorn. . .

If you're not going to accept scientific progress in one area, you have to be logical and reject it elsewhere. You can't reject experimentation with the building blocks of life and accept VCR's.

The only way to advance is to welcome the competition of ideas, of new things.

He appended a note to these lunchtime reflections: *Lighten it.*

Madsen's clinic. *Obstetricians and Gynecologists* on the door. Light always glowing warmly, welcomingly, behind the door.

Brand, in street clothes, said to Laura Phillips: "Dr. Madsen and I wanted to go over some additional details. You may have heard some of this, but you may also have some questions. He'd also like to start your tests."

She nodded. She had come to Madsen's clinic alone. The lab door opened. Entering, Madsen said, "Em tells me we've narrowed the field of candidates for egg donation to four. I believe he gave you the rubrics we--or he--applied in making these selections?"

"He did." She glanced at Brand. "I understand that part very thoroughly. I'm curious to know whether Susie Thatcher is one of the final four."

Brand said: "Susie is. You could select her as the donor without offending anyone at all. You can take these four applications with you when you leave if you like."

"Will the donor be anonymous?"

"Totally, if she wants to be."

"I only ask because Susie works, as you know, in Dr. Schofield's office. Would she have to take much time off? It might be hard to explain."

Madsen answered for Brand. "I doubt that she'd have to take more than an hour or two off from work. That would be at the beginning, for some tests. After that, we could do everything in the evening. We have evening hours."

"Can I talk to Susie and let you know how it looks?"

"Of course," Madsen said. "You're not under any pressure at all. We do have to synchronize your ovulation times, and would like to get started on that. That's our main consideration right now. Also, we'll run some routine tests. May I take a blood sample?"

"Of course." She watched while he prepared the syringe, then her arm. She twitched almost imperceptibly as the needle went in. "It'll sting only a few minutes," Madsen said.

"It never fails to make me wince." She watched the syringe filling up. "Can you explain synchronization to me?"

Brand watched Laura as Madsen explained. They were sitting in an office-examining room, Madsen at a small desk, half-turned to face Brand and Laura. Laura sat in a chair with arms, a captain's chair, Brand in a folding chair. A padded examining table ran obliquely out of a far corner. A wall cabinet with a glass front held hospital supplies; a standing low cabinet was crammed with books. There was nothing else.

"We'll need to know about your cycles," Madsen picked up. "Are they regular?" She was nodding without answering. "We'll have to do a hormonal evaluation. That's one visit to the hospital, brief." Madsen was watching the syringe, drawing slowly on the plunger. "We want also to do a chromosome analysis--both you and the donor. That tells us whether any dangerous defects are present."

"Huntington's?"

"No. Not that. Fractured chromosomes, other signs of potential problems. Since I'm a perfectionist, we'll test your uric acid level. You'll be the carrier. It'll be a lot easier and safer if we have the entire picture in advance."

He paused. He was speaking softly. His manner now belied the general impression he gave, Brand thought. You would have expected him to be overbearing, Jovelike with that head of hair and that mien. He wore a white hospital gown.

"We will synchronize to reduce the possibility of error." Madsen glanced at Brand, as if for confirmation. "If you had a uterus and we were doing an embryo implant, both your uterus and that of the donor would have to be synchronized as closely as possible. That's because the hormonal environment and the--let's call it the nutritional-- environment have to be the same in donor and recipient."

Madsen drew a breath. Gently but quickly he withdrew the needle, swabbed the tiny wound. "Changes take place during the cycle, as you probably know. In synchronizing we match the cycles. The first day of ovulation is, say, Day 0. If we take a five-day old egg, counting from Day 0, then we would have to transfer that egg into a uterus that's also at Day 5. That means five days after ovulation."

"But since I have no uterus?"

"It may or may not be academic. But we're convinced that it will be important to synchronize anyway. Typically, you would ovulate on the 14th day of your monthly cycle--counting from the first day of bleeding." Madsen took a pencil from a breast pocket and made a note, drew a design.

"I hope this isn't confusing. We have two different series of days here, as you can see from this diagram. The first day of bleeding starts one cycle--the monthly. The first day of ovulation, which we call Day 0, starts what is for our purposes a more important phase. This is the ovulation phase."

Madsen wrote quickly on a tiny label. Finishing, he pasted the label on the syringe, laid the blood-filled container on a sheet of paper.

"Since you don't have a uterus, you don't bleed. Special category. I'm a detail man, so I'd want to synchronize you artificially. We'd use estrogen for fourteen days and then progesterone and estrogen for fourteen days. At the end of the first fourteen-day cycle, you would be at the point of ovulation--theoretically. We would want the donor to be at the actual point of ovulation."

"You inseminate the donor at that time?"

"Yes. We have two ways to go there. Artificial insemination--with sperm injected into the donor by catheter--or in vitro insemination. In this one, the 'test-tube baby' way, we remove an egg and inseminate it in a petri dish."

"Which way is better?"

"I'd opt for the AI--the in vivo insemination technique. Injection of sperm into the living, breathing donor. I don't like to cut nature out any more than is necessary. If we find a healthy embryo in the donor, we'll transfer it to you within five to ten hours. We think you'll then, with some help, supply the hormones, nutritional elements, all the things that go into the embryo's support system."

"Susie, apparently, would be a different problem."

"If it's Susie, yes. But we expect no difficulty there, except perhaps in the matter of time. We would try one month and then know in a couple of weeks or so whether it took. Then if we failed, we'd try again after Susie again reaches Day 0. You've got me saying Susie. But we do have four very qualified donors."

Madsen glanced at his watch. As if in confirmation, a nurse leaned in through the open door. "Dr. Madsen?" she said, questioning. "Mrs. Brannigan is here."

"Could you tell her I'll be right there?" He turned to Laura. "You know how Em and I are going to divide the labor?"

"Yes, Dr. Brand has told me."

"I'll run." He took Laura's hand. "You're going to make history," he said. "You'll be written up in all the big medical journals."

"I'm not sure I care about that. Which reminds me--if Tim and I decide to keep it secret, or at least quiet, would that be possible? I know I'm sounding paranoid about this--asking endless questions, but I am curious."

"You can keep it as secret as you want to. And you should know the details. But at some date in the future Em may want to publish something on it. Em? What do you think?"

"The findings will be invaluable," Brand said. "But no, we wouldn't have to publish right away. Or ever."

Madsen left, the limp obvious as he left the room. "Any other questions, Laura?" Brand said. "And can we make it Em and Laura? Why stand on formality?"

"Em it is."

He drove her home and went on to work. The detour was minor, hardly a bend from his normal route back to the university. They talked more about the embryonation.

"You'd be able to brief Susie, I hope," Laura said. "If it's Susie." He could sense her smiling at the imitation of Madsen.

"I'd have to. I can do that without Madsen. We can then put her-- whoever it is--in Madsen's hands for the progesterone shots. He would be in charge of that."

"I have the feeling that he's magnificently competent."

"And I'm not?"

"Oh, Em, stop. You're the one on whom I'm depending."

She spoke with vehemence. They rode in silence a while.

"I'd have one concern about Susie," Brand said, "and it has nothing to do with her qualifications."

"I'd like to hear it."

"Normally the donor and recipient in these cases, as I understand it, would be strangers. The donor would be completely anonymous."

"It's something to consider. But I really feel Susie is something special. Honest, smart, you know?"

Brand nodded. As he pulled up in front of her house, she leaned over and kissed him. Her hand flicked across the back of his neck. Then she was gone.

21

It was a new sign. It read *For Admission to the Animal Facility Call 2423.*

Dressed in the lab-coat uniform of the Zoo, Vandorn studied the sign. *They were taking precautions.* He tried the door leading down to the subbasement; it gave, opened with a liquid tumbling of inner gears. He walked down, down. On the way he took out the mask that he had worn before.

"Can I help you?" The voice came from just inside the entrance to the Zoo. A young man's voice. Vandorn slowed, said: "I just wanted to see the baboon room again. I've been here before with Mr. Fenton. He said I could come back any time."

"That's okay. He just wants me to go around with anyone who comes in."

Be definite, wear the right clothes, look a part, and you could probably pick the locks at the Pentagon. Vandorn said: "Just the baboons. They're a special interest of mine."

They turned into the baboon room.

"Are they here all the time?" Vandorn had started to count the animals, making a ritual of it; some of them had apparently just awakened and were now prowling restlessly back and forth. All of them were emitting short, sharp, nervous barks. The sounds grated; some primordial fear seemed to inspire them. *Did they remember him?* He had counted nineteen baboons.

"They're most always here," the man said. "But one died. One's out for observation or something." The young man had a soft chin and the air of a person who respected authority, even feigned authority. "Some of them go up to the lab--through there." He pointed to the entrance to the connecting underground tunnel leading to the lab building.

"What's in there?"

"A kind of operating room. Table, cupboard, that kind of thing. We don't mess much with that room."

"It belongs to someone else?"

"Dr. Brand uses it mostly." The man had a slight speech defect that appeared in his s's. "Uses" came out almost as utheth," but not quite. It was not a lisp, more a sibilance. "He takes care of it. Cleans it up himself except when there's something special going on."

Avoiding the baboon dung, Vandorn walked along the cages. The man followed. The cages were not all full--again; the room could have accommodated as many as 30 animals. The baboons that occupied nineteen of the cages were scattered about, one here, one there. "These are ident numbers?" Vandorn asked. He pointed to a number on a cage.

"Oh yeah," the man said. "But they all have names. This one is Della." He grinned, showing gaps in his lower teeth. "Dr. Brand has something going with her. I mean she's in one of his experiments right now."

Vandorn came close. Della sat just behind the bars at the front of the cage. Her great eyes rolled. She was examining everything but Vandorn, yet she seemed to be totally aware of his presence. Vandorn had an uneasy feeling. *Brand's animals: Danger. How much can they sense? Understand?* "What's going on with Della?" he said.

"Oh, he's got her knocked up, I think. Look at her, bloating up already. Got her head in a bowl, just like my old lady always did." The man grinned again, ingenuously. He leaned close to the cage and tried to look Della in the eyes. The baboon only flicked a glance over him, restlessly; then she picked up a stalk of something that looked like celery and began to chew on it.

Della looked like the rest of the baboons. *No swelling that I can see,* Vandorn thought. "Has Dr. Brand been working on her recently?" he asked offhandedly.

"Oh, he's always down here. Days, nights. He's going to work himself to death, if you ask me. Always got those projects going. He's even got one at home right now."

"At home? What's that for?" Vandorn said. "Aren't they supposed to be kept on the premises? Or in the lab?"

"Yes, but you know how it is. Dr. Brand has privileges. They let him pretty much have the run of the place. He works on hormones, things like that. Some others use the baboons, but not near as much as Dr. Brand. He takes them out for a day or two or maybe a week at a time."

"And then brings them back?"

"Yes. He's had other animals out before."

"Do other people do that?"

"Yes. But not like Dr. Brand. It's slightly illegal. He's got to observe them or something." The man had moved away from Della's cage and was walking down the row, looking in where cages were occupied. "We've got a lot of males here right now," he said. "We usually have mostly females."

"What's the reason for having males?"

"Don't know. Brand's experiment, I guess."

Vandorn had started back toward the door. The feces on the floor looked like brown, dried blocks of some kind of breakfast cereal. Vandorn said: "How do these waste materials get on the floor?"

"Oh, the animals throw them there. They've got all kinds of ways to get at their own turds. Then they just toss them out. They find ways to unlock these--" The man pointed to two latches that were attached at the bases of the cages to hold in the waste pans. "--And then they just slide the pans out. You've got a holy mess in the morning. It's really clean right now. But I'll be sweeping up in a few minutes." He looked at his watch.

"I don't think I'll wait." Vandorn moved toward the door. He had learned what he wanted to know. But two men were entering. Both were tall, so big that each seemed to fill the doorway.

"Can I help you?" The man who spoke wore a white lab coat. He had a carefully trimmed mustache.

"I was just passing through," Vandorn said. "I couldn't find Mr. Fenton, so I thought I'd see if I could take another tour of the place."

"Do you work here?"

"Yes--at the University. But I've been visiting some of the labs, some departments."

"Well, our phone number is on the sign outside, in the hallway. You can feel free to come any time with Mr. Fenton's approval. If you could call first. . ."

The men were moving to other rooms. One of them had merely studied Vandorn, and had not spoken a word. Vandorn went out after them, forgetting the attendant. When he reached the first floor, he took off the mask and put it in his pocket.

Dr. Marvin Levenson kept a low profile, but sometimes he felt constrained to raise his balding head. As Deputy Hospital Administrator, he had more duties than the vice president of the United States; but not many more. He liked it that way. He was loyal to Schofield, and represented him honestly at all times: a team-player. But he was waiting for Schofield to trip on something.

Facing Schofield across the Administrator's desk, Levenson said: "We had a visitor in the Zoo today. I haven't yet found Fenton, but I'd guess it was unauthorized. I ran into him accidentally."

"Got a name?"

"Tyler said it was 'Vandore or something like that.' Called himself a doctor."

"Vandorn is the name. Dark, bullet-headed, cropped hair?"

"That's the one."

Schofield got up. He wore a suitcoat that could not hide a bulge at his midriff. "That man's got more nerve than a snake-oil salesman. Can you talk to Fenton? We may have to keep the Zoo door closed day as well as night--inconvenient though it would be."

"I'll check it out daily for a while. We've got too much invested down there to take any chances."

"You may want to establish some rules for the researchers using those animals. Maybe a reporting form or something so we'll have a daily check on all traffic."

"How about Brand?"

"We couldn't possibly make any exceptions."

22

The message from TV Station WNAV--"WORLD NEWS AND VIEWS"--arrived while Brand was making his morning rounds of the zoo. Playing the message off the recording device, Brand recognized the always modulated voice of George Broward, officially the WNAV station manager.

"Three days!" Broward said as recorded. "We're counting on seeing you and Dr. Vandorn this Friday, 10 a.m., Studio A. Give me a call?"

One more small chore, Brand thought, with a large chore as anchor. He had been reading and making notes in preparation for the "Genetics Debate," but had miles to go. At the least he needed to complete what he thought of as an essential keyword list. As an informal aide-memoire, a list would clue him to subject areas that should be parts of his presentation.

He was carrying the half-done list in his pocket Engagements book. Consulting the notes quickly, he ran his mind over both the items he had written and the things he still had to do before Friday. Realizing that some plans would have to be put off, he began to feel like a man gasping for air.

What would he jettison? He had already reduced his home-life participation to the irreducible minimum of time--except now and then on weekends. There was also Laura Phillips. He would see her at Dr. Madsen's this morning. With good fortune and some dazzling footwork, he might be able at last to pass her off to the gynie.

Much as Brand feared that Michelle might act to escape the hovering shadow of Baboon Terry, he harbored equivalent but different misgivings regarding Laura. The feeling that her faith in his judgment had become dependence had grown. He could recall only minute signs or signals that that was the case, but intuition, his pulsar monitor, was rarely wrong.

The rest of his agenda, Brand believed, would be manageable. He had all the baboons clearly catalogued according to the stage each occupied. He and Madsen were up to date, or would be once they had consulted with Laura regarding her next stage.

He was mentally allotting time for further prepping for the Debate when the phone rang. It was Alan Archer, editor of the newspaper *Gay Times*. He wanted to know whether Brand might visit the newspaper office and explain his "Mister Mommy" project.

Calculating quickly, Brand decided that he could go today. It would be two, two and one-half hours before he could get there.

As he hung up, Brand saw his day taking convenient shape. He could spend an hour with Dr. Madsen and Laura. He could use his appointment with Archer as the crowbar that would pry him free to leave Madsen's office.

Laura, Brand, and Dr. Madsen had hardly made themselves comfortable when Susie Thatcher arrived. For the first time Brand could observe her at close range. A strongly built young woman, she had an open manner and a smile that made the skin around her eyes crinkle. Brand knew her history from studying the questionnaire she had given him. She had musical talent, having studied the harpsichord for years. She had taken a bachelor of science in music degree.

Working as Dr. Schofield's secretary, Susie was working toward a master's degree in business administration. She was also studying hospital administration.

Susie had brought some of the forms that Brand had given her. She had questions about them, and Brand answered them. "They're legal things--releases," he said, "simple documents that you'll want to keep in copy form."

Susie nodded, then asked whether Brand could outline what she would be expected to do.

Brand took out a pencil, started making notes. The researcher's addiction, he thought: the occupational hazard of making notes. But he finished in slightly over a minute. Susie read what he had written:

1. Medical checkup (Madsen or family doctor)
2. Synchronize donor, recipient. Progesterone. (Madsen)
3. Start taking eggs; in vitro fertilization (IVF) (Madsen, Brand)
4. Embryonation within two to three days after fertilization (Madsen)
5. If first effort to implant fails, try again following month (Madsen)

The list resembled the one Brand had given Laura weeks ago. But this one was much simpler. The donor clearly had a minor role compared to that of the recipient.

"Is any of this--painful?" Susie asked.

"No. This is a prime concern, at least for me. It might be a little uncomfortable for you, for example when we flush out an egg. That would be about the only possible problem you'd face. And it's minor. A ten-minute procedure. If you ovulate on the 14th day, we'd try to flush out the egg on the 18th day. If that doesn't work we'd flush again on the 19th day. And again on the 20th if necessary. There are ways-- hormones--to increase the number of eggs you produce, but we don't think they'll be needed. If you tell us it's a wise precaution, we'd put some embryocidal agents inside you after the last try--on the 20th day."

"When would it be a wise precaution?"

"If there's a chance that you could get pregnant before we could flush again, about three and a half weeks later. The agents would kill the ovum."

Susie reddened. "There wouldn't be any need for that, Dr. Brand. I'm going to get married in a year or so--but, well, we're waiting. Old-fashioned, isn't it?"

"It's perfect for Laura's and our purposes," Brand said. He looked at his watch. "Time for me to cut out," he said. "I have another appointment. And Dr. Madsen knows more about this than I do."

Susie leaned forward in her chair as if she wanted to say something. But Brand was already on the way toward the door.

They sat around a table sipping coffee. Archer had poured some for Brand, who was letting it grow cold. In addition to Editor Archer, the group included reporter Brian Tarkington and a lawyer named John Quarles.

"We're interested in your project if we're understanding it," Archer said. "John here is going to keep us whole. He's also going to have some questions."

"What can I tell you?" Brand spread his fingers on the edge of the table. "I'm at your service."

"And we may be at yours," Archer said, smiling and touching the pearl that lay firmly affixed to his right ear. "Extrapolating from your note, we've figured out that you're planning on having a human male carry a baby to term and deliver it."

"Correct," Brand said. "I'm double-talking my way into the project to avoid problems in this preliminary stage. I'm busy professionally with genetic research, but this would be totally extracurricular. If we can work together, you and your paper would be under similar strictures, a sort of news blackout. That would be the case until we've actually achieved delivery stage. And probably later."

"Fascinating," Archer said. "Mind-boggling." He glanced at the other two men. "Am I right, gentlemen?"

Both nodded. "I'd have a few hundred questions," Quarles said. "But I'm sure you're prepared for that."

"Totally." Brand was about to continue when Tarkington spoke. "What a story," he said. "And we'd have it exclusive."

"You would want to hold on the publicity until we're sure that the candidate--the pregnant man--and the fetus are doing well. And thinking this over, we might decide on a permanent blackout."

"No problem." Archer was decisive. "You'd presumably give us regular reports."

"I would. I'd present the whole project as a genetic experiment."

The subject of strategies occupied more than a half-hour. But consensus and agreement seemed to pass like natural mileposts. *Gay Times* would conduct a carefully veiled search for a "candidate" to become the first-ever human male to bear and deliver a child. His role would have any limits that he wished to specify insofar as responsibility for the offspring was concerned; but *some* provisions for parenting once the birth was achieved would be a primary concern. Such post-natal upbringing would, of necessity, be arranged before embryonation occurred.

Lawyer Quarles agreed to research the legal status and the civil rights of the future neonate.

More coffee went around. This time Brand merely held a polite hand over his cup. Archer was talking: "I guess we're wondering why this hasn't been done before," he said. "This trick of having a male take the role of a mother."

"I don't know," Brand said. "It may only be that the technology and the interest and the candidate for embryonation haven't come together at one time in one place. I have a feeling it's as simple as that. The interest may be the key factor."

"Is your technology unique?" Quarles said.

"No. Everyone in embryology and most people in gynecology and related fields could devise it. I've developed some equipment that no one else may have. But that's not a world-shaking departure."

"What's the equipment?"

"For this project, a special kind of laparoscope." Brand pulled a pen from his shirt pocket. He had half a dozen writing utensils ready for instant use. "Can I draw you a picture?"

"It would help," Archer said. He shoved a ruled pad toward Brand. Standing up and leaning over, Brand drew the outline of a human stomach, including the navel. Alongside it he drew a diagram of the laparoscope.

"You can see that this instrument has three sections. You'd start with a local anesthetic. We'd make a small surgical incision here, just below the navel, then use this lap to implant an embryo. It's almost as simple as that. You flush the embryo into the omentum, the fleshy part of the stomach, by pressing this plunger. Some special fluid would go in with the embryo to give it a start."

"When would you know it worked?"

"In less than three weeks. You might know sooner if--as we expect--blood changes take place as soon as implantation is effective. After that, it's a matter of monitoring closely, imitating the female body chemistry, that kind of thing."

A tall, cadaverous but strong-looking man, Tarkington had greeted Brand with a vice-like handshake. Now he said: "Would the--subject--

undergo a voice change, grow tits, anything like that?" He was smiling but serious.

"It could happen," Brand said. "But I doubt that that kind of phenomenon would be irreversible."

"Only during the pregnancy?"

"Yes. Presumably. We're working with male baboons now and should have a lot of answers to questions like that in a few weeks or months."

"Ah," Quarles said, "you will have done it with an animal first."

"Yes. Animals, plural. Hopefully, several of them."

Brand sat down. His diagram lay in the middle of the oblong table.

Quarles had a sheet of paper in front of him. He glanced at it and cleared his throat. "I'm less interested in the technique," he said, "than in possible fallout from this project." His hands encircled the sheet protectively. "For example, is it hazardous for the subject--can you tell at this stage?"

"I frankly doubt it. If it were, I don't think I'd consider it."

"The male stomach isn't built to carry a foetus."

"I know. Some females aren't perfectly adapted to child-bearing either. They wear special supports, special clothing. They take medications to reduce pain and discomfort. You'll never get rid of those things entirely, but you can certainly minimize them."

"You'd obviously have signed releases, that kind of thing."

"Necessarily."

"Even more important, I can see big promotional possibilities in this. The first man to bear a child!" His eyes flared. He looked around the group. For the first time Brand had a negative feeling about the lawyer. *Mercenary*, he thought. "It would be worth book rights, TV rights, movie rights," Quarles continued. "Bigbuck Alley. The first carrier--what would you call him, Dr. Brand?"

"I hadn't thought of it. Probably a surrogate male mother. A woman who carries without contributing an egg is usually called a substitute uterine carrier."

"It sounds right. SMM. SUC for the female." Without moving his head, he glanced sideways at Archer. Both laughed. Brand and

Tarkington smiled. "The question is," Quarles said, "how would you want to distribute the spoils?"

"I haven't really thought of it in commercial terms. I know I'm going to run into some expenses, particularly if we have to use hospital facilities. And I'm facing expenses now, with the preliminary experimentation. If I could cover those--."

As if he hadn't been listening, Quarles said: "Who will be involved? You. Who else? Directly involved, I mean. Principals."

"A medical doctor. He'd do the medical procedures, the monitoring, that kind of thing. The subject, obviously. The paper, as discoverer of the candidate. That might be it." He paused. "But again, secrecy will be advisable."

Ignoring Brand, Quarles said, "And me as the agent for all of you. Can I take a whack at a contract, assuming that this search will succeed? There could be millions involved here. You, Dr. Brand, should be thinking long."

"I have to think safe first."

They talked longer, then Brand left. Quarles and the other two men were still talking animatedly when Brand reached the landing halfway down to the street. He could hear their voices.

The commercial part went against Brand's grain. But you did have to be practical. A contract might, after all, be a good legal cover: a protection against later misunderstandings.

Quarles had not mentioned the possibility of community resistance, of violence. For Archer and his staff that question might be academic in view of the publicity that the gay community could receive later. And none of them, obviously, had met Vandorn.

23

Debate day!

The audience parading to the 60-plus seats available as part of Studio A seemed pretty well divided between men and women. Watching from the offstage side of the set, Brand saw a relatively well dressed group that would very likely have thoughts of its own on the subject of the debate.

What thoughts? Would they be pro-lifers? "Well dressed" might mean "opposed to divorce, abortion, federal intervention on behalf of mere citizens in any way."

Would they deny the possibility that any child conceived through artificial insemination could be anything but a psychological eunuch?

Brand stood in a maze of cables. A few feet away, the cameras loomed like great skinny-legged birds. They were already focused, it seemed, on the set, a simple coffee table plus three chairs. Backgrounding it all was a blue banner with the name of the show in huge letters: "MIKE RAGALO ON CAMERA."

Brand felt in his shirt pocket. He had not forgotten the scattered notes that would guide him through the high points. But beyond the initial five-minute presentation he would be largely flying on instruments, meaning memory.

Ragalo tapped him on the shoulder. The TV host said, "We're just about ready. We're going to shut the door in a couple of minutes. You ready to go first?"

"Of course. I'm nervous as a whore in church, but I'm ready. I've done TV once before."

"Great. You remember the format? Opening statement, five minutes. Questions from the audience, alternating between you and Dr. Vandorn. Finally, questions by phone, again alternating between you and Dr. Vandorn. Two minutes the limit on all answers in the studio portion. Two minutes for answers in the final segment."

"Got it."

Ragalo stepped out on the set. First waving to the audience behind the huge glass window, he set some papers on the coffee table and rearranged the chairs.

Watching, Brand thought of the question at issue: "Is genetic experimentation justified on moral, ethical, humanitarian, or scientific grounds?" He, Brand, had insisted on insertion of the word *humanitarian*. Vandorn had objected at first, then had surrendered--with ill grace. "It's not that important," Vandorn had snorted. Then he had suggested a subtitle: "Pros and cons of the reproduction revolution."

It was Brand's turn to capitulate.

Brand saw Laura and Tim Phillips enter the studio and take two rear seats, almost the only ones remaining. They had entered just before the public entrance closed, just before a light went on over that door.

Suddenly a red light was flashing, on-off-on-off, on one side of the studio. Brand could now see Laura, in the back row of seats, directing a tiny finger-wave toward him. *She said she was going to come and watch this*, Brand thought, *if she could break Tim out of the work cycle*. Her presence gave him secret satisfaction. He would have support from one quarter, no matter what the rest of the audience believed. Michelle would be watching with her mother.

Ragalo was standing at the coffee table. "We're ready to go," he was saying to one of the cameramen. Brand could hear the words clearly. The cameras that had been standing alone and unattended a few moments ago now had escorts. A microphone hanging above the coffee table was bouncing up and down as someone adjusted it from somewhere.

Brand walked over and sat down in the right-hand chair. *For luck. Stay on the host's right*, Michelle had said. Brand had taken that right-hand seat at their one brief rehearsal and no one had questioned it.

Now he took it as if it belonged to him by right. Vandorn had entered, looking dark and dapper, and sat at Ragalo's left.

They were calling for silence. From the rear, someone counted down from 30. As he reached the end of the count--"Three, two, one!"--a man standing in front of the cameras pointed at Ragalo and immediately stepped back behind the cameras. The lights blazed. Ragalo began to talk.

Afterward Brand could not reconstruct details. Its outlines became blurred, all but the grand finale.

It started quietly, decorously. Ragalo gave a pleasantly smooth and innocuous introduction, stating both premises, naming the participants, having them shake hands, and ending on a light note. "But I know you're not visiting with us to listen to me. May I give the floor to Dr. Emlyn Brand of University Hospital? Dr. Brand will have five minutes to present his side of the issue."

Brand began, his notes lying in front of him, a comforting source of guidance. He hardly referred to them, as it turned out. "I'd like to scotch one rumor at the start," he said. "I'm pro-life. I have to work in a lab to make a living. But that doesn't dehumanize me. I believe in people, in families. I like my job. I eat food with a fork. My own family is the world to me.

"But I want you to think of this. Many people among us want to have families and can't. They can't for one reason or another. You know some of the medical or health reasons. They exist on both sides of the sexual divide. There are psychological reasons as well, equally serious reasons or bundles of rationales. One person may not want to pass on an unfortunate set of genes; another may decide that he or she cannot take the time required to bear a child--and may still want parenthood.

"Science has in this nineties decade begun to help these people. The woman who cannot conceive naturally can now conceive with laboratory help. In dozens of other types of cases help can now be provided. Yes, we will soon be able to develop human life, at least to a certain point, in a contrived environment.

"Look now at the question we have come to discuss. It touches on four aspects of genetic experimentation. From a moral point of view, can we deny to people the help that science is able to provide? From an ethical point of view, are we overstepping the bounds of the appropriate or the ethical if we give such help? I believe the reverse is true: ethically, we cannot terminate our experience or our experiments. We cannot withhold the fruits of those experiments if people need them. If they do not need them, they will not be used.

"The humanitarian aspect should need no illumination. Science can and should have a goal, or set of goals, that relates to the improvement of human life--of the quality of life, of the pursuit of life and of worthwhile human and social goals. One of those goals today can be the enrichment, the unique fulfillment that comes when a union of two becomes a family of three--or more."

Brand became aware that Ragalo was signaling him. His five minutes were ending. "From the science point of view, it's as simple as this: science cannot be neutral and it cannot be stopped. If we do not experiment, learn to control our environment, learn to help people in new ways and make sure that science retains its humanitarian content, someone else will do it and use it to move beyond us. Non-experimentation is ignorance, and today ignorance is self-destructive.

"Let me only add this: When you feel like condemning scientific experiments and solutions, think of how many other ways we already use them. We operate on cancer victims. We implant hearts. We put newborn babies into incubators if they do not appear to be viable on their own."

Vandorn was glib. Brand had to admit it. He came on powerfully. He might have been an old-time evangelist hurling thunderbolts at the devil. A listener wouldn't even realize at first that he was consumed by an all-devouring righteousness. He had The Word.

"I'm reminded," he began, "of the saying that used to be current about patriotism. You know: More crimes are committed in the name of patriotism . . . and so on. Can we change that word to humanitarianism? To science?

"We are talking about human life. That, I believe, is Number One. We're not talking about cattle or beetles or mice. We're talking about human life and the responsibility we have with regard to it. The *responsibilities*. As members of a society that is supposedly built on Judeo-Christian principles, our task here is very clear. We have to value and protect human life or we are denying the most basic precepts in our belief system. We are denying our heritage.

"I won't go into the cases that prove you can't make such a denial and retain the designation *civilized*. In the lifetime of a lot of people here in this studio, and of a lot of persons listening, we've had examples galore. The Nazis, for one. The communists, for another, in many of their incarnations.

"I would, however, like to talk about human life. You all know what happens in genetic experiments. You take a human embryo. You prepare it *in vitro*, in a dish, or you take it out of its natural environment, a mother's womb. What happens? As often as not, it dies. I would venture to say--and I think Dr. Brand would agree with me--that the embryo dies in the laboratory many more times than it survives.

"Think about that for a second. You have a human being in that tiny set of cells. You have a Michelangelo or a Shakespeare or an Albert Schweitzer. You have a human being, all programmed and ready to enter life. Do you really have the right to tinker with it?

"Think of where all this can lead. To cloning, where you may produce a monstrosity. Do you just kill it off and start again? Who says you are going to succeed in producing a musical genius every time? You may go farther. You may get into other things: as you lose respect for life, why not move into all the other things? Abortion? Why not euthanasia? Why not experiments on living subjects? After all, if they're just samples, to be dealt with as the science buffs would have it, they too can be the subjects of experimentation."

Vandorn took a sip of water, pausing briefly.

"I would appreciate it if you would take this thought away with you. Hug it close as we go on with this conversation: This is not purely a scientific problem. Nor is it exclusively a moral or ethical one. In no way is it a humanitarian one. It is a question of systems, ethical and moral, and of the directions in which society is to go: toward dehumanization or toward ennoblement. Science, sad to say, has no conscience. We cannot play God with human life or we are asking for a breakdown in all the values that we consider important.

"We are asking for--and justifying in advance--any and every state-controlled intervention in the role of the family. We are justifying cloning, genetic manipulation, xeroxing life and throwing away the bad copies. We are asking for dehumanization of our portion of the human race. We may be throwing away our greatest gift."

Ragalo was looking again at his watch, then at the studio clock. He had a finger poised.

"No one," Vandorn said, "denies that a child may be the fulfillment of a married couple's dream, a chance to reach toward immortality. But nature should be our path to redemption, not a soulless test-tube creature. Nature may receive aid, certainly, from medical people of one kind or another, of one specialty or another. But adoption has provided the solution for millions. Many others, facing infertility, have built careers working with children and in that way found their ideal."

Ragalo had raised his finger, and Vandorn stopped. "We have a minute to catch our collective breath after a wonderful beginning," Ragalo said. "In the meantime put on your thinking caps. The first question will go to Dr. Brand, and he will have two minutes to respond."

Brand heard some station-break filler music. It continued for perhaps half a minute, and Ragalo was talking again. "I see a hand in the second row already," he said. "May we hear the first question?"

A woman stood up. Tall and thin, she spoke as if she were making an accusation. "A lot of this seems to have to do with infertility," she said. "And the blame seems to fall mostly on women. My question to Dr. Brand would be, Is the male or the female more to blame in such cases? It always seems that the wife is barren, never the husband."

"It does seem that way," Brand began. "But I think the language is at fault. I'm not a gynecologist, but my researches would seem to indicate that the fault--if there is any fault--might lie on either husband or wife, or both, in any given case. In other words, it would be, in my opinion, a statistical standoff. I'm speaking, of course, of the physical causes of infertility."

Ragalo spoke as Brand nodded, indicating that he was finished. "Dr. Vandorn?" Ragalo said. "You have a minute if you care to respond."

"I'd only like to say, or hear Dr. Brand say it, that he brings technology to all these problems. Got an empty crib? He and his colleagues can fill it for you. All it takes is a Petri dish, an egg, and some sperm--anybody's sperm. Then a quick implant, with an embryo developing, and Presto! Science has worked another miracle. . . While ignoring the moral/ethical issues. And then there's the real problem--the techno age is taking over! We've got wombs to rent--."

"I'm sorry, your time is up," Ragalo said. And we have a questioner on the left side there."

A man was standing. "I'd only like to ask Dr. Vandorn if he really believes that the urge to motherhood can be placated through adoption, or working with kids."

Again Ragalo gestured politely to Vandorn. This time Vandorn stood up. "Just trying to eyeball my questioner," he said. "No, no surrogate exists, to my knowledge, that satisfies the maternal longing. That goes beyond sex, physical comfort, worldly honors, maybe even religion. But in our society motherhood has lost caste, or favor; it's something that happens, something that most people either avoid or ration.

"And here's where the technological approach to motherhood, or the problems it may present, helps to trivialize it, make it something for sale or rent. You can go to a reproduction center to become pregnant, or have your sperm frozen, or adopt an embryo or conceive without the intervention of the male of the species.

"We're well on the way to ruling out ethics or morals. We may be on the verge of eliminating marriage itself, the institution that works most directly to protect the nation's--or the world's--children."

Ragalo was signaling, but Vandorn continued in defiant tones. "As we move away from the old-fashioned family, we are more and more becoming a nation of single parents," he said. "That way lies endless social, socioeconomic, and educational problems."

A woman was already standing in the audience when Vandorn sat down. Ragalo said, "Let's hear from the lady toward the back." The woman began at once, speaking in a high-pitched voice.

"I assume that Dr. Brand represents the forces that are turning us into automatons or something. I'd like to hear in some detail how and why and what his research is about."

Brand paused. *Keep it theoretical*, Dr. Schofield had said. "First of all," he said, "It's pretty much what every other research hospital in the country does. That means we try to solve puzzles that the doctors encounter. These may have to do with diseases or sicknesses. They may have to do with medicines or medications. They may have to do with nutrition. An individual may be involved, or an entire population."

"We use animals, every species from monkeys or baboons to mice and rats. The animals make it possible to test things so new that we can't use them on humans first. We've tested combinations of bone marrow cells and specific virus genes to see whether the mix has curative power. The research initially may have aided one patient--but may over time help thousands of others with the same rare disease.

"I keep coming back to the same thing. We're in the business of finding ways to help people. And believe me, the field in which we operate is limitless. It has no boundaries. And the more we find or develop, the more there is to research."

Brand leaned back, relaxing. But Vandorn was again on his feet. "May I?" he said to Ragalo. The moderator nodded. "One minute," he said.

"I'd just like to point out what Dr. Brand won't." Vandorn was speaking more loudly than before. "All this stuff--he may call it genetics research, but I'd call it eugenics pure and simple. That means experiments designed to produce higher, more perfect humans that have less and less humanity. It means he and a lot of others--if we only knew about it--are working toward what I believe are clones. They're into embryo research!

"That means he's playing games with human life. An embryo is a person in microcosm!" he nearly shouted.

Ragalo was holding up a hand, and Vandorn went silent.

"We need a break," Ragalo said.

24

The studio audience buzzed excitedly. Unheard behind the huge glass window, people leaned forward and back, stretching to make points in support or rebuttal. Brand couldn't hear them, but he could guess at the comments.

The activity agitating the studio audience in *ersatz* silence filled Brand with unease. Vandorn's performance, culminating in a near-violent display of temper, had left a taste of doubt, a feeling of anxiety concerning the wisdom of this entire spectacle. Had Michelle been right to classify Vandorn as beyond fanatic, as deity-driven? As someone imbued with a prophet complex?

It was possible. But there seemed to be no escape. They had answered two or three more questions, all of them less incendiary than the first few. And Ragalo was cuing up for the calls from the home audience.

Suddenly they were into it. Ragalo was finishing his invitation to listeners/watchers to call in with their questions--and immediately accepting one.

"Our first question from the home audience," he said sententiously, "is on the way." Speaking close to his personal mike he added: "Speak up, please."

A melodious woman's voice came on. "Isn't it true that some faiths refuse to approve even the procedure that's so common nowadays--artificial insemination? This question is for Dr. Brand."

Vandorn had been sitting as if half-listening. Nodding as he heard the question, he sat straight, paying attention. Brand said, "Of course some faiths do--many do. The theologians and ethicists professing the

- 103 -

views of leading religious communities of faith also have thousands of followers."

As if announcing some new article of discovery Brand added: "Artificial insemination when accomplished with donor sperm has met with minor opposition. The opposite is true when the husband's sperm is made available. There's no possible cataclysm either way.

"In just a few years AI has become a major magic response to infertility. Hundreds or thousands of women are today gratefully experiencing the enriching felicity of motherhood and family life because of AI. We know about the famous Louise Brown in England. We don't know about the many others. But perhaps we should poll the mothers on this, not the few who oppose it."

Brand was not finished, but Vandorn broke in, forcing his voice on the conversation. "I'm in the loyal opposition," he said defiantly. "Did anyone count the embryos that were destroyed or thrown away?" he almost shouted. "Did anyone recall that each such project was cast in the mode of 1984--a Brave New World laboratory procedure? Has anyone tallied the additional abuses that have followed in the wake of AI--to the point, as mentioned, where cloning could be next?"

Ragalo had let both Brand and Vandorn finish. Speaking up suddenly, he announced that another caller was waiting. As the voice came on, Brand sensed that he had heard the voice and knew what was coming. But where? How?

"I'd like to get down to some specifics," the caller said in a hoarse male voice. "My wife told me to call, okay? Dr. Brand has a monkey in his garage, and all we hear is that it's part of an important experiment. Could I ask here--what is it doing there, and how long will it be there? A lot of people are scared."

Ragalo looked at Brand. "Dr. Brand, can you answer that?"

"Not easily. It's a baboon, and it's in a permanently locked cage. It's there because I have to check it, examine it from time to time. We have permission to keep it temporarily for research purposes."

Vandorn was making a note as the next speaker came on. "I'm maybe looking for a bluebird," the caller said, "but we keep hunting for magic bullets for cancer, pills that will restore memory, love potions, what have you? Why shouldn't we do whatever we can to produce clones or increase brain power, or produce people that can solve problems scientifically? What are we waiting for?

"My question is for Dr. Vandorn," the speaker added.

Again Vandorn was on his feet, waving his arms. "We're waiting for the threat of Doomsday to pass," Vandorn said. "Is it so hard to see that the road to mass psychosis runs alongside such suggestions? Brand is selling poisoned sugar plums! They will lead to more chaos than already exists in our research laboratories! In our lifetimes--please ponder this-- the things that will be possible will boggle your imagination. Forget clones. They're the prepping for the beginning. He will poison the ocean, envenom society!

"How about babies for sale? How about crossing humans and animals? How about down and dirty eugenics? How about men carrying babies--and yes, giving birth? These are the kinds of things that can creep out of laboratories when you push ethics and morals to the side!" Vandorn was almost shouting. "We are poking our noses into God's affairs, I tell you! As research goes for more and more bizarre goals, we get farther and farther off the track.

"It can lead only to one thing: A crisis of morality. We are almost there. . ." Ragalo was signaling, *Time up!* But Vandorn continued.

"The Brands of this world are the ones who will bring the Brave New World of monsters into being--unless he's stopped!" The last words came out as a shriek. At the same moment Vandorn lifted his side of the table and hoisted it, turning it over as Brand shoved his chair far back. He was out of the chair and on his feet, free, when the table crashed. The coffee cups and glasses of water flew and splashed. Papers went flying, and the gadgetry that Ragalo had placed in front of himself slid and crashed on the carpeted floor.

Like Brand, Ragalo had sprung clear of the flying debris. He had also shut off the station's transmitting equipment, terminating both sound and picture and automatically switching on calming music.

Brand could hear the deceptively melodious music. It had a restful effect. But considering the caller who had complained about Baboon Terry, Brand could think of nothing else. His inventive imagination could envision numberless unpleasant scenarios. A local mob could march on his home and demand that the baboon be removed. A neighbor given to violence could break into the garage and free Baboon

Terry. Anyone could bring the means to kill the occupant of the cage. There was nighttime fire. . .

Vandorn himself. . .

Ragalo was helping station workers to clean up the mess that Vandorn had created. To Brand he said, "That's a bad example. But my guess is we broke all records for listenership."

25

She dialed frantically, trying to reach Directory Assistance. After an eternity, a voice said, "May I help you?"

"I need the number of Channel 3." Michelle drummed her fingers on the small square table on which the phone sat.

"Here's your number. Hold on."

The mechanical voice came on. Michelle wrote down the number and dialed it. A switchboard operator answered. "My husband is there," Michelle said, controlling her voice carefully. "He was just on the Mike Ragalo show. Can you put me through to the studio?"

"Let me check." A pause. Then the woman said, "No, that phone has been cut off. The show is over."

"I know it's over. I'm trying to get hold of my husband, Dr. Brand."

"I can give you Mr. Ragalo's office."

"Please." In an instant another voice came on. Michelle asked again whether she could talk to Mr. Ragalo or Dr. Brand. It sounded strange to be calling Em *Dr. Brand*. As if he were a stranger.

Seconds ticked away.

"They're not here at the moment," the voice said. "May I take a message?"

Please--could you have Dr. Brand or Mr. Ragalo call this number. This is Mrs. Brand speaking." Michelle gave her mother's number, hung up. A minute, then two minutes passed while she stood next to the telephone table. A clutter of notes on tickets and slips of paper of varying sizes lay in disorder on the table. Her mother. Nearby, a core of organized endeavor resembling crewelwork in an ocean of random interests and projects, phone numbers and clothes and kitchen utensils. Michelle could see herself here: the apples don't fall far from the tree. Or horse, as Em put it.

The phone rang. It was Em. He was leaving the studio. Somehow, by some strange machination of Fate, the message had reached him. Yes, he was all right. Did she like the show? Of course. Michelle felt the pieces of her mind falling back together; fleeting wisps of guilt-sense floated like fog across the highway of her awareness.

"Did he actually try to attack you? It was cut off."

"Yes, in a half-assed sort of way."

"He's insane. Insane. Will you be home for dinner tonight?"

"Yes. It's been a rough morning. I've got a million things to do, but I've earned an evening off."

"After watching your debate opponent I took the girls to Mom's. That one call told the world that we've got a monkey in our garage, and that scares me."

"Well, they'll be okay at your mother's for a while. Your mother thinks she's on vacation when the girls are there."

"It's a vacation for them, that's definite." Concluding the conversation, Michelle felt better. Em had taken the news about the girls without argument. He sounded tired; in the wake of the debate he had to be dragged out. He would sleep at the dinner table tonight. "If you need me this afternoon, I'll be working at home," Michelle said.

The reactions came in, a call now and then. Congratulations to Em. Thank-God's. Laura Phillips for her and Tim. Susie Thatcher, Fenton, others. No Schofield. All the callers agreed: Brand had demolished Vandorn. Some wanted to know if "the madman" had actually attacked Em.

Some of the calls struck thought-provoking chords. Laura said, for example, "When Mr. God speaks through Satan, you really have to doubt the message. Not that anyone with a brain-cell functioning would believe that crack-of-doom pap."

Despite the calls, Brand felt soiled. Vandorn's accusations painted a different picture from the one Brand had of himself. Science had to be served, but science could not override humanitarian considerations. Was he guilty?

He had difficulty concentrating. He was making plans to embryonate two more baboons. But he could see Moke and Joanie in his imagination. They would not go away. Two little images that masked budding personalities. They had been embryos once. Now Michelle was "boarding them" with her mother.

Once born, they crowded into your psychological space. They belonged to you. They would, hopefully, never leave. They belonged to you and you to them. The mother who loses a son in war incarnates that son in memory; he cannot die. The daughter who succumbs to an early disease never passes; not in memory. Pain becomes sedation.

Had Vandorn thrown a tantrum to distract from the revelation about Baboon Terry? In reaction to that news?

"Let's have a drink. I need one after watching your friend Vandorn."

"No friend of mine. I do have one small chore."

"I know. Baboon Terry." She wanted to add: *Sometimes I feel as if I'm married to your animals.* But she refrained. This reunion was so fragile. She listened. From here, in the kitchen, she could sometimes hear Terry barking in the garage, or rattling his cage. But at night he slept for the most part. Always she listened, pathologically, absentmindedly, anxiously. Listening with an inner ear. That animal haunted her.

Em came back.

"We've had some complaints," Michelle said.

"The neighbors?"

"Yes."

Two neighbor-fathers had come over on an evening when Em was working late. They had been polite, but had wanted to know what kind of animal lived in the garage, brooding over the peace and balance of the area like some kind of forest god. They had heard about it from their kids. Michelle had taken them on the guided tour. They had been impressed with Brand's apparently escape-proof cage, but had asked routinely if the animal would be a permanent addition. "Lord, no," Michelle had said, "he's very temporary. Another week or two. Maybe a month. My husband just has to keep him under observation for a while."

They had gone then. But they had tried to get her to give them a date for Terry's departure. She had weaseled on that one. "Soon," she said.

The house seemed deathly still: time and quiet encouraging conversation. They could focus on Vandorn as a subject because he seemed so obviously obsessed, so *off the wall*. They had a second glass of wine: the sipping glass.

"Are you up to telling me what happened?" she said. *Get him talking*, Michelle thought, *get him relaxing. He seemed so perpetually tense these days.*

"I can. No problem." After a pause, he stood up, stretched. "What do you want to know?"

"I'd just like to know what happened today. After your smashing victory over the forces of evil. Details, please."

He stopped smiling. "The idiot overturned the table. That's most of it."

"Em, he is mad."

"Luckily Ragalo cut it off."

"Vandorn knew he'd lost."

"Worse than that, if you ask me. He thought I was making fun of him."

"Were you?"

"In a way, I guess. But that's all part of the game. He could have done the same thing."

"No, he takes himself too seriously." She swished the fluid left in her glass, reflecting: *And we are being swept into his crazy nightmares.* Should she tell Em what her mother had said? No. Not tonight.

He was staring at her. "You've got something on your mind."

"No. It's just that every time I see that man Vandorn I--you know, I've told you. He spooks me."

"Has he ever spoken to you?"

"I don't think so. But I've seen him up close, at the party. He seems like an avenging angel--or devil. He probably thinks he has the right to drop bombs on popes and princes, anyone who gets in his way. As if he had the only revealed word."

She was smiling and frowning at once. "Anyway, I think you won. I realize that his type always thinks they won. I don't even care."

She stopped; she was talking to herself.

Michelle glanced at her husband. He had slipped sideways on the couch. His breathing came deeply, regularly, the breathing pace of a deep sleep.

She would let him rest for a while. In sleep, even uncomfortable sleep, the tensions of the day would unwind, relax. Ensconced in an easy chair, Michelle picked up the book in which she had been browsing, feeling a twinge of conscience as she did. She had so little time for serious non-required reading these days.

She may have drowsed. How long had she slept? Em still lay half on the couch, still breathing the sleep of peace. But something had awakened her, and now she heard it again. Transfixed, she listened.

Angry barks were coming from the garage. They continued for half a minute, a minute longer. Briefly, the barks rose to a frenzied crescendo. There was a thump, like something heavy falling on a solid surface. And sudden brooding silence. Awaken Em? She hated to. Better to find a blanket and throw it over him.

Settling her internal tugs of conscience, she went to the couch. Dropping to one knee, she placed a hand on Em's shoulder. Whispering, she said, "Em, something's happening in the garage. The baboon. I think the baboon was barking."

He came awake struggling. Sitting up, he covered his face with both hands and rubbed. "Tell me again," he said. "Something about Terry?"

"It sounded as if he were fighting with someone. . . .I heard barks."

"Not the Pilchers' dog?"

"No, that bark is different. And he wouldn't be out at this hour."

"What hour?"

"A few minutes before eleven."

"My God. How long did I sleep?"

She received no answer. He was gone, heading for the back door.

26

From the TV studio Vandorn returned to his office. Because it was Friday, nearing noon, the campus and buildings were quiet. A lot of faculty members spent the last business day of the week in the library or in recreational pursuits.

Gustafson's phone rang 10 times before Vandorn gave up. Finding the professor's home number in the city directory, Vandorn tried that number.

Gustafson answered. Hearing Vandorn's voice, he began to laugh. "You had him on the ropes," the professor said. "I was hoping you'd keep at it another hour. It was better than a football game."

"He got me mad. All that bullshit about helping lonely women, nubile women. Sure he's going to find ways to populate the earth."

"What happened at the end? It looked like you were going to land on him. Old Ragalo shut it off just before the excitement started."

"I dumped the table on them. Simple as that." Vandorn picked up a pencil that lay on his desk and began to draw stick figures. From time to time he tried cartooning using these figures. "But that's over," he said. "I'm calling for help. As I recall it, you've got a little guy on your string of slaves. Am I on track?"

"You're thinking of Jeffords. He's so small he can hide behind a bouffant hairdo--and we have a few of those. But when do you need him?"

"Tonight. Maybe 10:30, 11:00 o'clock. For half an hour." Vandorn paused. Before Gustafson could comment, Vandorn said: "He should wear rough clothes. He may have to slither through a window. And I'll need half a dozen of your doctored fruits--same as last time."

"I'll see if I can find Jeffords. He can contact you?"

"He can. This afternoon at my place. I'll have to give him some simple marching orders."

"Where are you now?"

"In my office."

"Why don't you give me half an hour? I'll call you back, give you an update. That's if I don't find him right away. If I find him, I'll have him call you there."

"I'll wait here half an hour. And I'll be home after that."

27

In the afternoon Vandorn had time to review and plan the day.

The debate had gone pretty much as he had expected. Brand had spewed the usual malarkey, acting his old elusive do-gooder self. Science in the service of mankind. What bosh. The deadly hokum about making the world a better place--for women at least--no doubt sounded a saccharine note for female listeners. But the reality stood impenetrable and implacable: a verity whose proof lay in the sexual history of mankind and womankind. It lay too in the writings of philosophers and ethicists, students of the sister disciplines that serve always as the wellsprings of modern moral thought.

He found it comforting to know that he had won the argument with Brand. He had done it without adverting to Kant and his views on the categorical imperative: the rule, first, that we must act on maxims that can be taken as universalizable laws--and the principle, second, that we treat humanity as an end, not as a means. Bringing "science" into the process of reproduction violated both rubrics, in Vandorn's cosmology, by making both into phases of a purely mechanical function.

Sitting in his living room, one hand ruffling the back-fur of "Plato," the family lab retriever, he recalled Brand's look when the table had overturned. Vandorn felt that scene as a kind of recompense, a reward for all the nonsense he had heard. He knew that the Ragalo show produced far worse tableaux. On one recent occasion two adversaries had wrestled their way around the studio. Two burly attendants had finally separated them. But enough gloating. As if by instinct Vandorn had devised a way to dispose of the baboon in the garage.

Driving home from his office Vandorn had detoured past Brand's house. Just as he had pictured it, the garage opened on an alley that ran through the block. He had only to slow to a creep to have time to observe the side window, to assess what would be required to pry it open.

The day crawled along. With Jennifer working a six-hour turn at University Hospital, Vandorn realized that he would have the afternoon to himself until a few minutes after 4:00 p.m. By then, he expected, he would have heard from Dr. Gustafson, or Jeffords. He would be able to hit the gym, jog a few laps on the running track that circled the gymnasium balcony.

Gustafson called while Vandorn was finishing a sandwich. Baloney and cheese on rye. Better than you'd get at half the greasy spoons in town. Setting the sandwich remnant down, Vandorn picked up the cordless phone that they kept in the kitchen.

It was Jeffords. In a surprisingly deep bass voice the student said, "Dr. Vandorn?"

"Yes." Coming quickly to the mission, Vandorn outlined it. "It would entail climbing through the garage window and getting the food inside the cage. I'd provide the fruit. You would then exit the way you came in--."

"The window's open?"

"No, I will open it in seconds once we get there." Vandorn paused. "Come to think of it, the window might be open. But I can do that job in seconds."

"What's your plan?"

"First, you've got a car?"

"Yep. Eighty-five Chevy."

"The way I figure it, we meet in separate cars at the Walgreen's at 5th and Cypress. I lead you to about a block from the house. I drive you the rest of the way, park right behind the garage where my car can't be seen. I pry open the window, you take the food, climb in, dump the food into the cage, climb back out. Walk fast or run to your car."

"You'll be gone."

"Right."

The animal in the garage remained both target and conundrum. For Vandorn, it meant Brand was performing another genetic experiment, probably one involving impregnation. Thank you, Mr. Caller who told us about it over Mike Ragalo's phone.

Jogging in mid-afternoon, with the Jeffords assignment settled, Vandorn went in search of the tool he would need. He had borrowed tools here before. Finding the toolroom door unlocked, he entered. Minutes passed while he combed through the jumble of implements and garden machines. Finally he saw it: a crowbar perhaps two feet in length. Without trying to hide it, he placed it in the locker where he had secured his clothes.

The big clock high up on the lockerroom wall showed the time as 4: 25. Jennifer would be home, and Vandorn was planning a special evening for her.

She picked up on the first ring. "Jim! You were great," she said. Before he could say thanks she added: "Where are you?"

"At the gym. I'll be clearing out in a few minutes. But," he said mock-seriously: "First you've got a big decision to make."

"I do? What decision?"

"Whether to accept my invitation to dinner tonight or force me to eat alone at Del Greco's."

Relief rang in her voice. "I accept. We can talk about your new fame as a TV star."

"I did one thing right--I gave Brand a table sandwich. But yes, we can talk about it. I'll be home in half an hour, maybe an hour."

"I'll be picking out a dress." She paused. "And putting on my face."

It was a matter of minutes to go up to the chemistry lab, find the padlocked cupboard with the number 10 on it. Drawing the combination from his wallet, he spun the little wheel.

The lock snapped open.

The Mason jar with the fruit in it stood on a shelf almost at eye level. Vandorn picked it up, tried turning the cap. It rotated with the application of very little pressure. Curious, Vandorn smelled the contents with the lid off.

The jar gave off a pungent, gamey odor. Vandorn closed the container, then locked the cupboard. Rather than carry the jar exposed, he checked the waste-baskets. From one that stood under a table nearly covered with retorts and bottles, he took a brown paper bag that obviously had wrapped someone's lunch.

The bag was just large enough to hide the jar.

Jennifer fell into the spirit of the tete-a-tete. Since they would leave the home hearth late to avoid crowds, she selected her favorite dress and took her time "repairing her makeup." While she labored, Vandorn watched the evening news on television. By coincidence he saw clips of himself overturning the table in the Channel 3 studio.

He had to laugh. Brand eluded the falling table, but appeared flustered.

At dinner Jennifer seemed vivacious in a way that surprised and pleased Vandorn. Her obvious pleasure in the evening out put a mark of excellence on the outing and the entire day. *One more stage to go.* So Vandorn thought as he paid the check while inviting his wife to finish her wine at her leisure.

They were home at the exact time that Vandorn had mentally earmarked. It was 9:45 p.m., and the time for his rendezvous with Jeffords was 10:30.

At 10:15, having shared another sip of wine, he announced that he was going to take Plato for a walk. Before leaving, he complimented Jennifer on a marvelous evening. Would there be time later for. . .?

He let the sentence hang. She smiled and nodded.

Instead of walking, Vandorn put Plato into his car. In front of the Walgreen's, standing in front of a display window as if he were trying to decide whether to enter, Jeffords was swinging a key-chain.

It all seemed foreordained. Vandorn led the convoy of two cars to the alley behind the Brand residence. He picked up Jeffords. Behind the Brand garage he stopped and turned out his lights. In moments Vandorn was at the window that he had seen earlier. Finding a gap, he pressed the crowbar into it and used the bar as a lever.

The window swung inward from the bottom. As it did so, it struck some obstacle inside the garage. Vandorn reached in to grip the window edge and pry it free. Still the obstacle stopped the inward movement.

Hurrying, Vandorn pushed at the inside obstruction. He realized that he was trying to move the baboon's cage. Before he could pull back his hand, Baboon Terry had moved in the semidarkness. His razor-sharp teeth closed on the tip of Vandorn's left index finger, slicing it off while crushing the end of the bone.

By a miracle of self-control, Vandorn suppressed the explosive urge to scream. As the window fell inward, thudding, he wrapped a handkerchief around the damaged finger and said through gasps to Jeffords, "Your turn. Make it fast, for God's sake!"

He stepped to his car, still holding the handkerchief around the finger. With the car started and the lights off, he drove to the end of the alley and headed home. His face was contorted with pain. He couldn't banish the sound of the baboon barking.

Jennifer met him as he burst in the door. She wore a diaphanous robe that revealed the outlines of her figure.

Vandorn brushed past her, hurrying toward the bathroom, blood soaking through the handkerchief and escaping in drops that he caught with his free hand.

"We got in a dog-fight," he grunted. "The other one bit me. I'm going to have to hit the hospital."

To his disappearing back she said, "I'll drive you," and went to change her clothes.

28

On Friday/Saturday nights the flow of traffic to the Post Memorial Hospital Emergency Room was extremely variable. Feast or famine, ER personnel said philosophically.

This quiet Friday night East Indian surgeon-to-be Ramdar Singh had spent most of the evening in his cubicle. He had recently completed his residency. He was proud of his new American title of *doctor*. He had brought a couple of books to work, one on Anatomy/Physiology and the other on Physical Chemistry. But he had read very little. He had dreamed briefly about one of the Indian nurses he had encountered a few days earlier. He had fallen asleep.

Nurse Emily Parker poked her head into the cubicle. To Dr. Singh she looked as if she had seen the ghost of an ancestor. "Sorry to bother you, Doctor," she said. "But we have a real case here. A man who says he had a fight with a dog. He needs help real bad."

Dr. Singh roused himself. A dogbite case. *Rabies, shots in series.* "I come," he said in his formal, accented English. He pulled on a lab coat, wetting his fingers and smoothing down his hair, tightening his belt, and only then quickly washing his hands.

He had no more than 30 feet to walk: down a corridor and into the big reception room that had cubicles along one wall. Pull a curtain and voila!

Dr. Singh walked straight to the man who sat, head bowed, where the reasons-of-economy lighting was weakest. The man had his left arm folded up so that his fisted hand was just beneath his chin. The hand in the fist was wound about with cloths, some of which had red blotches on them.

"Mr. Vandorn," the doctor said, reading from the sheet the nurse had given him.

The man looked up without changing the position of his left arm. "*Doctor* Vandorn," he said. The shadow of an excruciating pain passed over his face.

"May I look at it?" Doctor Singh stepped close, examining what he could see as Vandorn slowly, grimacing, opened his hand.

"I will have to take the bandages off," Doctor Singh said. "I have to see it uncovered. But not here. If you will come with me, you can lie down and be more comfortable."

Vandorn struggled to his feet and followed the doctor into a separate curtained room. Nurse Parker had appeared and was following both Doctor Singh and Vandorn. In moments the ER doctor had adjusted the room's single hospital bed to the appropriate height. Vandorn first sat and then lay down. "I'll need wash equipment," Dr. Singh said to the nurse. "And please see if Dr. Follette is available. Quickly."

The nurse left. "Doctor," Vandorn said suddenly, "my wife is parking the car. Could you tell her I'm in here?"

"Of course." Hurrying, Dr. Singh stepped through the examining room door and called the nurse. He intercepted her and explained before she got out of range. Dr. Singh returned and began to unwrap the various clothes that Vandorn had wrapped around his left hand. Each little tug brought stifled groans from Vandorn.

Now there were two doctors hovering between him and the bright hanging lights. One of them was Dr. Singh. The other, apparently seeing Vandorn swimming through internal fog to wakefulness, introduced himself. "I'm Dr. Follette," he said. "Duty surgeon. We're about to fix up your finger. Your wife has signed the papers giving us the green light. Is that okay with you?"

"It's got to be fixed, and fast. I've got to get home."

Dr. Follette paused, as it were, in mid-flight. Vandorn became aware that the surgeon was standing on his left side. His left arm lay at full length in a kind of trough that seemed made for it. The injured finger hurt appallingly, but not at all as it had earlier.

"This will take a while--if you want me to proceed," Dr. Folllette said. "I have to clean off the end of the little bone, the phalange, at the tip of your index finger. Right here." He pointed. "Whatever bit you crushed that bone at its very end."

"How much finger will I lose?"

"Not much. At most half an inch."

"How long will it take--or how soon can I leave here?"

"If you insist, two-three hours."

Vandorn thought quickly. "What time is it now?"

"Eleven forty-five, almost."

"Let's get it done, if you're ready. You're going to use an anesthetic?"

"Absolutely. You may feel some minor twinges."

Over the next hour Vandorn passed into and out of the zone of unconsciousness several times. The episodes gave him merciful relief. While awake he was aware that Dr. Folllette was busy snipping, cutting, sewing. He deliberately fought off the urge to ask what was happening.

At some preordained moment he awakened to the instant realization that no one was working on his hand. It still lay where he had last located it--in the trough somewhere. His wounded finger felt bound, confined.

Vandorn lifted his head. The motion alone sent a charge of pain that seemed to moderate almost at once. Looking around, he saw Dr. Follette. The surgeon was bending over the small corner sink.

In his own ears his voice sounded hoarse to Vandorn. "All finished?" he said.

"Yes, finished. For now. We'd want to see you again in no more than four days." Dr. Follette spoke without turning his head. A moment later he straightened up and began to dry his hands.

"Is my wife still here? I've got to get home." Vandorn thought he remembered seeing a clock earlier; now he couldn't find it. Would you have the time?"

"In sequence, your wife is still here. And I'd advise you to make sure you can walk before you head home. And it's now about 2:20 in the morning."

"My God!" Vandorn tried to sit up but had to settle back while the pain emanating from his left hand passed in waves through his arm.

He winced, tried again, and this time, expecting the pain, he succeeded in sitting up.

"You'll need some help," the doctor said, and disappeared. In moments Nurse Parker entered the room. She was carrying the shirt Vandorn had been wearing. Half a minute later Jennifer followed, yawning.

"I'll wear the shirt," Vandorn said, speaking to the nurse. "If you'll help me into it." He examined the fabric closely as Nurse Parker held it up. "I must have lost a gallon of blood," he said as the nurse helped him push his arm through the sleeve.

The next stage seemed easier. Both women used their hands to stabilize him as he slid off the hospital bed to the floor.

"Got to get my sea legs," he said. An irritation verging on anger seized him as he stepped alongside the bed, holding on while he made certain of his balance. The goddam monkey had a bite like a stamping machine. Pregnant or not, the animal deserved to be in ape heaven.

With both Jennifer and Nurse Parker flanking him, he made his slow way to the reception room. The cushioned couches looked inviting, but he passed them. He could sit down when he got home.

There seemed to be an entire ball of pain in his left hand when he and Jennifer entered their living room. But once seated again, he felt as if he were wilting. He leaned back on the couch, feeling himself drowsing. "How about a double shot?" he said to Jennifer.

He had spoken like someone placing an order in a bar. Momentarily contrite, again feeling the throbbing pain, he added: "If I can try your incredible patience once again."

"You can," Jennifer said as she left the room. Returning with a half-full glass that tinkled, she said, "I added some rocks."

"You read my so-called mind." With the glass in his right hand, Vandorn shook the glass as if testing. He then drained the contents and held out the glass. Jennifer took it. She watched while her husband slumped down on the couch on his right side. Leaving the room quietly, she came back with a light blanket. She threw it over the inert form. "Crazy as a loon," she whispered.

His bandaged left hand hung over the edge of the couch.

29

Baboon Terry lay dying when Brand let himself into the garage. Evidence of a bitter struggle, with Terry's cage at its center, began on the shelf that ran along the wall under the window. Shards of window glass littered the scene. The cage had fallen to the floor. Still inside it, Terry lay on his back with his legs drawn up as if to crush a demon in his intestinal tract. Over it all hung the stench of vomit and feces.

The interior of the cage showed signs of Terry's initial enchantment with the food that had somehow entered the cage. Fragments of fruit, in some cases torn into strips or lumps, were visible over a rough circle on the floor. Some of the pieces were semiliquid regurgitations.

Holding a handkerchief to his nose, Brand inspected the shelf just inside the window. The window itself had crashed inward, smashing both panes. Some pieces were crunching under brand's slippers.

On the shelf--actually a part of a storage/work bench--Brand found dark spots and streaks. Some of them had joined, forming little puddles. All such traces were coagulating, becoming crusty. A few of the larger puddles remained liquid. Touching these and examining his finger, Brand decided that he was touching blood. Where his finger had made contact, the liquid showed deep red rather than black.

It seemed clear. Whoever had been here must have injured himself while delivering the doctored fruit. That was at least a hypothesis. Briefly, angered and disgusted by his incipient sense of helplessness, Brand allowed himself a moment of hatred.

Yet he had committed the basic error. He had assumed that he could keep Baboon Terry safe in this wooden shelter behind his house.

He had done so knowing that the enemies of his scientific research were dedicated to derailing whatever he attempted.

The animal's eyes, sunken and deep brown, gazed at nothing. Tiny movements of those eyes were evidence that Terry was still alive. Less definite as evidence was the drool that leaked from the baboon's partly open mouth.

Walking part-way around the cage, Brand was able to touch Terry's back. The animal felt warm to his fingers, and Brand, certain that Terry could no longer bite, let his hand rest for a long moment. At the instant of withdrawing his hand, it occurred to him that the blood that had dripped so profusely may have come from a wound inflicted by the monkey himself. Someone had reached into the cage. . .

What he was reconstructing had taken place hardly a half-hour ago. The thought put a new torch to his temper. He had, possibly, missed the perpetrator or perpetrators by minutes. If he were to look for someone, his search would focus on a small person--someone small enough to climb through the window and then leave by the same opening.

By daylight in the morning, he told himself, he would examine again the "crime scene"--as he had begun to consider it. The blood trail might lead somewhere. Tomorrow, too, he would return Terry's remains to the Zoo. He would first contact Fenton even though it was the zookeeper's day off.

He would check at both University Hospital and Post Memorial. If anyone had reported to an ER or clinic with an animal bite, some doors might open.

Michelle was still awake, still reading. Brand returned to the couch.

"Terry's dying," he said. "Looks like poison, same method used before."

"Same person," Michelle said, her voice caustic. "Namely Vandorn." She spoke as if she had certain knowledge. "No one else in this town would do a thing like that."

Studying her, Brand decided that the past few days had been an ordeal. "We have no proof," he said. "But it's entirely possible. Even likely. But if you're right I don't see how I can do much. Any publicity means trouble--for us as much as for him."

Michelle had been holding a finger in her book, keeping her place. Opening the book like someone reaching a decision, she inserted a small piece of paper between the pages that her finger had marked. "Will you tell Fenton?" she asked. "You can't just bury him here, can you?"

"No. No way." He thought of the blood that someone had lost inside and outside the garage. "After I clean up in the morning I'm going to take the body back. I'll have to make out a report, and think of an excuse for his death."

"Why an excuse? Just tell them someone killed him." She had spoken sharply.

He quelled an urge to respond as sharply. Like the kids, Michelle had been through her share of nuisance and confusion. "It may not be that simple," he said. "I have a feeling I'll be talking to Dr. Schofield in the next few days. This murder immediately after that so-called debate won't go unmentioned."

Michelle yawned.

"It's going on 2:00 a.m.," Brand said. "Time for some shuteye?"

"I'll read a couple of more pages and try to forget baboons. Then I'll join you. But I doubt that I can sleep. I can still hear your monkey shrieking and barking."

"You heard him?"

"I told you. I still do." She looked at him full-face. He could see that her lower lip was trembling.

"What if I whip up something that will put you to sleep?"

"I'll try anything. Or did I? But I won't sleep. Do you think your friend Dr. Madsen could prescribe something for monkey-nerves?"

"Now?"

"In the morning."

"I'll call him early. Would you see him if he wants you to stop in?"

"Certainly."

Slowly, almost painfully, Michelle stood up, then quickly sat down again. "I'm a little unsteady," she said.

Terry's remains were cold when Brand entered the garage shortly after dawn. The stench was stronger than ever. Brand had brought a green lawn and leaf bag. A dead weight and still somewhat limp, the baboon body seemed abnormally heavy; but exerting main force Brand managed to hoist the remains into the bag. He tied up the neck opening, working rapidly, and placed the bag in the trunk of his car. By similar means, he recalled, medical students of his years-ago acquaintance had made away with dead animals that they needed for experimental purposes.

Over the next hour Brand was able to rouse the girls, announce that they would be spending the day with Grandma Manley, and drive them to his mother-in-law's house. He had prepared the way by calling his mother-in-law first and explaining that Michelle was feeling "under the weather." She would be seeing a doctor that morning.

Instantly concerned, Mrs. Manley wanted details. Brand gave a few and added a positive prognosis. "The aftereffects of a heavy work schedule," Brand explained. "She just needs some rest, and today seems as good a time as any."

His chauffeuring duties completed to the excited cries of both girls, Brand returned home. Michelle was up but "dragging" by her own admission. "Dr. Madsen called," she added. "He'll see me in about half an hour. I should go to Emergency."

"I'm your designated driver today," Brand said. "Pickup and delivery on the customer's schedule."

He was in the car waiting when Michelle joined him. "I'm glad you're driving," she said. "I don't know that I could even drive to the grocery store."

To Brand, following the arrows indicating the way to Post Memorial's Emergency Room, the pleasant morning seemed wasted. Lightning and thunder weather should mirror the scares and alarms of the past 24 hours.

In particular the day should wear mourning for the pitiful burden in the trunk of his car.

He had not and would not mention to Michelle that the carcass of Baboon Terry, his experimental lost dream, lay there lifeless. He would in silence encourage Michelle to start a new chapter. Thinking such thoughts he stopped the car in front of the ER entrance. "This is where we find your doctor," he said cheerily. "And I should go and park the car."

"I'll go with you," Michelle said. "If you don't mind."

"I don't mind at all." He glanced at his wife, but she was staring straight ahead. For Michelle, the paragon of self-sufficiency, the request was unusual. Brand drove on.

Walking from the car to the ER entrance, Michelle held Brand's arm. Once inside, she took a seat. Brand went to the desk to explain that they were waiting for Dr. Madsen.

"He's here. Are you Dr. Brand?"

"I am."

"He said we should call him when you arrived. If you care to take a seat, he will be here in minutes."

Engaged mainly in research, Brand imagined a far more difficult role and challenge for medical doctors who were forever answerable to patients. Staying "on the clock," as he saw it, would challenge the best instincts of the ordinary mortal. Fitting the model, Madsen appeared only minutes after Brand's arrival with Michelle.

"I'll steal your lovely wife if she's willing," Madsen said as he emerged from the interior rooms. "I have some tests, simple procedures. And of course many questions."

Michelle was standing. Turning to leave, she said, "Wait for me?"

Brand nodded.

The time dragged, making Brand yawn. Reviewing again the events of recent hours, he could envision plots, conspiracies. At their epicenter stood Vandorn.

He was still musing when Madsen and Michelle returned. Unasked, she explained that she had already swallowed a sleeping potion. "Dr. Madsen wants me to stay a couple of days," she said. "But right now the order is sleep. Sleep before I fall down."

An elevator ride, a short walk down Saturday-silent halls, and they were in a room designated by Dr. Madsen. While Michelle dressed in her "sleeping togs," Brand and Madsen talked in the hall.

"Nature's cure" would bring Michelle back, Madsen said. His guess: she would sleep at least five or six hours. They agreed to look in on her in the afternoon. "I'll be back for other patients," the gynecologist said. "Shall we meet and see how she's doing?"

"Three o'clock, give or take a few?"

"Perfect."

"I have a few hundred things to do at the Zoo and the labs. But University Hospital has a few clocks to keep me on schedule."

"You should heed the words of counsel I gave Michelle," Madsen said. "Be warned. Don't take on too much." After a pause he added: "Let's talk a few minutes."

30

She had fallen asleep instantly. Brand struggled for answers.

Who could have predicted this? Who could have foreseen that the death of Baboon Terry would fire invisible darts into the Brand home? Where was the medical savant who would have said the darts would infect Michelle, exhausting her reserves of strength and placing her under a doctor's care while her children of necessity remained with her mother?

On the positive side, she liked Dr. Madsen, trusted him, felt positive about his ministrations and prescriptions.

She slept deeply while Brand and Madsen talked in low tones. By degrees they moved their conversation to the hall outside her room. "There's nothing organically wrong," Madsen said. "But we both know there's such a thing as stress and its sequels. So there are stress-related infirmities, but they're normally controllable, curable if caught in time. Bed-rest may be the treatment of choice in many cases."

"Removal of the cause of the stress should help?"

"It should."

From the doorway Brand could see Michelle's still form, outlined under a light blanket. "The cause of the stress is gone," he said. "I'll give you the whole story this afternoon if you'll be visiting again."

"I will be. I'll be checking between 2:00 and 4:00."

"Can I ask a favor on top of all the others?"

"Certainly."

"Have someone check, see if Dr. Vandorn came in here for emergency treatment either last night or early this morning?"

"Will do. I'll give you the results this afternoon."

Back in the overstuffed red chair, in Michelle's room, Brand tried to read the local newspaper he had picked up on entering Post Memorial a while ago. There were no reports of complaints about animal sounds in his Midtown neighborhood. He was still looking when sleep put an end to his search. The newspaper slipped to the floor.

A gentle hand on his shoulder brought him back to wakefulness. He found himself staring up at Madsen again.

"Take a minute?" Madsen was speaking softly, and Brand, nodding, followed him out.

A Saturday afternoon quiet lay over the visible stretch of hallway. "ER had what you probably expected," Madsen said. "A Mister Vandorn checked in a little after midnight this morning. He told our duty people that a dog had attacked and bitten him. He seemed to have trouble describing the dog."

"Vandorn?" Brand spelled the name.

"Yes. Then he said he had no ID on him. He had been out for a late-evening walk with his dog. He knew the kind of dog he owned--a lab--but that was about it as far as details were concerned."

"They got his address?"

"They did." Madsen pulled a small square of paper from the pocket of his white, hip-length jacket--his "working disguise." "They wrote it down for me. I can get a copy of the attending surgeon's report if you want it."

"I definitely do."

"There's been some talk about it apparently. The bite, whatever the animal, took off the end of the finger, including a little of the bone. Doctor Follette, who did the surgery, had a note in his report about the wound. To him it didn't look like a dog bite. It was some animal with stronger teeth."

"Prescient." Brand tried to recall the procedures appropriate to animal bites. "Was there antirabies treatment for the victim?"

"From what they tell me, he wanted no followup. But he finally agreed to the basic shot--rabies globulin, the traditional early safety treatment. Most of us would say the five later shots are just as important. Those are vaccine injections."

"He won't be back for those?"

"Not from what he said when he left."

"Anybody recall it?"

"Yes. He went out talking like a first sergeant, someone said--I think one of the nurses. 'I'm going to put you all in for medals.' That was his parting shot--pardon the pun."

Brand dozed again, awakening to see Michelle disappearing into the bathroom. He had been dreaming that he was physically pursuing Vandorn. As he returned to consciousness, he was closing on his quarry on a dark street. One of the baboons was riding his shoulder as he pressed the pursuit.

The images remained so clear that he could have sketched them out. One element puzzled him. Vandorn was wearing a priest's cassock--and running in spite of the hindrance it represented. Brand was still trying to interpret what the priestly garment meant when Michelle returned to the room.

She sat on the edge of the bed, swinging her feet comfortably in small arcs. "Well, I've slept the day away," she said, smiling. "If that's the treatment recommended by your friend Doctor Madsen, I'm all for it. But now I'm ready to go home."

"*My friend* Doctor Madsen would like to see you rest for at least two or three days." Brand spoke in a jocular tone that matched his wife's. If asked, he would have said she was fully recovered from her "attack of nerves." When she remarked that she felt rejuvenated and "ready to battle baboons," he admitted to himself that she seemed ready to go home. But he tried once more, feebly.

"What if I pull some strings and we have dinner here--and then you spend one whole night in Madsen's monastery?"

Michelle frowned, pretending to think over the proposal. "If you'll promise not to leave before 9:00 p.m.--and come back to have breakfast with me."

"It's a deal." Brand thought for a moment. "Now you should call your mother and tell her you're feeling like entering a marathon."

"Will do."

"And take another nap. I'm off to confer with Mr. Fenton. I'll be back for dinner."

He did not leave Post Memorial Hospital immediately. From Michelle's room he went down to ER. As Madsen had predicted Nurse Parker was already on duty and at the moment unoccupied. She remembered the "bullet-headed, dark-haired man" who had come in with a dog-bite. She had seen the wound uncovered and retained a mental picture. "It was mashed," she said. "Is he a friend of yours?"

"Not exactly. Let's say I'm interested in his case." As an afterthought Brand added: "Did he take away the wrappings that he came with--on his finger?"

"No, he told us to throw them away. I think it was a single handkerchief. It was saturated with blood."

"Thrown away already?"

"Yes, I think so." Nurse Parker spoke like someone discussing a mislaid family heirloom. "I could probably find it if you want. Dr. Madsen mentioned that it might be needed."

"I would like to have it--washed or not. But there's no need to go hunting for it now. I'll be back tonight and tomorrow morning."

"I'll leave it at the nurses' station," the nurse said, "if I can locate it."

"I'll be indebted."

31

Fenton was going over records in his Zoo office when Brand arrived. It was one of his strengths, for Brand, that the zookeeper never boggled at holiday or weekend duty. More than once, in his lighter moods, his philosophy would surface. "The only thing these animals don't know, or ignore," he might say, "is that they're supposed to observe weekends and holidays off."

He twisted in his chair as Brand stepped into the keeper's tiny office. "The monkey killer strikes again," Fenton said without smiling. He was pulling at his left ear, a cue that he was pondering his next course of action.

"The same killer if you want my opinion." As Fenton closed the ledger book he had been perusing, Brand continued: "And with a little luck I'll be able to prove it."

"That would rid the world of a curse."

"It would. It will. But what I came for--I've got Terry's carcass in the trunk of my car. I think we should put it on ice until we learn what the powers that be want us to do with it."

"If you'll give me the keys to your car, I'll bring him in."

Accepting the keys, Fenton left. Brand could hear him thumping up the metal stairs. He returned in minutes, and this time his footsteps on the same stairs sounded louder, heavier.

"In this condition Terry weighs a ton," Fenton said. He set the green bag on the floor. "But that's always the case. We get heavier when life ends."

"It seems that way. But other things happen. That's why I'm suggesting the refrigerator. Terry's been dead about 16, 18 hours. And we have no idea whether they'll want an autopsy--or when."

"We should preserve the remains. I agree."

Grunting theatrically, Fenton lifted the green bag and preceded Brand through the central hall to the locked door at the far end. A sign reading MORGUE identified the room. A smaller sign read, AUTHORIZED PERSONNEL ONLY.

"I hope you can stop these murders," Fenton said. He had set the bag down and was fitting a key into the oversized lock. "It's not only cruel, it costs University Hospital a small fortune."

He opened the heavy door and continued talking. "We should have our stories straight as to how Terry died, where he died, all that stuff."

"No question. In a nutshell he was poisoned while caged and held for observation in my garage. That sound official enough?"

Fenton was again lifting the green bag and walking it into the morgue. He had stopped before a great square, boxlike appliance that loomed black and forbidding in the center of the room. Cold air from ceiling vents filled the room, making Brand shiver. The cold reminded him that he had a mission insofar as Baboon Terry was concerned.

Broach it? Explain to Fenton that he wanted to remove the fetus that might be nestled in the dead Terry's omentum? Before he could pose the question, Fenton was placing the green bag in the refrigerator and talking at the same time.

"You remember you've got two new animals to replace this one?" Fenton said, only half questioning.

"I am aware of that. I haven't had time to get to really know them yet."

"You'll want to name them too. It's a great memory aid for me. Before you started naming them I had one hellova time keeping them separate. The names make them like people, sort of."

"They are like people in many ways. And I've been trying to figure out what new names we could use. I'd like to try a different approach-- no more T names for a while."

"And? I thought we were stuck on T."

"A few years ago we--the United States--was exploring Saturn. Remember?"

"Vaguely."

"They found something like 23 moons in the neighborhood of Saturn. I'd like to take a couple of the names they used on those moons. How about, for example, Rhea and Dione?"

"Those male names?"

"No. I don't think so. But who's going to know the difference? More and more as a society we're giving male names to little girls."

"It wouldn't bother me. So No. 3422 would be what--Rhea? And 3588 would be Dione?"

"Perfect. I'll write out the names. If you could put them on the two cages, I'll be able to get them straight."

They were leaving the Morgue. Fenton closed the huge door and tested to make sure it was locked. "One thing occurs to me," Brand said. "Is there a way I can get into this room for half an hour, maybe an hour in the next day or so?"

"Sure. Homer will have a key that will open it for you. We never know when someone will need those keys."

"I'll be going in there to do a quick operation on Terry. I want to make sure he was carrying a fetus--and remove it for examination later."

"You should do it now--before he freezes." Fenton had been swinging the keys like a jailer. Pausing, he deftly removed one key and handed it to Brand. "You can use this key. Will appreciate if you'll give it to Homer when you're done."

"Are there tools in there--knives, curettes, other stuff?"

"In the desk drawer."

A vague sensation hinting at illicit trespassing stirred Brand briefly as he went to work. The almost microscopic incision made only weeks ago remained visible beneath the naturally thinned-out stomach fur. Brand had only to repeat the earlier incision, slightly enlarged and performed with the utmost delicacy to avoid injury to the tiny shape.

He could feel it. Wearing a glove that he had also found in the desk, probing with his fingers, he was able gently to break the cord and free the fetus.

Holding the tiny form for a closer examination, Brand saw drops of fluid gathering and falling to the floor. The new implant had only recently completed the embryo stage of gestation and entered the fetal. With its minute legs extended, it would measure, by Brand's estimate, perhaps three and one-half inches.

Critically for Brand, the little ball of simian flesh represented success. Victory. He had impregnated Baboon Terry, had proved that a male of the monkey family was able to carry offspring.

His victory without living proof left Brand feeling painfully thwarted. The proof he needed would have to emerge from a male omentum as a fully formed, living neonate--it would have to survive. Anything less amounted to an automatic verdict of failure.

While he sewed and cleaned the small incision he had made in Terry's carcass, his mind and senses churned. His pursuit would continue. The Vandorns would find him on the front lines of his research.

Men would one day bear human children. Brand himself might some day test the same parental waters. Having lost a son to stillbirth, Michelle had announced that she "couldn't go through that again." Her child-bearing years were over.

Was it time for a new dispensation? Under any circumstances Brand was continually registering new findings about pregnancy and childbirth. Would Archer come through?

He left with a small jar filled with water. The jar, wrapped in a plastic bag, also held a tiny baboon shape. Brand was carrying the prize in a plastic bag.

As he locked the door to the Morgue, he recalled that he wanted to check his office for recorded messages.

Dusk was softening the black outlines of the campus trees as he walked to his office. Inside, he found the recorder light blinking five times. One call was from Dr. Lovenson, deputy hospital administrator; another had come from Archer, editor of the gay newspaper, and a third had originated with Laura Phillips.

A fourth had come from Vandorn. The fifth was garbled and not understandable.

32

Brand had no interest in returning a call from James Vandorn. He had no need to call Dr. Lovenson. The deputy had left a polite message asking Brand, "if he was free," to stop in at Dr. Schofield's office on Monday morning--"maybe about 10:00 a.m."

He dialed Laura Phillips' number from memory. She answered immediately, as if she had been sitting at the phone. "Em here," he said without preamble.

"Oh Em, thank God. I've got to see you--talk to you. Would you-- are you busy?"

"I guess I could say my work never ends," he said gently. "But I can certainly answer questions."

"This is--it's more than sensitive. From my view it's borderline disastrous. And very personal."

"If I can help--? Is it possible to explain over the phone? I'm supposed to be at the hospital in a few minutes, so this wouldn't be a good time."

"Someone is in the hospital?"

"Michelle--but just for what we are calling rest and recuperation."

"I'm sorry, really sorry. But maybe later? Is later possible?"

"I'll be home by 9:15, 9:30. We could talk then."

"Marvelous. May I stop by?"

Stop by. Marvelous. Estimating times, visualizing possible delays, Brand said, "I don't see why not. Let's see how it looks when you call."

Time-passing kept betraying Brand. Thinking he would run home, shower quickly, change clothes, and make haste for the hospital, he checked the clock after talking with Laura Phillips. His target time for reaching the hospital was 5:00 p.m. When Brand hung up, it was already a quarter of 5:00.

He had promised the hospital visit and their tete-a-tete, and Michelle would be waiting. Instead of going home, Brand washed as well as he could in the office area washroom. Minutes later, the big clock in the lobby at Post Memorial Hospital told him it was almost five minutes after 5:00.

Michelle was waiting and reading when Brand entered her room: waiting and robed comfortably for a husbandly kiss and a relaxed sickroom visit, not sitting on the bed but ensconced in one of the room's two chairs.

"I'm going to change family doctors if he'll have us," Michelle said. "And I do mean your friend Dr. Madsen. Look what he brought me--us." She gestured, and Brand noticed for the first time a bottle of red wine that stood in shadow on the floor next to Michelle's chair.

Examining the bottle Brand found that it was corked but not sealed. He poured small glasses for each of them and, acting the gallant, toasted his wife: "You look like a million, really. Here's to your new lease on life."

"Thank you. And thank your doctor friend. He's had me sleeping all day." She held up her glass. "This is called healing the spirit to heal the body--phychosomatism at work, if that's a word. Are you up to telling me about your day?"

"Thought you'd never ask."

Together they moved toward lifting and obliterating the spiritual weight of Baboon Terry's brief tenancy in the garage. They made no mention of that interlude by common, unspoken agreement, leaving Terry's fate to the irrelevance of total silence.

By some quirk of influence Doctor Madsen had the kitchen prepare specialty dishes for the celebratory dinner. Brand would never forget the beef filet. Buoyed by two glasses of Burgundy each, they made the evening a partytime. Michelle continued in her high spirits until the clock neared 9:00 p.m.

"You'll sleep again," Brand said as he was leaving a few minutes later. "And I don't expect any problems in that department myself." His good-night kiss was warmly reciprocated.

Laura was sitting in her darkened car waiting for him. Expecting both Laura and her husband, Brand crossed his recently cut lawn to the driver's-side window. A hand inside the window moved, made a gesture, half-wave and half-signal, indicating she was alighting.

Inside the house, Brand felt the silence almost like a living presence, one positioned to observe this Saturday evening consultation. While he suggested she make herself comfortable, his curiosity ran unchecked. Why had she come? Why alone? Women like her, in his experience, were many-sided, sometimes capricious, always high-strung. Always adjusted to *now* and the ensuing layered future.

Yes, she would appreciate a dollop of wine. It would "calm her nerves."

With the wine served, Brand took the easy chair across from Laura in the corner of the living room. Some five feet separated them; Brand could trace and recognize her scent. She began to talk without setting her glass down. More wine, he thought. *Go slowly.*

"It's about Tim," she said. "Or rather, first about Mr.--Professor Vandorn. He called earlier today and reached Tim. He sounded either drunk or under great strain."

"What did he tell Tim?"

"That I was risking all kinds of things by going ahead with my--our plans. He said I was risking my life. I was breaking the law. I was insulting the community. He had half a dozen things to pin on me."

She paused, took a sip of wine. Noting that her hand trembled, Brand said:

"Did he sound as if he was feeling great pain?"

"He was unnatural--yes, it could have been interpreted that way. His voice was, can I call it tight, cold, maybe angry?"

"As far as I'm concerned, yes; and you could comfortably forget everything he said. His great cause, or vision, or crusade, has unbalanced him, that's what I believe. He plans to purify the community."

"I have the same feeling. Have had it since I saw him in his office."
She paused, drew breath. She had another sip of wine. "The problem
is," she said, "that he's spooked Tim."

"He's taking Vandorn seriously?"

"Yes." Her voice sounded close to breaking. "Tim thinks we should
give up our__."

She made a little choking sound. Very carefully, she set the wineglass
on the small end-table. "And--pardon me and try to understand this--
the whole project is part of me. Or I'm part of it." She dropped her
head, causing her lush hair to fall partly over her face. Her voice became
a guttural whisper. "Does it all sound hysterical?"

He paused. Subduing the riot of thoughts that the name Vandorn
conjured, he controlled his voice. "It's not hysterical at all. I'll go farther
and say your feelings are completely justified."

There was silence. The image of Vandorn as it had invaded his
imagination this afternoon returned, moved, held a weapon, slashed
with it. Brand shook his head. He wanted no mind-phantoms. On an
impulse he moved quickly to the couch, taking a seat next to Laura.

His hand massaged her back. "What if I talk to Tim?" he said.
"Would that help?"

"I hate to bother you. I know how busy you are." She lifted her
right hand, let it fall, a gesture of surrender. Looking straight at Brand
she said: "You're the only one who could--what shall I say?--rescue me.
And it's purely selfish of me to bring you into it__."

"But it's logical, inevitable. I'm the culprit who got you interested,
convinced, converted. Unless you tell me to forget the whole thing, I'll
see if Tim will talk to me."

A new silence, more stillness than silence, crept into the warm
corner where Brand liked to read, study. Stepping back to his chair, he
took a sip of the tiny pool of wine left in the bottom of his glass.

"Another dollop?" he said.

"Yes, just a drop, please. I have to remember that I'm driving."

He set their two glasses side by side on the end-table. "How serious
is Tim?" he said, "Or how seriously is he affected?"

"With me he's a rock of obstinacy. Dead set against going through
with what he calls pseudo-motherhood."

"That means it's not real any more? For him? Because the method of delivery is not the natural way?"

"Yes. I think it has something to do with his family. He had five siblings and can't get over it. His mother is a fine woman, but she must have been a baby machine. She also lost two children."

"You think he's comparing you and his mother? You aren't measuring up?"

"Yes," she said in a strangled voice. "I can feel it--but I'm feeling it now more than ever because of that mad fool!" She breathed deeply, exhaled, breathed again and took another sip of the wine.

"Vandorn is the mad fool?"

"Yes."

Laura was no longer lowering her head. She was leaning forward, jaw clenched shut. "Em," she said, "I've been thinking divorce if I can't go through with my. . .project. Does that sound insane?"

"It may be premature. It would hand a bad message to Professor Vandorn. He would become more unbearable than he already is."

"You're right. But just maybe alone I could go through with all that I've been planning." She sat silently; Brand waited while her thoughts jelled. "But how do you raise a child without two people to help?" Her voice shrill again, she said, "It's such a mess. You can't imagine--." Another pause. "Yes, you can imagine and understand. I think you feel what I feel."

"I do."

She was getting to her feet. "I could bend your ear through the night," she said. "But you've got problems of your own."

"And they focus on the same madman."

"Together we'll--." She stopped.

Her arms went around Brand and he returned the embrace. Their mouths met, held for a timeless moment.

Then she broke free, turned away to hide the tears on her cheeks, and said:

"Walk me to my car?"

33

Brand brooded in his sleep. Burdened with a generalized tension on awakening, he felt as if his eyebrows had been sewn together, forming a permanent frown. At a basic stratum of being, he needed simply to relax.

A cup of hot tea helped. But deeper still, a buried epiphany lurked and sought egress. He had dreamed of a spectral Vandorn, seen him, shouted at him--some current banality like "Get a life!"

An impatient irritation had haunted Brand's night hours. In some appropriate venue, imagined vaguely, he would prove that ethicist Vandorn had either personally or through a confederate killed Baboon Terry. Just as viciously, Vandorn was actively, deliberately destroying a woman's heart-deep ambition and perhaps her life and marriage. *He had forgotten to leave the remains of Terry's fetus in his office.* Or had he? Hastily, interrupting his shaving preparations, he sat down and wrote a list of things "to do." "Breakfast with M" stood at the top of the list. As persons to be called he included Archer and Tim Phillips. Behind "Pick up kids" he placed a question mark.

There were several other items. Finding himself basically organized, he realized that he had moved toward a program for action. He had subordinated, contained his rage. He was gauging his chances of encountering Professor Vandorn when he recalled another item. "Check at Post Memorial for V's bandage," he wrote at the bottom of his list. Below that entry he wrote: "Visit kids, report to M."

Mrs. Manley opened the front door only after a substantial pause. Brand was about to ring again when the front door swung open as if operated hydraulically. Inside, Brand saw instantly what had caused the delay. Joanie and Moke were undergoing final wardrobe preparations for church.

Distracted happily, the girls shifted their attention to their father. Moke ran to seize his hand. "Can we go home?" she cried.

"Not yet," he said. "Maybe later today." To Mrs. Manley he said, "I think they'll release her today. This morning." While Moke tried to swing from his hand, he added: "She just needed some rest."

"Well, my girls have kept me entertained. And I think they miss their mother." She was watching Joanie button her light coat. "We'll be back from church in an hour or a little more."

"Need a ride?"

"No, we really need the walk."

"I'll be on my way then." He knelt and exchanged hugs with both daughters. To Mrs. Manley he said goodbye. "I'll call you in an hour or two," he said, "and let you know how your daughter is doing."

"Fine." In a stage whisper she said, "If you can stop here on the way home, we would all welcome a visit."

He entered Michelle's room smiling. This time she was not only awake; she was dressed in street clothes. Her outfit was complete to her "practical" shoes. Her purse lay on the bed.

The breakfast hour had nearly come to an end, Michelle said. "But they're holding some for us." She pressed a button on a small signal mechanism. Almost at once a voice emanated from an unseen public address system. "It's on the way, Mrs. Brand."

Michelle began to explain that Dr. Madsen had already been in to release her. Remembering his "To-Do" list, Brand said, "I'll be back in one minute."

At the nurses' station he asked whether a small package had been left for him. "Yes, Dr. Brand," the duty nurse said. Her eyes searched the cluttered desk. "Here it is." She handed Brand a plastic bag such as he and Michelle used at home to wrap small portions of leftover food.

Inside, Brand could see what appeared to be a bloody rag. Manipulating the contents as he walked back to Michelle's room, he made a discovery. Having isolated a corner of the scrap of cloth, he saw three clearly distinguishable initials: J. B. V.

The scrambled eggs were cold, but Brand couldn't remember when he had enjoyed a better breakfast.

34

Passing through the administrator's outer office on Monday morning, Brand received a nod and a bright smile from Susie. Both Dr. Schofield and Dr. Levenson were in the administrator's inner sanctum when Brand made his entrance.

Dr. Schofield opened the conversation. "Dr. Levenson and I can't agree on what effect, if any, your Friday TV appearance will have," Schofield said. "Frankly, he thinks the publicity will help us fill beds here--and will in fact put our name and services before the public in a positive way. I'm not sure I agree, and we don't really have any way to obtain answers."

Brand was about to speak, but Schofield added a question.

"Would you have heard or read anything in the way of feedback from the public?"

Brand thought of Archer and the Gay Pride: out of bounds here. "Not really. I have been the target of some congratulations. But those are mostly personal friends who would feel duty-bound to compliment any effort."

Schofield was nodding as if to say, "common sense." "But we are in total agreement that the animal mortality rate is unacceptable," Schofield continued. "And there's now the possibility that the debate and the death of a second baboon are related."

"That possibility exists, of course," Brand said. "But the two murders--probably by the same person--are the acts of someone with some marbles missing. That's putting it mildly."

Schofield reddened slightly. "The world is full of nuts," he said loudly. "Nuts with causes. Nuts with weapons. People smear blood on abortion clinics, or bomb them. Or shoot abortion doctors. All we'd need would be a bomb in the Zoo."

Brand leaned forward. Very softly he said: "All that is true. No doubt about it. But I believe we have a special case here."

"Vandorn?" Levenson asked. Noting that Brand was nodding, the deputy continued. Where Schofield's voice had grated like sandpaper, Levenson's had a conciliatory timbre: "Granted," he began, "it's hard or impossible to establish a connection between the debate and the death of a baboon. But we've been thinking that you might at least consider, er, going somewhat underground."

"That might be the answer," Brand said. Speaking deliberately he added: "But offhand, it's hard to picture."

As if he were reading Brand's mind and next remarks, Levenson said, "We've been getting some calls from newspapers about your research work. We've been answering simply that it has to do with hormone research, reproductive problems, that kind of thing. Nothing about genetics, nothing about embryonation, stem cells, DNA--nothing of that kind. You can see our purpose. We'd like to make the work we do here sound as if it's all patient-oriented and relatively straightforward."

"I think that line is not only simple but eminently advisable. It seems especially appropriate now that we're sure that there's at least one rather vocal university faculty member who represents a very conservative set of views."

"Our albatross," Schofield said. "We heard and saw him in action Friday. But right now the real question is, *can* you—euphemistically-- go underground? Or are too many people involved? Would there be other problems? Are we in an unquenchable spotlight?"

"I think it can be done," Brand said, thinking: *Go slowly. There may be a trap here.*

"If that's settled, we should move on," Levenson remarked quickly, as if he wanted to shut off conversation on that score. He waved a sheet of paper. "This is Fenton's report on the death of No. 3381. He mentions that he has ordered an autopsy. It's to be completed as soon as possible. This your understanding, Dr. Brand?"

"It is, yes. That may still mean four or five days. With all the issues hanging by a thread in the meantime."

"We don't expect them to do the impossible." Levenson blew his nose noisily, then smiled. "Only the inconceivable."

Schofield was not quite done. "I have to say it: Things are tight these days, and it's largely because of our competitive situation. So my feeling is that we should lock lips on the loss of Baboon 3381."

"Good idea," Levenson said. "After all, it's a University Hospital problem. But truth to tell, I've seen nothing in any papers about it. Nothing new."

"My neighbors may have their suspicions," Brand said. "And of course the perpetrator knows about it. But if he talks, he's dumber than we thought." Levenson was standing. With a final thought crowding imperatively, Brand continued: "One thing does concern me. If the perpetrator isn't done--if he starts to go public with charges and innuendoes like those Professor Vandorn aired Friday, I think we should counter. We can do it in a civilized, rational way that should keep the public informed and convinced that we're on the right side."

"Good idea--." Levenson began and stopped as Schofield broke in.

"Can we do that without pouring gasoline on the fire?" Schofield asked. "Or would we be better off to ignore any wild theories, let them die of their own weight, their own insanity?"

"It's an automatically explosive subject, it seems to me. It arouses interest no matter what approach a speaker takes. All he has to do is shout loudly enough."

"The sex-family-community morality aspect," Schofield said. "But I don't see how we can counter everything Vandorn might say."

"No, and I don't think we should try that. But I suspect he's plotting some new blockbuster attack. He won't be satisfied with Friday's performance."

The tenor of the discussion was tending in his favor; Brand could feel it. But Schofield spoke almost at once. "Can we stay in contact on that question in particular? Confer?"

Both Levenson and Brand nodded. Brand, moving slowly, followed Levenson out. He stopped at Susie's desk.

A brief conversation told Brand that Susie Thatcher had not heard yet about Laura's new source of discouragement. It was not the time or place to discuss it, Brand decided, and left with a generic goodbye.

35

Meetings nearly always did unwelcome things to Brand. Left him feeling futile, for example. Or wound up his biological clock, bringing on bouts of frenetic action. Or simply made him sleepy.

Wound up in the wake of his session with Drs. Schofield and Levenson, he found that his day already had a truncated feel. He would not finish all that he foresaw as essential in the time allotted. He could work himself into normal fatigue, then return home ready for a drink, dinner, an hour with the girls, an hour or more with Michelle.

All to the good. He would rid himself of the last shreds of the weekend's empty-nest languor.

He picked up the office phone to which he had affixed a 2x3-inch photo of the two girls. Susie Thatcher answered, as Brand had hoped. He had seen Susie, heard her cheerful voice not half an hour ago. Excusing the unusual followup, he asked whether she was alone in Dr. Schofield's outer office.

She was.

"I have a peculiar request," he began. "I'm wondering whether you know someone in the Personnel Department over at the University. I'm wondering secondly whether that someone could 'borrow' a copy of a particular personnel file. I'm looking specifically for the part of such a file that pertains to the subject's early-adult record. That means experience well before joining the University."

Susie's voice had a different timbre; it came over the wire so softly that Brand initially had trouble hearing what was said. Then it became readily audible. "I believe those files are permanently available. That's because people like the heads of departments or the provost or the president himself refers to them quite often."

"I'm presuming that you can pick out of the air the name of the man whose papers I'm looking for."

"Dr. Brand, I was able to see most of your debate Friday. I'd guess that Dr. Vandorn would be the party of interest."

"Right on. But you'll want to let your friend know that if risks are involved, he--or she--should forget it. If it's a situation where these records lie around anyway, then onward and upward."

"I understand. I don't believe they have any high-alert security."

Brand's second call went to Dr. Madsen, bringing another lucky moment. Madsen answered, and Brand went straight to the question. Would the gynecologist care to take part while Brand operated to terminate what appeared to be a successful implant pregnancy? "It's a female baboon this time, Al," Brand said. "You might find it interesting. Obviously, it's a caesarean delivery."

"I'm interested. Are you getting signs of life?"

"For weeks. A few days ago I thought the little guy would break out without my help."

"Is this the Baboon Della you mentioned a few weeks ago?"

"It is. A natural mother even though she's a little long in the tooth. A placid type. You've seen it: adjusts to pregnancy without a fight, without sickness."

"I'm looking forward."

They agreed on the next Saturday, 10:00 a.m. Conferring on Michelle, Brand said his wife had taken one more day off but was "back on her feet" except for a little residual weakness. The weekend as Madsen had organized it had provided the ideal corrective. Thanks were in order.

Concluding, Brand mentioned what Laura had told him. "I'm taking on the Homeric task of trying to bring Tim, her husband, back into the stable," Brand said. "In the meantime she's holding her breath and waiting to learn what I can find out. If anything. Say a prayer. If she has to drop her project, I think it could affect her health, not to mention her marriage."

"My wife had similar problems. We wanted to adopt, but her health has been too poor. We've had to give up."

"Sorry to hear it."

"Thanks. I'm working my way through it."

Before calling Tim Phillips Brand ran mentally through the possible approaches that might bring Laura's husband to renewed acceptance of his wife's project. He would have to rule out mention of such things as her ingenuous reference to a possible divorce. Other talking points:

-- Let Vandorn's influence win? He will never stop if this becomes a victory.

-- To surrender to Vandorn's lies and exaggerations would be the height of folly. It would also, in a critically important sense, mean deserting Laura in a unique kind of life-crisis. From another point of view, the physical, Tim's withdrawal of continuing support could conceivably ensure her failure--or loss of an embryo.

The worst case scenario might be Laura's attempt to "go it alone," without Tim's participation in any way. Failure to begin gestation or to carry initially, then to lose the new life might well scar her permanently. Musing, Brand sought to put words to a long familiar aphorism that began, "Where hope is lost. . ."

The final phrases eluded him, and Brand decided that he had the appropriate tack. The crux would be surrender because of Vandorn.

He dialed Tim's work number, a combination written down weeks ago when he first encountered the Phillipses. A secretary told him that "Mr. Phillips was out." Might she have him call?

Yes, of course.

Brand was gulping fragments of a "roast beef and Swiss on rye" when Tim Phillips returned his call. From Tim's first words forward, Brand could recognize the signs of a man whose mind was set, fixed. What the true "beneath the prattle" motivations were, Brand could neither find out nor hazard a guess.

He decided to probe, to see if he could dig beyond the words planted by Vandorn, and if possible to plant some of his own.

"You're aware, of course, that your wife has her mind and heart set on her plans to have a baby," Brand said. "And I presume you know that in planning and trying--disciplining herself toward that end-- she is answering an instinct that makes your most treasured ambition and mine a juvenile whim." Picking up quickly, he went on. "And in stymying that instinct we--you, I, anyone--is probably killing that instinct. What else we kill when we do that we don't know. The worst part is this--."

"Dr. Brand," Tim broke in, "I've heard all this. Womanly instincts, the momma quotient, the complete family, spiritual growth, all that stuff. But the fact is that she'll be violating human reproductive norms-- actually offending against the natural laws governing morality. Sexual morality of course, but morality, and social morality as much as any other kind."

"I don't really want to argue. But that, Tim, is hogwash. You don't violate morality by having a child--you assist nature. To call it a violation because we've found new ways to assist nature is to say we sin by using new, problem-specific techniques.

"There's no morality involved in unnatural conception?"

"There's response to need." Shifting the perspective, wondering how long Tim would continue to talk, Brand said: "We're not discussing Vandorn stuff here. The eugenics or selective breeding business. We're even farther from talking about a baby without a future or an oddity--a woman giving birth to her own grandchild. We're trying to give life that would have a decent existence after birth. We're--."

Again Tim interrupted. "You can't change the rules of the game and not pay for it. It's as simple as that. Laura--well, she sees only a little kid running around the house. There's no awareness that something could go wrong--."

"Something could go wrong when you're driving to work."

"I know. But my answer is to drive more carefully. Laura's going gung-ho for something she doesn't understand--something she could regret the rest of her life. She could adopt and be done with it."

"We both know that isn't the same."

"The same or not, my mind's also made up. She'll get used to it."

"Will you think of what she must conclude and feel?"

"I have already. But yes. I'm sure not blaming you. Or her. But we have to move on, find other ways to go. Legal, moral ways."

With a brusque "Talk to you later," Tim Phillips was gone. And Brand went to the lab, where work was waiting.

36

Coffee talk with Eldy Dennington equated in Vandorn's mind with fencing with chopsticks. A parry meant the same as a swing and a miss. The man thought big thoughts that were original with him but had no immediate relevance. At one moment he talked of his collection of guns, antique and modern, while wondering whether they could be used to advance the cause of CAP. Answered with a soft but faintly dismissive negative, Dennington became querulous.

Vandorn turned the conversation toward more practical considerations. "What we have to do," he said, "as I see it is get your steering group together in one room and see what we can come up with." Adding an innocent-sounding codicil that he felt was critical, Vandorn said, "We've got to make a few waves. Give the newspapers the stuff of headlines. Act legally, but raise a few eyebrows."

Sounding doubtful, Dennington scratched the bald spot on the back of his head. "Legally?" he said. "Will anybody notice?"

"I think people can be coaxed or persuaded to notice. Curiosity is the identifying characteristic of moderns everywhere, so it shouldn't be so hard, really." In talking out his thoughts Vandorn was feeling increasingly sanguine. But he felt also that progress toward the reality of an effective public splash lay with a group approach. With as many as could be dragooned into participation.

As if sensing what Vandorn was thinking, Dennington picked up where Vandorn had started. "We could probably get our steering people together on a Thursday," he said. "People are always going places on weekends, so you can't find 'em."

"Can you send out a notice? Or call your steering group members--however you notify them? Make it for a week from tomorrow, a Thursday?"

"Sure." A spark flared in his voice, a scintilla of the triumphal enthusiasm Dennington had originally exhibited on meeting Vandorn.

"We'll make it the most important caucus of the year. Big Program Session! I'll balloon it. And if you can give us a pep talk, we'll be off and running. All we've needed is a little leadership."

"I'll come with a full tank. You needn't be concerned."

"We'll meet at my house. My wife won't join us. When we're done maybe I'll show you my gun collection."

The part that Brand could not forget, and that kept intruding on memory, had occurred Saturday evening. The moment defined itself. It had begun with Laura's tears, intensifying into poignancy as they continued--for how long he could not say. With her stunning revelation of the quality that Brand read as artless love--her spontaneous desperate embrace--she had invaded his most vulnerable core.

And the memory lay there, an obstinate reminder that she was woman first, semi-client second.

The fact was that the heart-deep hug had opened a hazy vista of unspoken favors. All that while he knew he had to try, would honestly try, to maintain his concentration on established goals.

Beginning a new day or a new week, his habit had always been to attack undesirable or distasteful tasks first. The Monday meeting had already circumvented that practice. But logically he could shift blame for his minor delinquency onto Dr. Schofield. From there he had no more room for procrastination.

He dialed Alan Archer's phone. He instantly encountered a spontaneous wave of enthusiasm. "River City, man!" Archer nearly shouted. "You zapped him! I hope he didn't cripple you with that table stunt."

"I survived," Brand said. "But you can see what a gentle soul Professor Vandorn is."

"An example to us all! But we're sitting here with news for you. We've made contact--*sub rosa* contact--with three different candidates.

One we're discounting. He falls outside what we would consider a suitable age group, like over 50. Are we reading your mind correctly?"

"You are. The physical demands on the adult body aren't enormous as far as we can tell. But they are substantial. I'd say the 30's would be the limit."

"The thinner the better also?"

"Thin to medium would be most appropriate. But females of all body types experience pregnancy successfully. There once was a theory that the woman could and should be at least plump--not grossly fat, but somewhat heavy."

"On the theory that the fetus would need and consume plenty of the mother's bod?"

"Exactly. But those days are gone forever. Nowadays thin or medium build seems to make the whole process more comfortable. We're still guessing a little, but I'd say your choices of candidates should be pretty much what you've described."

"We can introduce you with fanfare any time you're available."

"Can you call them in on short notice?"

"Short or no notice. The two that we've tabbed live in town, not too far from us. Give us a few minutes and we're in business."

"I'll try to get time this week. Otherwise next week. I can talk to both candidates at once."

"I'll forewarn them."

37

"It's like something out of a Tarzan film," Madsen said. "The part on the cutting-room floor." He was modulating his voice to avoid awakening Baboon Della.

"You can speak in a normal tone." Brand lifted the straight, sticklike extension arm and tested the needle that he had already attached to it. "She's sound asleep, I believe. I'm only giving her another shot to make sure she doesn't wake up 'til we're done."

He could just reach her with the oversized needle on the extension rod. Standing close to the cage but remaining carefully outside it, he plunged the needle into Della's right buttock. The animal twitched and then lay still again. Her paws together, she lay on her side facing the rear of the cage. She might have been praying.

Quickly Brand looped a short wire around Della's feet. He knotted the wire carefully. Taking another syringe from Madsen, Brand gave Della another half-dose of lidocaine. "If it seems like a lot of sedation, I'd have to answer, Better safe than sorry," he commented. "We could ask Professor Vandorn about the strength of simian teeth."

"Speaking of your Nemesis, I saw him a couple of days ago," Madsen said. "He was carrying his left hand in a sling. That hand was invisible."

"It must be costing him a ton of sleep."

With Madsen helping, they hoisted Della out through the open door of the cage and into the tiny operating room. Together they placed her on the informal "operating table." Brand tied Della down with her feet in the dangling stirrups and her spine comfortably planted in the table's lengthwise slot.

Della's breath came normally. As well as Brand could tell, her heartbeat was steady. Her belly region rose grotesquely, a mound of flesh and bone.

He was prepping her, shaving and cleaning the area above the pubis, when the bell in the outer room rang. Madsen went to open the locked door. Fenton walked in, dapper in light Saturday togs. "Just stopping in to see if you need anything," he said to Brand.

"I think we're fully equipped. But thanks."

"I'll be checking around if you need me."

"We'll holler."

Brand was working on Della's stomach. "Life signs and everything else normal," he said as Fenton left.

"She needed a general?" Madsen asked. "We'd usually use a local unless the patient has a different idea."

"I would too. But I hate to take a chance. It's the Vandorn syndrome, I guess. And I don't like tying my animals down like Gulliver in the land of Little People."

"Any signs of sabotage in your Zoo recently?"

Brand struck his forehead with his open palm. "I never even thought of it. Good God. Give me one minute."

He went out. Fenton was pushing a broom in the baboon area and muttering under his breath. To Brand's question whether the night man had reported any visitors, Fenton answered emphatically, "Nossir. He's got instructions to report *anyone* to me. You're the first ones since yesterday afternoon."

"Thanks. Sounds under control."

Back in the operating room, Brand said "All clear," and asked Madsen if he wanted to remove Della's fetus. "Watching, I could learn something," Brand said.

"I'll try it if you're okay with that. I'll just have to get used to the smaller monkey dimensions as compared with the human."

"It'll come naturally. It has with me."

Brand handed Madsen a pair of rubber gloves. The surgical instruments that Madsen would need lay within easy reach on an open area of the table.

Beginning, Madsen made a shallow horizontal incision and then pulled back the folds of skin, locking them open with clamps. Della bled profusely. Handing the clamps to Brand to hold, Madsen felt inside the belly with a pair of forceps. "There it is," he muttered after a moment.

Carefully, searching for a firm grip, Madsen maneuvered the fetus to the surface. Brand could see a tiny, lightly furred head, still covered with blood. Using the forceps again, Madsen took hold of the tiny monkey head and lifted the animal out bodily.

The newborn squirmed. Mouth open, it sucked in air. The tiny chest began to heave. Then the new arrival emitted a raspy cough. There was no followup sound.

Brand held Della's offspring in the palm of his hand. "A perfect male," Madsen said. He watched as Brand laid the infant baboon on the sideboard next to the sink. "If you could sew Della up, Al, I'll clean this one off and give it some milk. Then he goes to one of the other females for breast-feeding."

"The surrogate mother doesn't mind?"

"They're pretty responsible. Or responsive. Mothering instinct, I'd guess. Our baboons seem to have it pretty much as humans would in the same circumstances."

"I've run into cases," Madsen said, "where a new mother wouldn't touch someone's else's neonate. Milk avarice, perhaps. Or self-protection. Nature's defenses."

Madsen was cleaning up around the incision in Della's midsection. His hands moved slowly and gently. "Everything's still in here," he said. "Fetal epithelium, the rest of the placenta. Take anything out or leave it in, Em?"

"My guess is that we can leave it in. It should resorb."

"I'd go along with that. No reason why it shouldn't, since it's abdominal. We did take out that residue when we had that abdominal pregnancy a few weeks ago."

"Precautionary?"

"Yes."

They worked in silence for a while. Again Brand debated inwardly and decided again to maintain silence on Laura's quandary. Then Madsen said, "I thought at first that you'd have fetal rejection if you implanted in the omentum," he said. "You know, no cooperation at all. Obviously I was wrong. But how can you explain no immune response?"

Brand was carefully cleaning the newborn baboon. "We had apparently viable pregnancies when I first contacted you, remember? I can only figure that the fetus grows a layer of epithelium. The antibodies in the omentum can't penetrate that wall."

"That's got to be the case." Madsen was finishing the resection.

"You know," he said, turning to look at Brand. "This is amazing. Everything here's exactly as you'd find it in a human."

"When you get into the details, it's even more amazing." Brand finished the cleaning and set the bloody wads of cotton in a waste bowl.

He cradled the tiny baboon in his two hands. Moving close, Madsen examined the new life. "What's your guess? Viable?"

"I think so," Brand said. "These animals are tough."

The baby baboon stretched, as if luxuriating in a new, free environment.

"Birth weight, by estimate?" Madsen said.

"Smaller than usual. Probably a pound to a pound and a half. Maybe a little less."

"Well, congratulations. Your new day is dawning. I never thought I'd chortle over the birth of a baboon."

Brand named the newcomer Tethys. Thinking "father instinct," he decided to make sure the infant received--and retained--food before going home.

It became an unexpected ordeal filled with irksome detail. Unable to arouse a female baboon to rise to her nursing functions, Brand went in search of cow's milk. He found none until he went up to the ground floor and aroused the nightman, Andy Garrison. As Brand learned quickly, Garrison had sequestered some milk for his own early-morning snack. He found it downstairs in Fenton's cooler. The zookeeper kept it stocked with a variety of foods for emergencies.

Finally equipped, Brand found that the feeding of a newborn monkey went agonizingly slowly. That meant drop by drop. But he made sure Della's issue received its first nourishment. Brand found it reminiscent of his nights with his daughters in the immediate aftermath of their births.

When he finally left the little one with its mother, it was nearing 2:00 a.m. Michelle was awake and reading when Brand arrived home. "I know I shouldn't worry," she said. "Especially since you called last night. But I keep thinking of that night prowler Vandorn. And the one thing your friend Dr. Madsen didn't give me was sleeping pills."

38

Eldy Dennington called the meeting to order, then went silent. In the pause it became clear that he had nothing to say to the five other CAP members present. They sat across from him at the dining room table. Dennington had appropriated one whole side, making space for Vandorn by planting a chair next to his.

They had almost no time to wait. They had hardly arranged themselves in their straight-backed chairs when Vandorn walked in. Dennington slammed a welcoming hand down on the chair he was holding, indicating it was reserved for the guest of honor. Vandorn sat after first nodding to the others. He was carrying his left arm in a colorful tartan sling. He could thank Jennifer for that. She had suggested something "decent but sort of garish" to distract people from devoting too much attention to the limb that hung in the tartan.

Dennington stood, staggered almost imperceptibly, and spoke. "You've all met Dr. Vandorn, I believe," he said. "Our newest--and most famous--member. A teacher at the University. A great speaker. A gentleman who can be our guide as we move forward. I suggest that we welcome Dr. Vandorn by joining in our battle cry!"

The assembled heads were nodding. Dennington raised his hand, held it up briefly, and sang out while the others formed a chorus:

"Welcome, welcome cohorts all!

Vict'ry's ours--sound the call!"

Half-standing and half-sitting, Dennington continued: "And now I yield the floor to Doctor Vandorn."

Vandorn stood. "I have to say first that I'm happy to be one of you," he said unceremoniously. "You are the present and future force that this community needs. As the CAP steering committee, what's at stake in our deliberations--if I can use the possessive *our* at this early stage--is nothing less than the general tenor, the general level of decency, even the liveability of this community that we all love." His hand had started pulsating painfully. He sat down.

"The problem is one we're all familiar with--one that holds the threat of degradation of the moral climate in Franklin as if its practice and message were a contagion. A plague!" he said, raising his voice. "And you--we--hold it in our power, once we design a program and bring your--our--total membership into the picture. . . We can turn this tide of what its leading exponents are calling 'medical experiments!' We can actually stop the bleeding."

He stopped, made eye contact with the five people on the other side of the table. "But here I am, banging my gums when you all know what the threat is. You know that this 'medical experimentation' is--bunk-- precisely what all the so-called 'advances' in the cause of reproductive science really amount to." His voice rose again. "It's hogwash," he finished.

"Hear, hear!" Dennington said. "We're looking at another time bomb under our community. But we're mostly looking at action to prevent the plague from taking hold. To keep everyone from going crazy. To build on our record. We've made our point with the town's drugstores. It took a lot of work, but none of them show those pornographic magazines on their open racks anymore. We can do the same for Mr. Brand and his clique!"

"I agree that we have to do something," George Rhodes said from his chair on the right flank of the group of five. A short, broad-shouldered man, Rhodes operated a gas station at a busy intersection near the university grounds. Vandorn bought all his gas there, and that had established an instant bond when the two men had first met. "But the question is, what? If one of us owned a newspaper or a radio station, we'd have a way to get the word out. But we don't. At least I don't."

Vandorn cut in, interrupting Barbara Dee, who had just raised her right hand, asking for time. "We can't let that stop us," Vandorn said. He was finding kinship in this group; now, slowly, he would take control of their group destiny. *Slowly.* "We could, for example, go in a body to the editor of the *Palladium*. Ask him if he stands rock-solid with us in this, er, crusade."

"What if he says no?" Rhodes asked.

"He won't. He'll engage in some gobblegook and then come down with something like--." Vandorn's voice rose: *"Show me some news. We cover everything newsworthy that happens in this town."* Again Vandorn let his gaze circulate. "After that, we'll have a commitment, even if it's a vague one. But we have to inform him before we take any public action."

Seizing her opportunity, Barbara Dee spoke up. A secretary in a law office, she had a thin, handsome face. She spoke with precision. Her hands moved perpetually, weaving invisible tapestries. "I wonder," she began, "whether even after we confront an editor or a radio or TV programmer, we couldn't figure a way to generate real news. Something they'd have to send someone to cover." She smirked. "I'm not thinking of something really incendiary. I'm thinking of some public event-- something public but legal. Something my bosses wouldn't boggle at."

"Exactly right," Vandorn said. "Something public but legal." He would coax and coax again; Let them name the first group exercise. Then, once named, and agreed upon, it's theirs.

"What I'm suggesting is a protest march," Barbara said. "We could get a bunch of our people to join in. We could carry placards, signs, flags. We'd notify everyone in advance, of course--radio, TV, newspapers."

"And no violence," Vandorn said. "No broken store windows. But I'd say it would be fine to pass out leaflets, or have resolutions that people could sign. That kind of stuff makes for good pictures, and that's half the battle, a few pictures that tell our story."

Dennington had been listening with his head tilted. Now, alive again, he said: "We could pick a day when everybody's out and around. Go where the crowds are. Maybe the University Mall. Maybe the Joyline Flea Market. Some place like that."

"All great ideas," Vandorn said. He jotted some notes on a small yellow tablet that he had brought. "For me," he said while continuing to write, "I'd like to see a march go through a busy shopping area and a residential area also."

"Way to go." Rhodes seemed suddenly to awaken from a shallow nap. "Give everybody a chance to see us with our best regalia, our best signs. I'd help make new signs if we need them."

"Would we notify the gay newspaper?" Dennington had hardly asked the question when the second woman present, Georgia Andrews LeBaron, placed her right-hand fingers at her mouth and stifled a giggle. Immediately, joining the conversation for the first time, LeBaron said in a voice that oozed contempt: "I'd hate to get mixed up with those people. They're all, I presume, *homosexual*." A resident of the "official" Franklin municipal gold coast, Georgia, according to rumor, "had money." No one in CAP doubted it because Georgia was always the first to respond to pleas for funds for group projects.

"I doubt that we'd want to contact the homosexuals at all," Vandorn said firmly. "They're part of the problem in this town. I'm even hearing at the University that they're recruiting secretly. They may give us a writeup or two, but I can guarantee that what they write won't be favorable to CAP."

"Hear, hear," Dennington said loudly.

"Which reminds me," Vandorn resumed, "I think we should set a date for our protest march--if we all agree." As he paused and looked around, as if counting votes, there was a small chorus of "Ayes" and "Yeses."

"--And I'd also like to suggest that you--we--change the name of our group."

"We talked about that," Dennington said. "Some of us think we need a better name."

"I'm suggesting CITIZENS against MORAL POLLUTION or some such name," Vandorn said. "Make it a little more comprehensive. Pornography in all its forms is of course part of it--a big part. But so is reproductive experimenting such as they're doing at the hospital."

There was general agreement that Vandorn's suggestion was welcome; it would "Do the trick," and the meeting adjourned. Out of the bustle as the meeting dissolved came a suggestion on a date for a protest march. They would also call their group CAMP.

It would be a Sunday, early afternoon, two weeks down the road. As the steering committee members moved toward the door, Eldy Dennington tapped Vandorn on the left shoulder. Vandorn released a kind of snort. With his right hand he gestured toward the tartan sling.

Dennington said "Sorry!" In the next breath he asked Vandorn if he wanted to see a great gun collection. Vandorn nodded *yes*.

39

Once deciphered, the papers couldn't have been more damning. They began with a form indicating that James B. Vandorn, Candidate, had been terminated in his third year as a scholastic. His academic standing had not come into question. On the contrary, he had shown himself to be an outstanding student, especially in the critical disciplines: Philosophy, Theology, Apologetics.

Brand read the form twice. He had begun a third reading when the document suddenly shed its apparent pointless nature and became clarified. In a critical line the Latin word *Casus* appeared. Next to it in a space for an answer of some kind Brand saw the abbreviated word FELL., and following that the lower-case initials i.f.d.

Minutes passed while Brand let his mind range over the possible meanings imbedded in the partial word and the three initials. The word *Casus* was clear; it was a Latin word for *cause*. But FELL, and i.f.d.?

The first of those might be fellatio, he decided. The initials, again, had to stand for the legalistic Latin phrase *In flagrante delictu*, meaning "redhanded," or "in the act."

The attached papers ran a gamut of surprising extent. They included lengthy typed statements from the prefects of Discipline and Charism. Also attached by a large paperclip were three handwritten reports from persons who, from the tenor of their comments, had to be students.

There was no statement from Vandorn. What seemed undeniable was the reality that Vandorn had not become a priest. On the contrary, the seminary had expelled him while he was still pursuing his undergraduate studies on the way to the graduate or postgrad studies that would have directly prepared him for the rite of ordination.

Struggling through the long-hand documents, Brand found references that awakened fresh memories. If he was decoding it accurately, one comment read: "Subject tends to consider himself the ultimate arbiter of right and wrong, of the ethical and unethical, the moral and the immoral or amoral.

Another had different critiques: "James has this idea, it seems to me, that women are the sole sources of evil in the affairs of men, in particular of sexual evil from which all other evils proceed."

"My frank judgment would be that Candidate Vandorn seeks to become a wearer of the cloth as a way to gain superiority over his fellowmen--not merely his fellow candidates but all his fellowmen, which includes women."

Brand made notes rapidly, carefully, then filed the whole package where it would remain under lock and key. In that file he kept notes on his baboon experiments.

He had also begun a new file on his notes taken after the fact on his televised debate. He recalled now that he had asked the station for a transcript of that encounter, but had not yet received it. He would ask again. A transcript would be a mine of statements, words, phrases that he had possibly forgotten.

You never knew when Vandorn would be back in the attack mode.

40

The hesitancy in Laura's voice could only mean that she had unusual, perhaps negative, news. Similar significance attached to the fact that she had tracked Brand to the lab. She would have tried calling his office and the Zoo first.

"I'll go over to my office," Brand said, noting with a strangely disconnected curiosity how mellow his voice sounded. "We can talk more comfortably there." Also, he thought with an access of soft exhilaration, meeting there transforms what may be a simple exchange of information into the facsimile of a tryst.

Following the Quadrangle sidewalk to the Professional Building, he walked with a vague sense of expectancy. Was that the word? Guilt was more accurate? With an effort of the will, he channeled his thinking to Al Madsen and his role in Laura's case.

Case sounded in his head like something that involved an unknown, a stranger, an unperson.

He had not seen or talked to her since *that* Saturday evening. Nor had he heard her voice, the voice that had won a permanent place in his catalogue of treasured accents.

He hadn't been in his office five minutes when she entered silently. Hunting in his PROJECTS file for some papers, he heard her speaking his name. "Em," she said, "am I interrupting you?"

"Nothing that I couldn't joyfully break off," he said.

"I'm glad, I keep running into these dead-ends, or unsolvables, or whatevers." Responding to his hand gesture, she sat down. Now as she leaned forward, he had a view of deep cleavage. "I got a call from your marvelous Dr. Madsen," she continued. He told me one of our potential egg donors and I are about to be matched--timed precisely. It will happen in the next few days."

"And you're wondering--."

"I am. If I go ahead now, I'm working directly against Tim's wishes. He's determined--well, you know all that. He's determined that we won't have any more 'frivolity.' But I feel just awful. Look at all the people I've brought into my case. . ."

Case again. Brand made a mental note: find another word.

"If I just drop the whole project now, I'll be making Tim happy and alienating maybe half a dozen other people. Worst of all, I'll be terminating what I've started with Dr. Madsen."

She stopped. Leaning back in the office chair, she took a deep breath, as if recovering from her presentation. Watching, Brand could sympathize, even feel her pain as the pain of surrender. But she hadn't yet come to the phase of her "project", as she called it, to taste the sweet fruit of imminent or approaching victory.

"I've tried interceding with Tim," Brand said. "And I struck out."

"I know. And that's not what I'm asking. Or would ask."

"Something else? Something I could do?"

"Yes. I know you're busy beyond my even imagining. But I'm finding that I can't just stop, drop the whole thing, call everyone and say the experiment is over. Finished."

"You're going ahead with it? Keeping Al--Dr. Madsen--on the project?"

"I'm going to," Laura said in a firm voice. "On one condition."

"Which is?" Brand said softly, his curiosity outstripping his reasoning processes.

"That you stay with it. Be there when he performs any procedures. Follow what happens."

"A tall order," Brand said, buying time, earning a pause. He could easily picture the occasions on which Laura would have to undergo "procedures," and how long each might take. Even more simply he could visualize the travel time that would be part of his sideline participation in the embryonation attempts. Some of Dr. Madsen's work could, and undoubtedly would, take place in the evening, when the day patients would have gone home. On those evenings when Dr. Madsen had late hours for Laura, Brand could be there.

He thought of home. He would see less of it. Michelle would notice. But for Brand the looming problem might be Laura's husband.

"Is there a chance that Tim might come after me with a shotgun?" he asked, intending that the facetious phrasing would place a humorous patina on the question and the possibility that it raised.

"He's not that type--if you're serious. But I would also say I'm taking a class or some such thing."

"If I had to miss an appointment or two, assuming I can find a way to be present as a monitor--." Brand let the question hang.

"I would be thankful for the other times when you could be there."

They sat in silence. Brand could hear the murmur of voices. That would be coming from an office down the hall, Dr. Stapleton's office. A cardiologist, he had advised Brand more than once.

"I'll find a way," Brand said.

41

Brand settled against the red leather of the circular restaurant booth. Music sounded unobtrusively from unseen loud-speakers. Across from the booth, over a row of bare tables, the long bar loomed against its backdrop of mirrors.

Gay bar at midday. Like the title of a painting.

"We had a call from your Mr. Vandorn," Archer said. He had taken a seat between John Gennett and Martin Adamson. Introducing Gennett, volunteer for the role of first Pregnant Man, had in jest given him the title "First Fother."

"He's not my Mr. Vandorn," Brand said. "He's his own self-appointed savior of the world." Briefly he considered adding "from people like us," but stopped at the realization that he was dealing with three homosexuals.

"I still think he's got his jeans in an unnecessary uproar," Archer said. "He's going to die of unfulfilled Quixotism."

They talked about CAMP and its depressing campaign. A waiter came and took their orders. In an accent betraying a slight foreign flavor, the man recommended dishes, sandwiches. "You can't possibly go wrong with the double cheeseburger," he said. To Gennett he added immediately, "Kir, Mr. Gennett?"

"Not now," Gennett said. "Later."

With the orders placed, Brand said, "I'm sure you've got questions." He was looking at Gennett, noting again the rounded shoulders, the incipient paunch, the large eyeglasses that gave the wearer an owlish look. It was a searching, scholarly look, seen from an angle.

"A million of them," Gennett said. "Like, what bodily changes can I expect if we can pull this off?"

They'll probably replicate what happens to the female of the species-- as far as we can read it now," Brand said. "That means some weight gain over gestating time. It means, or can mean, variable attacks of appetite. We doubt that your voice will change, but it might. Remember you'll be a first. A trail-blazer."

"How about chemistry? Don't you have to make allowances for the male hormones, that kind of thing? You know I've been considering a sex change anyway. Would that make it better or worse?"

Gennett was staring large-eyed at Brand, thoughtful behind the glasses.

"I'm guessing that it would be worse because now, as you are today, we can simply control the testosterone. We also have to administer some female hormones--but those would be required in any case."

"Where do you find those?"

"Practically any drugstore. They are just about the easiest things of all to find. We'd have to have your hormonal profile right from the start, of course. Then it's up to us to keep the level where it's supposed to be."

"How do you find where it's supposed to be?"

"It would be a pretty general norm. But we'll be testing steadily."

The waiter returned. Balancing a tray, he passed out the dishes from memory, murmuring the specific order in each case. No one spoke until the waiter asked if anyone had any further wishes; no one spoke and the man moved off. John Gennett spoke again to Brand.

"I've been hearing a lot of stuff about this. But what actually happens?"

"It's as simple as planting cucumber seeds in the spring. We have the subject--we hope that will be you. The doctor makes a little needle puncture in the subject's belly. He makes that puncture in the fleshy part just below the belly-button. The trick then is to wash an egg out of the donor female--if we haven't done that already. You transfer that egg into the recipient male, the subject."

Brand paused. His three listeners were ignoring their food and listening intently. Brand had given lectures at which he had observed lower levels of attention.

Resuming, he said, "That spot where the egg enters is the omentum. Once there, of course, the egg has to meet a seed, a live sperm, to become an embryo. The doctor does that too. In many cases, of course, the two are brought together before going into the omentum. That's the better way, actually. You create the human speck, the living embryo, then implant it."

Silent since the food had arrived, Adamson now spoke. "It still seems strange. You can do that without all the apparatus that a woman has for first conceiving and then carrying a baby."

"You want to remember that we have enough studies of the baby environment that we can duplicate it in a male."

"You're sure of that?" Gennett asked.

"We are. Those are details. There are indispensable hormones that change to accommodate a female pregnancy. They're HCG--human choreonic gonadotropin--prolactin, others. But that's not all. There are also some minor hormones that also do some changing." Pausing again, Brand took a sip of water. "Examples would be pituitary hormones and some growth hormones. Since this is a first, we'll probably keep tabs on them too."

Speaking to Gennett, said, "Once you're into this and go to the gym for a workout, they'll be telling you to lay off the milk shakes."

A general laugh went around the table.

"That reminds me," Brand said. "You won't want to be entering marathons, playing tennis, or helping your friends to move. That would be pretty much the way a woman would normally react. She'd limit herself on the strenuous exercise front. Protect the fetus."

"How about boobs? Will I develop big floppers?" Gennett said, directing an eloquent look toward Adamson.

Adamson laughed as though he were sharing a private joke and Brand said, "You could have some growth there. No question. We had some in a couple of baboons that we impregnated. What happens in one species like that will usually repeat in the human counterpart."

"I think you should give us a rundown on the behavior John should expect or would be allowed," Archer said. "We know about the strenuous exercise, that kind of thing. But how about appearing in public once he starts to show. That's a pretty compromising picture, as I recall it."

Brand helped himself to another sip of water. Gennett, with his pragmatic demeanor, was impressing him favorably. It was time, however, to appraise the candidate's feelings about the potentially monastic life of a pregnant male.

"Our experiences of the past weeks and months have convinced us that there's serious sacrifice in what you'll be taking on," Brand said. "Graveyards don't yawn, as Shakespeare would have it. There wouldn't be warning signs. But there are people who see our experiments as stamping on some deity's big toe. They've killed a couple of our most qualified baboons, as you've probably heard--."

"The debate nut," interpolated Archer. "The crack-brain that I told you about."

Gennett was nodding his recollection. Again, Brand returned to the subject, the one that might spell mortal danger for the expectant male.

"Your possible sex change wouldn't be nearly as important as your tolerance for lying low," Brand said. "Some 5,000 men are now known to have undergone castration and other changes, accepting surgical procedures. But that's a 'bag o' shells,' as some comedian calls it, compared to entering an imaginary monastery. That's what we're recommending."

"What could they possibly do, these crackpots?" Gennett spoke from curiosity more than disbelief, as Brand read his question. Responding in kind, Brand said:

"I'm afraid they can kill. From some source they have an arsenal of deadly potions, if you don't mind a poetic term."

I love it. But have they killed humans--or only animals?"

"No humans that we know of. But it seems that they're currently riding a tidal wave of fanaticism. They think the morals--and probably the economic future--of the municipality of Franklin is being endangered."

"Sounds like the way out for me would be to leave town."

"No," Brand said. "You'll be under pretty regular surveillance--by us. We'd have to take blood from time to time, give shots. You know, monitor generally."

"Our food is cold," Archer said. "Let's take a break while we think of other questions."

Folding his cloth napkin carefully, Brand toyed with the impression that Gennett had already, in effect, accepted the challenge of becoming the pregnant man volunteer. He had shown no hesitancy during the question-answer session just completed. He had asked sensible questions. Neither of the other two present during the conversation-- Editor Archer and Gennett's friend Adamson--had shown negative attitudes or issued warnings of lurking dangers. In fact, it had gone the other way: the two members of the audience had helped the discussion along.

Time to settle the question of secrecy. "There might actually be different ways to meet the need for secrecy," Brand said to Gennett, who had himself pushed his plate away. He had left part of a grilled cheese sandwich.

"I think it'll be easily arranged," Gennett said. "We've got this little place outside town, just far enough off the beaten track. We could use it." As he finished he glanced at Adamson; the latter nodded.

"Sounds ideal," Brand said. "And don't forget there's always darkness now that the days are getting shorter. Some or most of your appointments with Dr. Madsen and me will be in the evening--another advantage if okay with you."

"It's ideal with me," Gennett said. "In fact, when do we start?"

"I think we have to figure two to four weeks. In the meantime, aren't we expecting a contract? Mr. Quarles mentioned it when we met not long ago."

Gennett was smiling. "The distribution of the spoils," he said. "That's the way Quarles is looking at it."

"He's talking about a book, a movie, talk shows, what-have-you," Adamson said. "Sounds like a star is born--or maybe star delivers. Something like that."

Brand held up a monitory hand. "You'll want to cover all those possibilities. But I don't think you should forget Vandorn, the mad ethicist, not for a second. If he sees some wealth coming to John here and others, he's going to have a shit hemorrhage."

"Maybe that's when we go totally underground," Adamson said.

"You'll have plenty of time to figure that out," Brand said. "I only advise caution even if things look pretty quiet."

"I'll get on Quarles and find out what he's got as far as a contract is concerned," Archer said. "Once we have a copy, I'll send it over to your office. Okay if I send a copy also for Dr. Madsen?"

"Definitely. We'll be working on this project together, the way we've talked it over." Brand smiled. "But he's leaving to me any contacts we get from Professor Vandorn."

"We're back to work on that note," said.

"May I leave one thought for Mr. Quarles?" Brand said.

The others were standing. "Shoot," said.

"He should include in the contract your own thoughts about *post partum* nurture of a new baby."

42

The 24 CAMP volunteers could no more march in formation than they could grow wings. Walking at their head, Vandorn could only hope that they would not wander off, depriving the protest march of one more link. The "crowd" was already small enough.

Vandorn had given up trying to organize them. Starting as the self-appointed drill sergeant, he had quickly noted that the protest was more lark than demonstration. The weather had to accept part of the blame. This Sunday was a technicolor 75 degrees with just enough breeze to stir the scent of lilac. The marchers were serious about making a splash for community purity, but not at the cost of having a good time.

Some of them were passing out leaflets. Others now and then waved their little slogan-bearing flags. "NO MORE MORAL POLLUTION IN FRANKLIN" read the slogan on the flags. More than once, looking back to check his marching legions, Vandorn had experienced a surge of fear that someone would poke a fellow demonstrator in the eye.

Walking next to Georgia LeBaron, Vandorn by an act of will restrained the urge to criticize his fellow demonstrators. Rather than sound negative, he sought and found words of praise. He also dropped hints regarding Brand and his work at University Hospital.

Georgia had heard much about Brand, from whatever unmentioned sources. The word had been both laudatory and harshly accusatory, and Georgia admitted that she could not reach a conclusion. "I have friends," she said, "who think he's the thirteenth Apostle. Others think he's the devil in human garb."

"He's the latter," Vandorn said before considering the effect his words might have. "He's really the primary polluter in this town," he added.

"The people who have had him consulting on their medical cases are the ones who praise him," Georgia said. "They don't even care that he experiments in reproductive areas."

For Vandorn the conversation had become confusing. He had no room for middle-ground attitudes toward Brand. His association with CAMP had no other purpose than termination of Brand's career as a known betrayer of traditional values. Yet, he thought as he slowed his steps, letting Georgia catch up with him: yet he was seeing harmony with Georgia as a key to extending his influence over the CAMP members.

Their eyes met. Hers were semi-lidded, his, expressive of a will to rationalize, to avoid disagreement. "We'll be getting into this pretty deeply over the next few weeks and months," he said. "No need to try to settle it here."

"I agree." She spoke readily. "I agree," she said again.

Vandorn was anticipating his opening. They were leaving the mall area and starting along a tree-lined street with small, well-tended lawns. From driving past and checking the house numbers, Vandorn knew which homes belonged to the Phillips family.

As he had planned, he could now present Exhibit One to Georgia. Show her one of the women who took roles in Brand's hocus-pocus with live human beings in the form of embryos, who sought out Brand as the magician who could provide egg and sperm with a magic word, who could juggle male and female hormones and other elements to produce parentless offspring. "There's a woman living along here who's been in Doctor Brand's clutches," Vandorn said, "If you'll come to the door with me, I'll introduce you."

"Color me curious," Georgia said.

They were in front of the Phillips house. Turning to face the marchers immediately in his rear, Vandorn said, "We're pausing to leave a brochure here." To Georgia he said, "This lady was once a patient of Doctor Brand's. She's recanted--changed her mind. Seen the error of her ways."

He started up the walk with Georgia close behind. Reaching the porch level first, Vandorn pressed the bell. He had a brochure--his brochure, with his words in it--in his right hand.

Half a minute passed before the front door opened. Laura, dressed in a plain house dress, stood behind the screen door. "Dr. Vandorn?" Laura said. "What are you__."

"We're marching with a group of citizens," Vandorn said. "And I've brought you one of the brochures we're passing out. It explains what we're doing to clean up the community."

"I think I've heard it all," Laura said. "I don't really need anything more." She made a move to close the door. At that moment Tim called from the deeper interior of the house.

"Who is it?" Tim said in a semi-bellow.

"Doctor Vandorn. You remember."

"Of course I do. Tell him we don't want any."

Laura was closing the door. "I'll put this in your mailbox," Vandorn said as the door clicked shut.

"What in the living hell was he doing here?" Tim said. "In other words, what's he selling now?"

"Some literature. He's with a bunch of people, walking around apparently and purifying the community. That's what it sounds like."

"We must be on his guest list. That must mean we'll never get rid of him. If he stops or calls again, you can tell him we're converted. He should find other suckers."

"I'll get rid of him. But I don't think we'll hear from him again," Laura said. From the hallway inside the front door she watched Tim as he peered out a living room window. Vandorn's appearance unannounced had left her feeling uncomfortable; the man carried his zealotry like a poisoned dart. He would fire it wherever he suspected deviation from his vision of societal morality.

"He's walking at the head of a bunch of people carrying signs," Tim said. "But at least they're moving down the block. I hope they stop at old man Travister's."

43

Eagerness met opportunity.

Donna Mallory had impressed Brand, during his "inquisition" period, as a donor candidate of special promise. She seemed appropriately curious, yet showed no signs of hesitation or fear. Her motive for volunteering to donate eggs seemed basically humanitarian; the mother of three, she was willing, even anxious, to spread the good word of motherhood in any safe way. Even better, she understood and sympathized with Laura Phillips' situation as if the two were old friends.

Mallory's systemic timeliness became Laura's opportunity. Both women expressed unalloyed eagerness. Mallory jested about "mothering in absentia."

Responding to the call from Dr. Madsen's secretary, Mallory reported to his office on time and prepared for the vaginal search that would hopefully bring out a healthy egg. It would then be up to the Madsen-Brand team to join the ovum with the sperm Laura had secretly obtained according to Madsen's instructions. She had insisted on such personal participation.

Delivery of the capsule containing the sperm had evoked what she interpreted indifferently as the wages of stealth. It was for her as if part of her marriage had disintegrated under the impact of this simple act: removing the capsule from her secret P.O. box.

Madsen set the procedure in motion. His next method called for explanations to patients or volunteers of what they faced and what instruments would be used. With Brand observing, he held up the small pump that had become integral to his examining-room equipment. Mallory watched, entranced.

The pump looked like nothing more than a miniature generator.

"This is the key to today's procedure," Madsen said. "It's a pump that we'll use to push the medium inside. Later, with luck, we bring out an egg."

Mallory smiled, raising her head from her supine position to see the instrument better. As she lay back, pulling at the light blanket to cover her near-nudity, Madsen showed her Exhibit 2. "Dr. Brand invented this one," Madsen said, "the special catheter that we will be using to perform the final magic to capture the egg."

"What makes this one different from other catheters?" Donna's grey, intelligent eyes held curiosity unmixed with anxiety.

"It's got a double barrel, so to speak. Double tubes. The lavage fluid goes out through this side and is sucked back in through the other one."

"Sucked? Do I feel it?"

"Yes, slightly but not painfully. This works with the pump and we can regulate the strength of the suction."

"I'll be praying that it works on the first try."

Brand and Madsen went to work. Brand loaded the catheter with the liquid medium and handed it over at a signal from Madsen. The rubber gloves felt clumsy on his hands; he was not used to them, but Madsen's clinic required them.

Brand moved the couple of steps to the foot of the elevator bed. He would activate the pump on signal.

Madsen made the vaginal insertion. The catheter entered slowly. Donna twitched slightly as the catheter moved.

"Sensitive," Madsen said matter-of-factly.

"Very."

"Now for the pump," Madsen said, nodding. At once Brand turned on the tiny machine. It made a steady whirring sound.

Moments passed. Madsen used hand signals to Brand, controlling the pump action. Minutes passed and Madsen withdrew the catheter. "Lavage complete," he said. Brand accepted the catheter. Looking at Donna, who had been lying stone-still during the purging action, Brand said, "I hope you've just helped us make history."

Donna was smiling. "That's if we have an egg?"

"Yes. This is one of the first uses of this instrument, among other unique things here." Brand held up the catheter. "Now it's up to me to see if we have a live one in here. I'll use a microscope to do that."

Donna sat up holding the light blanket over her upper body, covering and warming simultaneously. "Will you let me know if you captured one?"

"You'll be the third to know," Brand said. "But right now you're done."

As Brand and Madsen left the room, Donna was starting to dress. Brand first checked the incubator in the adjunct "Equipment Room," noting the settings: atmosphere, oxygen, carbon dioxide, relative humidity, temperature, pH or acidity. All stood at the required levels.

He went to the microscope and began the search for an egg in the culture medium.

Brand had called home, telling Michelle that they were in the midst of an experiment that would take another "hour or two." Michelle took the news with a small groan, but recovered rapidly. "Make it as soon as you can, Em?" she said. "The girls are jumpy. They want to wait up to see you. And I'm holding dinner."

Brand said he would break away as soon as possible.

"Mating time," for Brand, began with placement of both Donna's egg and a donor's sperm in a Petri dish. That done, the passage of more than three remaining afternoon hours gave the microscopic actors in the drama--egg and sperm--the time and opportunity to join forces to become a human being: an embryo.

Brand had time to return to the hospital lab to resume his day job. Time for a home dinner.

Madsen's Clinic, 6:30 p.m. Laura, dressed in light, removable clothing, arrives at Madsen's. The clinic seems to hum with subsurface excitement. Already on the premises, Brand is making notes.

Clinic, 6:35 p.m. Alerted, Brand moves to the Examining Room, meeting Laura who is already virtually ready for her "operation." Brand tells her he believes they have created an embryo. "A sturdy-looking egg," he announces. The mood of high expectancy intensifies. Brand wonders if he is the only one experiencing it.

Clinic, 6:45 p.m. Dr. Madsen enters with a tall, grey-haired nurse. Brand and Laura have just touched hands--for luck in what is about to happen.

Talking to Laura, Madsen explains again. "All the conditions seem to be right," he says. "Your hormone level is exactly where we want it. Estrogen the same--about 400 picograms per millilitre. Progesterone the same--about 1,000 picos per millilitre."

Laura lies on the adjustable bed, a picture of total comfort, back flat, chest out. Brand could see faint pinkish flush spots on each cheek.

"Picograms?" she said to Dr. Madsen.

"One millionth of a millionth of a gram."

"Best of all," Brand added, joining the conversation, "it looks as if we have an embryo." He realizes he is repeating himself.

"Obtained today?" Laura's question communicated a soft strain of excitement.

"About two, three hours ago," Brand said.

"I'm not a praying person, but I've been praying that it works the first time--the implant. I've even convinced my mother that she should say a few 'Hail Marys'. She started out dead determined to talk me out of the whole Frankenstein project, as she calls it."

"You're the second one today who has said she's praying for quick results," Madsen said, smiling and showing small, even teeth. "The egg donor, Donna, mentioned the same thing." He slapped his powerful hands together, exulting. "Shall we give it a go?" he added. He was looking at Laura.

"I'm as ready as I'll ever be." She smiled, looking somehow girlish and yet more mature, more womanly, than Brand had ever seen her.

Can even the prospect, the thought of motherhood, work a change? Brand could see it, sense it. *Does part of the apparent change lie in the woman's new aura of fulfillment, or self-confidence? Of independent decisions in Laura's case?* Of owning your body?

Could others detect the new Laura? Brand wondered. He was still puzzling when she turned slightly and wiggled her fingers in Brand's direction, a parting signal that also invited him to join in her magical adventure.

Lying on the adjustable bed, Laura had questions. About the incision: how big would it be? Would it heal quickly? Would it show, disappear? If the first embryonation attempt failed, would a second incision have to be made in the same place?

Madsen answered thoughtfully as he laid bare the site for the implantation. Her legs flat, pubic mound visible under the sheet that covered her lower body. A hospital gown, worn backwards, covered her upper parts.

Madsen and Brand readied their instruments once Laura had received her answers.

Brand told her more: what he had seen in the microscope had certainly looked like an embryo, "at about the 100-cell stage." It was stored, for the time being, in the laparoscope that Brand was guarding.

Madsen was deep into his work: parting the cloths over Laura's middle, swabbing, using a syringe to administer a local anesthetic. He talked at times, explaining as he worked. "Some people like sheets with holes in them here--to work through," he said. "It seems confining to me. Or falsely modest." He had pinched up some stomach skin with his gloved fingers, giving the anesthetic needle a target. As the needle went in, a tremor passed almost imperceptibly over Laura's body--and she laughed.

"Surprised me," she said.

"We'll give it a couple of minutes. This lidocaine works pretty quickly, but we want to be sure it's taken. . ." To the nurse he said: "Curette ready? We'll need a couple of those hooks too."

Now they stood over Laura, two on Madsen's side, Brand alone on his. He had a guardian role here, an assistantship. He was Laura's *vademecum*, her insurance. Not that his presence would do more than ensure that this beginning would not be bungled: that described his entire role. Or did it?

He was also on Laura's mind; he could sense it. Her request that he join Madsen bespoke faith in his skill as a practitioner. He could not yet fathom the deeper narrative.

Laura's relaxation seemed complete. Madsen took the curette that the nurse held out and instantly, expertly made an incision. It was perhaps an inch long. It bled lightly. "Just right," Madsen muttered. "Em, would you apply the hooks, hold it open? I'll need the lap now."

Brand gave Madsen the laparoscope and maneuvered the hooks to hold open the incision. Madsen watched as a gap became visible, widened; selecting his moment, he inserted the lap, pressed slightly and pushed down on the plunger to discharge the medium inside. The lap emptied.

"That's it, young lady," Madsen said to Laura after a long pause. He was grinning; she smiled back, broadly, eyes flashing, teeth brilliant in the overhead light. "Couple of stitches and you may be a mother." As he removed the lap, he added: "But it may take more than one try. Many more."

"Thank you, doctors," Laura said. Brand heard the plural "doctors" and felt his chest muscles tighten.

44

The letters on the frosted glass window read "HOMER L. KELLER, MAYOR."

In smaller letters the citizens in the waiting room could read "City of Franklin."

Prof. James Vandorn had read both levels of print several times. He had examined them to what for him was surfeit. Avoiding a third reading that might again provide hope that the door would open *at last*, Vandorn leaned over to Eldy Dennington. The president of the civic organization CAMP responded by leaning over to hear what Vandorn had to say.

Now Dennington and Vandorn were tilted across the front of Georgia LeBaron, who sat between the two. Georgia didn't have to move to become a participant in the conversation.

"Just to make you feel good," Vandorn said, "I've heard that Mayor Keller has a door and a special passage leading to the outside. When he runs out of time for an appointment, or just doesn't want to see someone, he does a disappearing act. His secretaries then announce that 'the Mayor was called away'."

"That's all we need," Dennington said. "Write letters, get an appointment, and then he's flew the coop."

"Flown," Georgia said. "And I think someone in the opposition party is spreading stories like that--that he runs out on appointments. I have more faith in him than that."

"I don't believe it myself," Vandorn said. "But I've heard supposedly knowledgeable people remark on it."

"Well, we should set a deadline and not wait beyond that--," Eldy began as the door to the Mayor's office opened. The Mayor himself stood in the doorway, beckoning in friendly fashion.

Vandorn let Georgia lead them into the inner sanctum. According to rumor Georgia had political ties to the Mayor, ties that overran strict boundaries to become social relations as well. Georgia had in fact found her way onto a gossip column's roster of those who attended the wedding of one of the Mayor's daughters.

Georgia had never spoken of it, leaving the report to others to interpret, digest, or simply reject.

Seated across from the Mayor, again with Georgia in the middle of three chairs, Vandorn deferred to Georgia to open the dialogue.

"Mr. Mayor," Georgia said formally after he had greeted her by her first name. "We're members of the civic improvement group that we call CAMP--Citizens against Moral Pollution. That means moral pollution of the kind that has turned other communities in this state into sewers."

"We're hoping to prevent that kind of thing," Vandorn said, "and we believe we can do more--keep property values stable, provide a wholesome environment for the children of the community, keep unsavory characters from setting up shop here, and so on. When I say setting up shop, I mean all the typical ones and a few others. These others don't work in stores. They ply their immoral trades in sterile laboratories."

The Mayor spoke, picking up on Vandorn. "You're referring to this doctor at University Hospital? What's the name?" The Mayor spoke gently, almost inaudibly. He gave the impression of one who was innocently, curiously, seeking answers.

"He's the one. Brand." As if he were awarding her a laurel wreath, emblem of victory, Vandorn added: "I've just been telling Georgia that the real threats to community morals are coming from people like him. His name is Brand, Doctor Brand."

"The one you faced in that debate on Channel One." Again the Mayor sounded meek and cooperative.

"That one," Vandorn said. He was about to continue when Georgia spoke.

"We're keeping all our work practical, down to earth, Homer. We've gotten some press that you may have seen--the drugstores and their cruddy magazines. We thought we had made some points with right-thinking movie house owners. But they kept saying, 'Come back when everybody's agreeing to boycott the X-rated stuff.'"

"We plan to keep after them," Vandorn added. "Despite the odds. We have more than four dozen active members, so we figure we can start exerting legitimate pressure." He had taken the number "four dozen" out of the air.

"The Mayor's office isn't exactly looking for work," the Mayor said. "But we've put our blessing on things that were less desirable than your work. I must admit that we'd like to avoid violence--violent confrontations, street disorder, that kind of thing. But. . ."

"We're absolutely dedicated to staying cool, Homer," Georgia said. "We do think our efforts would have more effect if we had your backing."

The Mayor steepled his fingers. His voice became firmer. "What exactly would you expect from us?"

Vandorn took the floor. He had mentioned to Georgia that he would "give his eyeteeth to pin the boss-man down on something meaningful." "If it's not too much, Your Honor, we'd like to go before the assembled City Council, give them all a rundown on the various projects we're undertaking. They're all community things, like our March for a Cleaner Franklin a couple of weeks ago. You may have read about that."

"I did. It seemed to go off quietly enough."

"We made sure that it did." Hastening on, Vandorn completed what he considered his minimal wanted list. "If the council could pass a resolution of support, it would be a major victory for us. If you could also issue a proclamation, that would sort of crown the climax."

"All that would take some thought," Mayor Keller said, speaking slowly. "I'm basically in favor, but I'd bring down my happy home here if I didn't give the known opposition equal air time." The fingers of Mayor Keller's right hand began to drum lightly on the desk-top.

Georgia spoke during the brief pause. "That would only be fair," the woman said. "And we would certainly be happy to go along with it."

With a glance from under his thick eyebrows the Mayor addressed Vandorn. "My recollection is that that TV tete-a-tete turned a little topsy-turvy," he said. "The papers said no one was injured, but the scene looked more than a little hazardous at the end. The papers may have dressed up the pictures a little," he added lamely.

Picking up the conversation, Georgia again took over from Vandorn. "That was sort of a special situation," she said. "We've studied ways to prevent such confrontations in the future--and I think we could give you scout's honor that there wouldn't be a repetition. Am I on target, Jim?"

Vandorn nodded affirmatively.

"Eldy?" Surprised by the question, Eldy Dennington spoke with forced emphasis. "Darn tootin'," he said. "Like our meetings, just as smooth as pie."

As if Eldy had settled everything, Mayor Keller swiveled in his chair, making a quarter-turn and using his hands on the arms of the chair to lever himself to a standing position. "I'll be checking all this, and will go over it with the entire council within a week."

"It will be their decision?" Georgia asked.

"It will," the Mayor answered. "I'm pretty certain that the council will want to hear what you and your group have to say. I'm also pretty sure they'll want to hear Dr. Brand's--, to hear what the other side has to say. Can we leave it at that?"

Georgia answered instantly. "Yes, you can, Homer." She turned to Vandorn. "Fair arrangement, Professor Jim?"

Vandorn felt upstaged, less the great oracle to whom all questions could be directed than the caboose on Georgia's train. Well, he would live with it.

But angrily.

45

Myrtle Keller had a mind of her own. The fact that her husband was the mayor of Franklin neither impressed her nor convinced her that she should bear herself like royalty. She would simply be, do, think, and say what seemed to her appropriate. If her idea of the appropriate deviated sometimes from her husband's concepts, so be it. She was not above saying, with vulgar finality, "Up theirs."

Having by chance seen Georgia LeBaron and Vandorn entering City Hall, she was prepared to grill her husband at dinner. She would ask what in hell that snooty broad was doing in the temple of civic power and influence.

The mayor had hardly sat down when she began. He hadn't had time, even, for his first sip of Merlot, the wine that everyone hailed as a cancer preventative. Or a weight--loss agent. Or. . .

The question she asked from the far end of the table, her chosen seat, gave Homer forewarning that she had much on her mind. "What was good old Georgia L. doing in City Hall today?" Myrtle asked, keeping her voice down. That way, she thought, the young man who doubled as a butler in the evening wouldn't overhear. But he was entering from the kitchen as she spoke, and may have heard.

Not to be denied, Homer took his first sip. He delayed putting the glass down until the young man had left, then responded.

"She's got a deal going with that mad psychologist or whatever he teaches. The two of them have taken over some group that wants to purify our fair city. As if I haven't done enough in that direction--or at least pretended to."

"You've done more than enough. And frankly, Homer, I'd be happy if you'd put the clamps on Miss Georgia and that crowd of do-gooders. After that TV spectacle I've done some phoning. I think Georgia and her group--but mostly including that madman Vandorn--are after that handsome Dr. Brand. They want to put him out of business, that's what I'm hearing."

"How can I 'Put the clamps' to those people? They're putting on airs as if they were the last, best hope of the community."

"I know." Hearing the "kitchen aide" entering the dining room from behind her, Myrtle wagged a single finger that indicated both she and Homer needed a wine refill. When the young man finished pouring and had left, Myrtle said: "And you have to act fair no matter what you think. But one thing you've got to promise me."

"Which is?" Homer said.

"That I can sit up in the nickel seats at your council session and just listen."

"If you'll just listen. We're going to have the entire 28 council members there. And probably the press. Both radio-TV and print, I'd guess. So I've got to make sure we keep order. If it gets out of hand I'm going to gavel it to a stop."

"You might save Dr. Brand's life, judging by the shenanigans at the TV bout."

"'Bout' is the word. I'm also going to have a few of Franklin's finest there."

"And the public?"

"I think we're going to have to let people into the balcony on a first-come, first-serve basis. That's what I'm going to do, anyway. That way I don't have to worry about friends of the ald--, of the council members. I've got to avoid that like the plague."

"I'll be the first one there. I'll just pretend I'm the hostess."

"And then sit in your favorite chair."

"Of course."

46

The phone rang in the late afternoon. Deep in his "catchup mode," Brand first debated the wisdom of answering. It was the time of day when an action response to most calls was impossible; callers would almost without exception wait until the next day. Importantly, too, Brand's overdue attention to his case reports was showing results.

Curiosity and his innate sense of the work imperative convinced him. He lifted the receiver. A cultured, faint voice asked, "Dr. Brand?"

"Yes, I'm Dr. Brand."

"I'm Brother John at the St. George Seminary in St. George, Indiana. I'm--."

"Excuse me," Brand said, interrupting. "Could you speak a little louder, please?"

"Yes, of course." The soft voice rose in volume. "Did you understand where I am?"

"I did. I wrote to you--to your institution--a few weeks ago."

"Yes, I have your letter in front of me. You express interest in one of our former student scholastics, Mr. James Vandorn."

"I was trying to establish some facts for institutional and professional reasons."

"May we talk confidentially? We hesitate, for obvious reasons, to give out information on former students, whatever their vocational status. You can understand why. Cessation of or failure in the very difficult behavioral and academic regimen that most young men face here may have many causes. These can range from the simple desire to adopt another lifeway to acts or activities that for us may indicate unsuitability to the demanding priestly career toward which most of our student-scholastics work."

"Confidentiality on specifics--that I can guarantee. But I may need answers to some broad personal questions if this exercise is to be even minimally productive."

"Perhaps it would serve both our purposes better if you were to ask your questions. If I can answer them without violating any of our policies or protocols, I will."

"Fair enough. As I may have mentioned in my letter, my overarching question is very straightforward. In view of the fact that Dr. Vandorn has been passing as a former priest, I'd be interested in knowing whether he was actually ordained."

"That I can answer. He was not to my knowledge. I can say that he did not enter the Roman Catholic priesthood at St. George."

"That's clear and definite. Could he have entered the priesthood elsewhere? At some other seminary?"

"No. That would be impossible. True ordination could only have been possible if the ordaining agency--seminary, university, or whatever--had contacted us first. They would do that to confirm his academic credits. Most important among the areas of greatest interest and concern would be the disciplines of theology, philosophy, and what we call apologetics."

"That settles one question. May I ask another?" Brand had been standing; now he made himself comfortable in one of the office chairs that he himself had chosen.

"You may," Brother John said.

"Can you tell me whether you, whether St. George awards degrees, and whether Dr. Vandorn received any such while at your institution?"

"We do confer degrees as symbols of completion of the particular courses required for specific awards. The constituent courses are almost entirely the same as those required for degrees at public universities or colleges. In fact, our requirements are generally more stringent because of the focus on religion that we have to maintain."

"Am I to understand that Professor Vandorn didn't complete the courses of study required before ordination?"

"He did not finish, correct."

"May I ask just one more?"

"Of course. I will answer if I can."

"Did he leave for his reasons or for yours--the seminary's?"

A pause began, lengthened somewhat; then Brother John said, "I will answer that if it's your final choice in this line of questioning."

"It will be."

"He left at our request."

The line again went silent. No sounds invaded the receiver silence except for noises that Brand could hear: employees bidding others goodbye, a distant car horn, and down the hall from Brand's office the noise made by a filing cabinet drawer that had been shut violently.

"Brother John?" Brand said. "Are you still there?"

"Yes." The voice had returned to its barely-audible level.

"I want to thank you. You've answered some questions that have concerned a number of people here."

"Glad to be of help."

Hanging up, Brand began to jot notes on what he had heard. He would wager, given the chance, that Vandorn had been dismissed by the seminary for violent behavior. But he had learned enough.

47

The idea hit him as he was leaving Eldy Dennington's bungalow-style home.

It hit him because his temper had caught fire during the "summit" session with Georgia. Truth was, as he saw it, that they didn't have the single, explosive issue that would lodge in the busy memories of the City Council members. No bombshell had appeared in any kind of concrete form. Had one come up at all? Had anyone even mentioned Brand's capital offense, male impregnation or embryonation?

He couldn't remember. Memory flagged when his mind seethed.

He stopped in a drugstore that he knew had a public telephone. He dialed the number of Dr. Lee Gustafson.

The phone rang six times at the other end. Eight. Ten. And suddenly Dr. Gustafson was speaking, his voice hearty, the volume near a shout. "Yes sir or madam," he boomed. "Speak or forever."

Vandorn smiled to himself. Some things never changed. "Jim Vandorn here," he said. "And as usual I'm looking for professional help. A different situation this time."

"Can you give me some details over the phone? I'm in the midst of correcting late papers and it's running me ragged."

"I can tell you in a few words. We're trying to get some information on Dr. Brand's activities, on Brand's friends. You'll remember that name. What I'm asking is whether one of your galley slaves might be able to take a part-time job in a gay bar."

Remembering where he was, Vandorn lowered his voice. Speaking *sotto voce*, he explained the rumors he and his fellow CAMP members were receiving.

He had a willing and surprisingly informative audience. To Vandorn's astonishment, Gustafson reported that some of his students were discussing the PG man case as if it were "old hat" news. One of the students, in fact, had a part-time weekend job in the East Side's Kitkat Lounge.

"The lounge, of course, is a gay hangout," Gustafson said.

Elated, Vandorn probed. Could he drop in at the Kitkat himself? Could Gus find out whatever hours the student worked? And did he work the bar or food service or both? His name--and would he respond if Vandorn asked for him?

Completing the call, Vandorn was feeling a surge of optimism. He would do his own undercover work this coming weekend. He could hardly wait.

He considered taking Jennifer to the Kitkat as an "adventure." Almost at once he decided against that plan. She would not enjoy it. Like other women that they knew--faculty wives for example--she found it unnerving to associate in any venue, for any purpose, with homosexuals of either gender. Equally disqualifying, she had never found it possible to disguise her feelings. If she had buried them, a social event might prove salvageable. But he, Vandorn, had watched her struggling. Her discomfort, and resulting social awkwardness, made Vandorn's decision for him. He would go alone.

They talked it over without ever discussing the true purpose behind Vandorn's "'Kitkat Plan."

"Why can't we both go to Smithson's?" she asked with unimpugnable logic. If he wanted to go out, so did she--but in a way that included her.

"It won't work." Before she could ask why not, he provided the rationale, the best he could devise. "I've got to check out the lay of their land."

Her voice shifted into lament mode. "The lay of their land! What does that mean? You joining them?"

"Don't make me laugh. I'm doing research there for our morality group--and I have to do it when somebody's there."

"While I sit here."

He suppressed his impatience with an effort. "You and I can go out tomorrow night--to Smithson's. Or later tonight. I'll call when I'm leaving there."

"You'll probably think of some other excuse--or maybe decide to spy on Dr. Brand. I've waited before."

"This time I'll make it."

Vandorn stood up and walked into the small room where he did his reading and thinking. Here, too, he kept his journal, making daily entries and keeping the notebooks locked in his desk. He began to make notes; they included the name Brownlee, the student who worked at the Kitkat. Brownlee would know who drinks what. . .

He also remembered the name Jeffords. But he had forgotten to ask Gustafson whether the lithe little man might be available for other, more interesting assignments in the future. He would ask later. CAMP was turning out to be less of the terrible swift strike-force that he had hoped. And that meant the time for more lethal action might be nearing.

The interior of the Kitkat Club lay in near-total darkness despite the sun-bright brilliance outside. Pausing just inside the door, Vandorn waited while his eyes grew accustomed to the shadows. As sight returned, he could see that three of the booths along the wall opposite the bar were occupied. No one sat at the bar.

As well as he could discern them, the patrons appeared to be uniformly men.

He went to the bar and sat on a stool that had a supportive back. Once comfortable, he relaxed. He would listen. He quelled his inevitable impatience, stopped the fingers of his right hand, which had begun to drum on the varnished surface of the bar.

The bartender appeared, a tall man wearing a clean white apron that seemed too small for him. He stopped in front of Vandorn, saying, "Something cool, sir?"

"Yes. Can you recommend something? No beer, no boilermakers, no rum and Coke. Something maybe just a little exotic?"

Vandorn wanted conversation that would lead--where? "Suggestions?" he said.

"Well." The bartender smiled. "We can satisfy just about any taste. Think Bloody Mary. Grasshopper. And aperitif. Kir, though that's mostly wine. You name it, I'll guarantee that we can serve it. For something like a Scotch and soda, unless your thirst is really menacing, we can whip it up in seconds."

It occurred to Vandorn that Gustafson had mentioned Kir, the drink favored by the candidate for embryonation.

"I'll try a kir if you'll show me how you mix it," he said to the bartender.

"We have it ready-mixed." Almost before Vandorn could track the bartender's hand movements, he had poured an unmeasured dollop. He stirred the drink carefully. "Ice?" he asked.

"Yes, please."

"Shall I keep a tab?" the bartender asked, setting the drink on a napkin in front of Vandorn. As Vandorn lifted the glass, it left a damp circle on the napkin over the words "Kitkat Klub."

"A tab is fine," Vandorn said. "Assuming that this doesn't knock me over the bar. This time of day I have to go slowly or it hits me."

"We've got some muscle-bound types over there." The bartender nodded toward the booths. "They could pick you up and set you right back on that stool."

"I'm in the midst of a bunch of weight lifters?"

"No, they just try to stay in condition. John over there is training for some wild project--I don't know exactly what it's about. But he works out twice a day. Also, he's drinkin' pop right now. He calls it pop but it's Kir."

"Must be an important project."

"Sounds important at least. They keep kiddin' each other about gettin' rich, buyin' the Lounge--this place. Doin' everything you can think of. They've got their drawers in an uproar."

"Where's this big fortune supposed to come from?"

"What I hear, movies, books, all that stuff." The bartender had been leaning on the bar. Now he stood up straight and began to wipe it clean. He was wiping where Vandorn could see no evidence of use.

"If that's an investment scheme, I'd like to know what paper is writin' it up."

"No, no investments, nothin' like that--." He was opening his mouth to continue when one of the men at a table said loudly enough to carry throughout the room, "How 'bout some service, Mattie?"

As if he was glad to have other work, the bartender walked rapidly around the end of the bar and went to the table. Vandorn could hear muttered comments--but nothing that sounded like an order.

The conversation went on, the words indistinct, for another minute or two. Making up his mind, one of the men said with falsely heavy emphasis: "And I'll have another of the same."

"Anyone else?" Audibly.

"Okay, same all around," the bartender said. In moments he was back behind the bar and busy setting out bottles and glasses.

Vandorn mused. The bartender had poured the kir from a partly empty bottle.

48

Mayor Keller's gavel commanded order, silence. But the council members behaved as if surprised. Finishing conversations, they meandered shuffling toward their assigned seats.

The gavel finally stopped. The buzz of voices continued, but at a much reduced level.

The Mayor was still standing. As the hum of conversation dwindled, he picked up the gavel and hammered again, three times. Again the room seemed to become quieter.

The Mayor seized his opportunity. Leaning on the lectern that also held a microphone, he read from a sheet that lay on the lectern's slanted surface.

"We've come here on a very important mission today," Mayor Keller began. "It's a mission that can, and probably will, affect all of us one way or another." He took a deep breath. "In a few words, we'll be deciding between what we've come to call--for lack of a better term--a community morals question.

"I don't think I have to explain this in detail. That will be the role of our, er, opponents in this discussion. And notice that I'm calling it a discussion, not a debate."

He was smiling sheepishly as he added, "It passed as a debate a couple of months ago and some furniture began to fly." A ripple of laughter stirred both the council members in their comfortable chairs and segregated area and the visitors filling the upper-level balcony.

"I'm honored now to give the floor to our guests," the Mayor said. "And we have their assurance that only words will fly today." He paused.

"Now, I'm told that our first speaker will be Mrs. Georgia LeBaron, an officer of the civic organization Campaign against Moral Pollution."

Mayor Keller looked around, smiling. "Georgia?" he said. "The lectern is yours." Georgia stood up and walked with determination to the podium. For perhaps half a minute she paused, arranging her papers on the shelf-like lectern.

"Fellow citizens," she said finally. "Fellows both in and not in the City Council of our fair city. I'd like to make it clear at the outset that I'm talking to all who are here--and equally, all who are not here.

"As members of CAMP we feel strongly that our work involves every single citizen. The reason is simple. In a community sense, in a moral or ethical or even cultural sense, we all breathe the same air. We call--or I call it--our moral air. This is what many define as the moral or ethical *climate*."

Georgia lifted one page and slid it under the others. "We face a difficult task as we try to cleanse this climate," she continued. "And we apologize for that. We are working for your good--for your children-- for those, yes those, who wish to have nothing to do with us. We would rather stay at home watching television than go knocking on doors. Or passing out leaflets of our own creation. Or calling on druggists who purvey pornographic materials. Or engage in letter campaigns.

"And most important of all, we've become the baby-watch.

"As the baby-watch, we see our work tending toward a distasteful task. More and more we have to harp on what we see--and most sensible authorities agree--as the healthy, natural way to bring families into the world.

"Having said that, we are not closing our eyes to the things that are going on in hospital laboratories and operating rooms. We are not unaware of experiments that seem sometimes to deprive children of their true heritage. To create embryos that are in every sense already *People*--but are in too many cases ending up in garbage cans.

"I fear for the future of these new children. We all fear the climate, the circumstances these parentless children grow up in."

Georgia paused, moved another sheet of paper to the bottom of her shallow stack. "Now," she said with a half-smile, "I just committed a capital crime--ended a sentence with not one but two prepositions. Will those who noticed it please forgive me? We'll say it adds emphasis."

Serious again, she said: "Right here I have to address myself to the City Council. We can't reach into the doctors' precincts to change minds and end abuses. We can't really pass laws or regulations. But the council can. And we hope it will. The time has come, we believe."

With a new burst of intensity, Georgia said: "The abuses are what you'd call part of the script. They're in all the papers. A woman's eggs were stolen. And she learned only later that the child she might have had was born to another woman in the same circle. Doctors were charged with theft and fraud. There were reports of unapproved fertility drugs. *Fertility* drugs! I have to say this. I fear not only for the moral climate in Franklin; I fear for the futures of our new crop of citizens: for what they will grow up with.

"The two, of course, go together. One causes the other. We are unashamedly producing what some have called 'designer babies'-- neonates who are supposed to have certain characteristics. If that isn't eugenics, I don't know what is.

"But that's not the only thing that is becoming commonplace in our laboratories. As if babies were Barbie Dolls, the new-mode baby may be borne--gestated--by a surrogate mother. Ponder this: some women nowadays--yes, some who live in our midst--are renting their bodies to produce babies for other women.

"The *other women* then sometimes take over as the self-proclaimed mothers. For the services of a surrogate mother, the buyer-mother may pay $10,000.

"You know about these things, many or most of you. But have you pondered how things like that affect our young people? Do you wonder that there's an 'anything-goes' attitude among young adults and teens?"

Georgia produced a frilly handkerchief from an invisible pocket. Using it briskly, she mopped the palms of her hands.

"For those who haven't encountered the possible accidents common to the New Age," she said, "I'd like to enumerate just three or four. Remember, these horrors occurred when people played God, never thinking of the consequences.

"In one case a husband and wife--seeking parenthood--paid to have the wife impregnated. The embryo represented the seed of an unknown father. The egg was also the 'gift' of an unknown woman.

"The couple separated, then divorced a month before the baby entered the world. When the mother went to court seeking child support, a judge denied her request. The former husband was not the child's father, the judge said. In fact, the child had no legal parent at all.

"Other problems make the newspapers almost daily. A surrogate mom who also donated an egg for fertilization decided to keep the baby that was born later. As the biological mother, she finally was able to keep the blessed event. In other cases of embryonation, babies born with major birth defects were rejected by the eager parents. We now have homeless, parentless babies.

"What concerns us is the fact that these things are occurring in Franklin right now. In this community. They are occurring even while our statistics on unwed motherhood are steadily rising.

"We hold that the high-tech abuses of the moral law of conception as meaning a union of a man and woman are multiplying. We also find from research that new abuses are appearing almost daily.

"It all looks so simple. But we are defying religion and basic morality.

"We are really playing God when we cross species--in what some call an 'experimental' procedure.

"Some scientists are even talking about 'genetic commerce'-- building businesses on commercial exchanges or transplants of genes, eggs, even children.

"Thanks for listening."

Mayor Keller stood, hands clapping. Some among the balcony crowd were also applauding. As Georgia sat down, the Mayor said, "Thank you, thank you. We now are warned. And if my schedule here is correct, we will now hear from Dr. Emlyn Brand, our second speaker."

"Good morning," Brand said. "Good bright sunshiny morning. Isn't it invigorating to walk out into a day like this? Isn't it even more energizing when we remember that even if it rained for 40 days and 40 nights, we couldn't do much about it?

"When it comes to welcoming our children, it used to be that we were just that helpless. Remember? A child might be born with Down Syndrome. Or spina bifida.

"We were helpless. We watched children die. In many cases we knew there was a family tendency toward early deaths from a specific disease or ailment. We could see the offspring of such a family suffering from the known problem and be unable to help.

"Remember? Can you imagine what it means to be discovering cures for diseases that may have been killing young people? At one time pneumonia could be fatal. In the late teens and the early 1920s the White Lady, influenza, took 20 million lives around the world.

"I want you to think about this. The advances that have been made in medicine in the past half century have in many cases been discovered because someone was searching for an answer. The cure for one thing proved to be a gratuitous answer to something else. Penicillin has proved to have multiple uses, meaning at least some other maladies have been brought under control."

Brand took a sip from a glass of water that stood unused on a low table next to the lectern. His throat felt dry still, and he took another swallow. While talking he had noticed Laura Phillips in the gallery. He had not seen her come in. In the few seconds during which he was directing his gaze toward her the fingers of her right hand did a little dance. A finger wave.

"May I cite a quotation? It expresses well how far we have come with our 'wild' experimentation, our 'immoral' testing, our 'inhuman' scans and Petri dishes and so on. The quotation states a new reality: For the first time, people who are carrying a. . .genetic disease *can start a pregnancy from the beginning, knowing it will be normal, and not have the specter of a termination of the pregnancy.*"

As Brand concluded the quotation, there was scattered applause in the gallery. He glanced again toward Laura. She was clapping more enthusiastically than most of the others.

Briefly it occurred to Brand that he might invite Laura to step to the microphone and give her own future-mother testimony regarding her efforts to become abdominally pregnant. As quickly as he considered it, he rejected the notion. Laura, he remembered, might be proceeding clandestinely in that undertaking. And he would see her this evening as he and Madsen made their fifth try to embryonate.

Buying a moment of respite, he helped himself to another sip of water. As he did so, he saw Vandorn sitting in a platform chair near the mayor. "With your kind indulgence," he said, "I'll take a timeout and give the stage to my esteemed colleague Dr. James Vandorn. You'll note that the forces he brings to the fray here are double ours. I think it's only equable that I be allowed to appear twice."

Vandorn had been leaning forward, his gaze focused on the papers in his hands. Hearing Brand as Brand passed him the gavel, he rose quickly to his feet. The two men passed as Brand left the lectern.

49

Vandorn walked to the lectern like a man just freed from prison. He had brought notes, all newly minted. He didn't intend to use the notes; he had brought them in case he needed a reference.

The Mayor sat somewhat behind Vandorn and the lectern, occupying a low platform with four of his aides. Seated, the Mayor was beyond the reach of Vandorn's peripheral vision. A small table stood next to his mayoral chair.

Vandorn had hardly taken his position at the lectern when Mayor Keller made a hand gesture. At once a second, larger gavel appeared, as if by prearrangement, on the little table. The Mayor let it lie there.

"Ladies and gentlemen," Vandorn began. "Council Members." He paused, then added: "Mr. Mayor."

"At the risk of repeating myself," he continued, "a community is known by the company it keeps. By the people it harbors. By its products and works. By its moral and social tenor.

"All of those elements contribute to the community's standing and quality of life. If the elements are of dubious value or virtue, the city or town--the community--will struggle. Its quality of life will be inadequate or nonexistent. It may acquire a name as a place to avoid or as a desert of iniquity.

"Am I sounding too theoretical? We can boil these statements down, make them simpler or more understandable. The elements I'm referring to are in part those that Georgia alluded to. They are also the Sodom and Gomorrah types of things *that catch the public eye*. The violations of common decency or morality. The things that go into our courts and from there into our newspapers."

Vandorn cleared his throat. Resuming, he was speaking more loudly.

"We're talking about two things--what a community presents to its citizens and what it projects outside its own boundaries. But the two are really different faces of the same things. We in CAMP have analyzed what's going on here and have found that we are today--as a community--projecting a negative image."

A murmur of voices uniting in mutters of disagreement became audible in the gallery. It began in the back of the public area and moved toward the front.

Vandorn ignored it. "I'm sure you all know what I mean," he said. "We now have places of entertainment that cater to our lowest instincts--or that feature these so-called 'alternative life styles'. There's increasing drug use. Gangs--and, yes we have our first gang. We have also our first house of prostitution."

The murmur became a low rumble. Without speaking, Mayor Keller hit the table next to him twice with the bigger gavel. The murmuring dropped off but didn't end.

"There's more," Vandorn said. "We have organized gambling, prostitution--and you already know what we will soon have--a homosexual male who will bear a child. He wants to become the first male to carry and deliver a human infant."

The muttering increased briefly in volume. It dropped as Mayor Keller reached again for the gavel.

"What we are calling for screams for city action as well as citizen action," Vandorn went on. "Our churches, our various institutes and protective agencies can't do their jobs without council assistance. Without local legislation. When I was in the priesthood it became clear that the absolute best efforts of the faithful in any kind of civic campaign were doomed to failure without the help of the police and other civic groups, always backed by the law."

Vandorn developed his theme for several more minutes. In emphatic but moderated tones he painted a picture of community economic decline following moral decay. Of encroachment by undesirable elements, of declining property values, of homes going to ruin because of neglect.

All this could and would take place, he maintained again, unless the city government took the lead and joined its citizens in prohibiting the practice of genetic experimentation "and the pollution of unrestrained, unregulated homosexuality." Children would find attraction in the wrong models; adults with families would succumb to the temptation to leave Franklin.

"Believe me, as a priest," he said, "I saw it happen in two communities. It's like poisoning--poisoning a mind. Once started, it can't be stopped without coordinated effort. And sometimes not even then. Such is the power of moral plagues."

He sipped at the water. "I submit, finally--to make this completely transparent--that the city government has no alternative. It has to terminate the mad experimentation now going on under the auspices of a local homosexual newspaper. The pregnant man experiment simply mocks our mores, our standards, everything we hold sacred.

"And unless we act now, I can promise from experience that worse scenarios will follow. You can imagine what these may be. Human clones. Cross-breeding of humans and animals--to allegedly distill the best characteristics of both guinea pigs. And all along the way to further monstrosities there would form a trail of live embryos. Tiny human beings. I'll leave you with that picture. Those human beings will be discarded."

Vandorn was gathering his papers. He had hardly used them, but they lent a semblance of official gravitas to the proceedings. As Vandorn wound down, another man stepped behind him and went to the lectern.

"May I seize the moment?" the man said. "And introduce myself?" He paused and looked around, swiveling his gaze across the entire gallery. "I'm Allan, editor of *Gay Community*, the local newspaper." There were snickers and, again, the murmur of low conversation in the balcony.

"We've been here for seven years," Archer went on, "and in that time we've performed invaluable services for our clients. I should say our readers," he added. "I would like to have it understood that we feel we are members of this community in good standing. We live and work here. We--some of us--have homes here. We pay taxes and buy in local stores."

He was talking now to a silent audience.

"We don't feel that we in the slightest degree represent a blot on the community's escutcheon. We also believe that putting Franklin at the cutting edge of scientific endeavor--in whatever way--can only reflect credit on the community."

"What garbage!" a female voice said loudly. Seconds later Mayor Keller was hammering with the gavel. "Sergeant-at arms." the Mayor said, "please remove the lady who just spoke."

Again total silence ruled. The sergeant-at-arms, who had been sitting unidentified behind the mayor, made his way off the dais and disappeared toward the stairs to the gallery. In moments he was leaning politely over the woman who had spoken out. Head bobbing, she got to her feet and followed him. Some two minutes later the sergeant-at-arms returned to his seat behind the Mayor.

The chamber seethed with barely audible noise. Vandorn was exchanging glances with his fellow CAMP members and smiling.

Brand wanted a second turn at the mike as a way to equalize the time allotted to each side in the dispute. Or to attempt to equalize to the extent that such equalization was possible.

While Archer had been making his unprogrammed presentation, Brand had moments to consider and reconsider the stance he would take publicly on the issue of the pregnant man. He had decided to minimize his role. He would give thankful credit to "a qualified physician, a specialist in gynecology and obstetrics," who would manage the entire effort. He, Brand, would be that physician's "water carrier" when necessary.

His testimony, he believed, would prove acceptable to Drs. Schofield and Levenson. They undoubtedly had representation in the gallery audience; so he believed.

More problematic was the City Council. How would it react to a bald announcement that the rumors were true? You might not really care how the citizens reacted, but the official consensus had or could have the power of interdiction: the City Council could legislate. The experiment, and Gennett/Adamson with it, could be run out of town.

Brand, speaking again, decided merely to inject reason into the debate and leave it at that.

"I was going to bend your collective ears with some basic facts about scientific inquiry," he began. "I was thinking how mankind had to move forward despite any consequences. In nearly all cases, the consequences were more beneficial than otherwise anyway.

"When man first discovered fire, somewhere and at some time, community tongues must have wagged. A prehistoric city council must have explored the reality of fire and decided whether it would stay or come under a ban, taboo, or simple prohibition. Then perhaps the inventor of fire may have treated the council members to roasted mammoth steaks."

A generalized titter ran through both the gallery audience and the assembled council members.

"It was probably the same when man discovered the wheel, paper, vulcanized rubber. There were questions, there was opposition. And in the sequel, human society benefited."

Brand paused, took a sip of water. Rather than continue on the *science in the service of man* line of reasoning, he decided, he would introduce Madsen. He and Madsen had considered that possibility.

"But let me introduce a colleague who feels much as I do about reproductive science. He is, in fact, the skilled practitioner who is devoting time to helping two persons to enjoy man's supreme moment-- parentage."

Madsen stood, but remained in place smiling. "Dr. Albert Madsen," Brand said. "He gave me permission to call on him." As Brand stepped away from the lectern and microphone, Madsen moved to take his place. There was scattered applause as he did so.

"I won't take much of your time," Madsen began. "I only hope I can describe my own approach to the work of collaborating in the divine plan. From my experience over more than 25 years, it burns in all of us--but in some more hotly than others.

"Some people, unfortunately, face barriers to fulfillment of their natural need to procreate. In situations where I can bring some specialized knowledge and technique to bear to help them, I do it. I see my small role this way: that this may be the most important service I can bring to others who share this life and community with me.

"You've probably heard all this, but it's something that's easy to overlook, or forget. In parenting, in particular by carrying one's own fetus and delivering it, we achieve a kind of immortality. We climb to the level of the saints and angels, but do so while still on earth.

"I've seen this phenomenon at close range, and it never ceases to astound me. The mother who five minutes ago felt terrible and didn't think she could tolerate life any longer--all of a sudden she is rejoicing, smiling, cooing and hugging her newborn.

"She has done it. She has stepped across the threshold into the Land of the Lucky, the parent club.

"She has become a mother."

Watching Madsen, hearing his words, Brand wondered how or why he had never seen this side of the gynecologist. It had the effect, for Brand, of sealing their collaboration--of turning that collaboration into an association of the heart.

Madsen was winding down. "That's pretty much where I am," Madsen said. "A man lucky enough to work where life becomes tangible, palpable--and inspiring. May we all be so lucky at some time in our lives! Thanks for listening."

Vandorn had risen to his feet before Madsen had resumed his seat. Speaking softly, Vandorn asked Mayor Keller if a dissenting voice might once more be heard. The Mayor nodded.

Taking his place again at the lectern, Vandorn watched while four or five members of the gallery audience rose to their feet and made their ways to the exits.

He began when the gallery had settled down.

"I asked for a few more minutes because we are hearing one highly dramatic, even lyrical, version of what is at issue here. I feel it my duty to remind the assembled councilors and interested citizens that we are in reality talking about an ugly phenomenon.

"It's a phenomenon that, as far as the annals of medicine are concerned, has never before occurred. Never. Humanity, insofar as we can gather from its history, has never witnessed male motherhood. In fact, we are unquestionably referring to a monstrosity of the abnormal in discussing such a possibility."

He pushed his notes to one side as if ridding himself of the mere notion of a pregnant male.

"Think for a moment. Put yourselves in the position of a priest. I had to do this; you can imagine yourselves into the basic situation. A man comes to you and says--confesses--that he has become pregnant.

Now, belatedly, he is filled with remorse. He has no idea what he will do if he delivers a viable baby. He wants to abort even though he can feel life.

"As a priest, I would have had to tell that individual what I would have had to tell a woman, a girl: that we can't take the life that is stirring inside your body. You have to continue, bear the child, find a way. Find someone who will adopt if no other solution is practical--if, for example, starvation faces the child."

Vandorn let his gaze rove over the gallery. He could see Laura Phillips in the front row, on the left. Alone.

"What we end up with here," he said, "is a violation of the natural, a Frankenstein monster, as we've pointed out--such a violation as is inherently, by its own nature, wrong. May I use the word sinful? That's what our Dr. Madsen is talking about in idyllic terms. Something so unnatural that it cries to Heaven, not for vengeance but for eradication, for denunciation, for legal or legislative prohibition.

"I have no hesitation in calling on the honorable City Council to take appropriate prohibitive action in this matter."

Vandorn, clutching his notes, took his seat.

A glance from the Mayor was all Brand needed as approval to take the microphone once again. While listening to Vandorn he had not merely paid close attention; he had also scribbled some words. Five of them faced him as he laid one sheet of his notes on the lectern. The five were *ugly, monstrosity, abort, unnatural,* and *priest.*

"My colleague Professor Vandorn has indulged his skill at slanderous oratory as only he can," Brand said. "He finds some scientific findings and experiments to be unjustified and unjustifiable. In fact, he finds the very subject of maternity--of one approach to maternity--as ugly.

"Is it truly possible to have normal instincts and still find maternity ugly? Or to find wholesome ways to achieving motherhood are *unnatural?*

"We have different outlooks, obviously. We take the position that maternity--motherhood--by right merits a special place in society as in the family. We cannot quarrel with the law of the land, but a companion growing belief holds that violent termination of pregnancy should be outlawed as murder.

"Yes, there are circumstances under which abortion may be justified. Everyone knows what they are, so I needn't go into them. But I could see--even though I could not perform--abortion to save the life of the mother.

"I feel that I have to present the truth on another aspect of this discussion. Largely to prove that he speaks with special authority, Professor Vandorn keeps referring back to his days as a man of the cloth. As, in fact, a Roman Catholic priest. You've heard it today. 'When I was in the priesthood. . .' That kind of off-the-cuff mention.

"I have it on unimpeachable authority that he is not, and never was, a priest. He did study at a Catholic seminary, but the institution terminated his studies for reasons that cannot be divulged."

Vandorn was on his feet. Mayor Keller had likewise risen to a standing position. He stood holding the larger gavel as if it were a weapon.

In the gallery a tide of rapt attention was keeping people in their seats. But everyone, it seemed, was whispering to his or her neighbor.

But there was one other item. Raising his voice so as to recapture the attention of everyone still in the council chamber, Brand said: "We also have very convincing circumstantial proof that Doctor Vandorn ended the life of one of our experimental baboons. In his misplaced zeal to purify this community, he and a confederate found a way to poison one of these valuable animals.

"What do the animals do? They contribute in many ways to our work of finding solutions to difficult health problems. The beneficiaries are, in the main, women of this community, wives and mothers.

"The murder of this baboon was an act of simple depravity. In perpetrating it, Vandorn made a mistake: he got too close and the animal bit off part of one of his fingers.

If you'll look at the index finger of his left hand, you'll see a bandage. The bite that took off part of that finger hasn't totally healed yet. Two-three months later he still bears the marks."

Brand wanted to end on a positive note, but decided that he would omit the oratorical flourish that he was contemplating. It would likely not be heard--or if heard, it would be wasted.

He returned to his seat and made himself comfortable. The chamber was seething with excited, whispered conversation. Mayor Keller was pounding with the larger gavel.

50

Brand was readying the "Operating Theater" in Madsen's clinic when Laura arrived. He heard her cheerful greeting as she passed the front desk and the late-shift receptionist. An interval of womanly chit-chat followed, a murmur of warm voices.

A week earlier she had greeted Brand with a sisterly hug and a joyful smile. For Brand, that experience had left a question that he hesitated even to formulate. It related to her future intentions. If the hug and smile became ritual, Brand would not object. *Where was the harm?* But what did it mean?

She responded to his curiosity as if she was aware of it. Entering the Op Room on her way to change for another implant, she gave Brand an open-arm hug that seemed to presume a relationship. Brand remained professionally cool.

"Negative news," Brand announced as Laura freed herself. "With tonight's embryo we are out of the male element. We have no shortage of eggs."

His euphemism, "male element" for sperm, brought a smile. "I'll figure something out," she said. "If we don't catch the brass ring tonight."

"We can't keep missing the target. If I were one of these little guys, I'd make sure I started growing. After all--." He let the thought die, concluding with a smile.

In part because they were using the last of the mail-order sperm, Brand had a "feeling." This implant, he felt strongly, would "take," then turn into the "charmed new life" that they struggled toward. Laura would absorb, adjust; her instinctual need would morph under the spell of the female reproductive magic. In nine months, give or take a few days or weeks, she would deliver from her omentum.

During Madsen's expert manipulation of the implant instruments nothing occurred to negate Brand's hunch. The preparatory incision opened as if forewarned. The infinitesimally tiny embryo slid without a problem from the Petri dish to the Brand-devised implantation device.

The post-op, as Madsen called it, went as smoothly. Once again the incision closed as if zipped. Brand was preparing to leave when Laura emerged from the dressing room. "You'll let me know yes or no?" she said. "Whether I'm a mother-to-be?"

"I will, definitely. But you'd be wise to start thinking about more of the male element."

She was smiling. "I'm already on the trail of a new supply."

"A sperm bank?"

"No. You." Briefly, her gaze held his--focused unwavering on his eyes. "Oh, Em," she said, "that's how I've wanted it from the beginning. Can you understand this? You would be the father as well as the architect of this whole new life that you're building. You would be part of my life. Of *our* lives as soon as I make it to motherhood."

"It's not something I can even--."

She interrupted. "No one would ever know. You can believe me. It would be *our* secret, *our* private covenant. *Our* compact."

"No, I'm sorry, but that would violate every known protocol. Every single ethical standard. Here I am, sounding like someone in Professor Vandorn's shoes. Or Vandorn himself. Playing the ethicist. But it's definite, no, and I am sorry."

She was standing close to him, her scent fresh, stimulant. "Will you at least think it over? Or *talk* it over with Dr. Madsen?"

"I can't--I don't need to. I can help you in many ways, but not that way. Will you try to understand?"

Her answer came in a whisper. "I'll try."

51

Vandorn took a backward look. . . . A retrospective. A self-administered kick.

You couldn't win them all. At best you could only chip away at a target, persist, plan and replan, and accept outcomes.

By luck Vandorn had learned volumes during his private eye visit to the Kitkat Club. He had found, among other things, where Brand's nominee for Pregnant Man hung out. He had seen the crowd with which that gentleman, Gennett by name, associated. He had seen the kir bottles and knew now where the bartender kept them.

They were visible on the shelves behind the bar, ready to be tapped.

Leaving the Kitkat after an hour and a half, he had arrived at home in time to treat Jennifer to dinner at Smithson's. In alley-level chitchat he could lose himself, entertain himself while thinking his way through the rat's-nest of details that he had absorbed. At the same time, seated happily near a fireplace, he could observe how his wife preened at the realization that they were "out."

He made a resolution that he knew he would forget: to do this more often. His mind wrestled with possible ways to rid Franklin of Gennett. He would be awakening in the night to struggle with that conundrum.

In the meantime he would listen to Jennifer as she talked about the new novel she was reading. He listened, asked questions in the hope she might inadvertently drop a clue to an idea. Sipping at a Scotch on the rocks, he was imagining that the glass held poison. He was carefully avoiding talk about the City Council session. He had earlier sequestered and destroyed the daily papers that had covered the "tattle-tale" allegations that Brand had disgorged.

Similar ruminations occupied his mind while he waited for Eldy Dennington and Gus Gustafson. Several days had passed: a period filled with random mental sketchings that might lead to Mr. Gennett's exit from the Franklin stage.

The City Council's verdict on the pregnant man issue had left Vandorn with a garbagey taste. It added up as a travesty, a means of kicking the question onto the endless belt that ran into a legislative sump. Appoint a committee to investigate indeed!

The revelation of his failure to achieve ordination, on the other hand, began as trivium and ended as broad-ax insult. There had been a time when the seminary's termination of his studies had pained; he hated to have to surrender a program once pursued so diligently. But they had left him no choice; there was no reprieve, no extenuation in the God-business these days.

In the present, having climbed some ramparts of time and rage, the whole affair, including the fellatio incident with the pipsqueak fellow novice, could no longer make ripples on the sea of his indifference. But more than anything he felt that he owed Brand some recompense.

The City Council? Basically he had drowned out their brayings. Thank God for Keller and his frigging gavel.

Vandorn looked at his watch. Both Eldy and Gus Gustafson were late. But he had a reason for waiting--seeing a fellow instructor, an adequate recipe for continued chair-warming.

Vandorn sipped at his coffee. As usual, he could find comfort at any time in the fact that he held tenure in the University. If he wanted to look further for destiny's favor, there was his record as a teaching, publishing ethicist. The University wouldn't find a degree-holding ethicist on every street corner, that was foregone. And truth to tell, admitted publicly or not, ethics as a subject for study had many too many byways and contradictions. Even the ancient Greeks had problems with the ideal and the material. And they had invented such concepts.

The Greeks also--the greatest of them--had their own unique and often disregarded theses and theorems. And whatever the historic abstraction or thesis, it underwent change sooner or later. Would anyone need further evidence that "permanent truths" were no more permanent than the *Zeitgeist* in which they were spawned? As change took place, thus, it could subsume extremes of attitudes toward both morality and immorality.

Neither, in fact, had any more permanence or validity than the reputation of the founder of any particular school. From the Greeks to Augustine to Kant, Mill, and their fellow theorists, all underwent interpretation and reinterpretation. In the process they defended their own divergences, their own nonconformism.

Vandorn had begun to doodle, make notes. Seeing Eldy Dennington enter the Golden Horseshoe, the extravagantly named off-campus coffee shop, he put his notesheet away.

"Georgia thinks we should have an emergency meeting," Dennington said as he sat down. "I think she suspects that we're favorin' some pretty tough action."

"I don't see that we have much of a choice, do you?" Vandorn said. "We get the group together--the steering committee--and we end up with a lot of talk, no solutions, no decisions. We steer into a swamp of conflicting ideas."

"It nearly always happens. We start with big intentions, then the air leaks out."

"So it's really up to you and me." Vandorn took from a shirt pocket the sheet on which he had been making notes. That way, he could look official. "And here's what I'm thinking. We find a way to get at the kir bottles in the Kitkat Club. The bartender showed them to me the other day. And as I was told, that's the future Pregnant Man's favorite drink-- he apparently slugs down gallons of it."

"And you're figuring on tossing in a little poison."

"Exactly. I haven't figured out how we do that yet, but it's got to be possible."

"I can figure that out for you, I'm pretty sure. I think I could get a weekend job there. I was a bartender once, got used to it. Amateur level, no career stuff."

"You could be the answer to a jailbird's prayer. Have you talked yet to the boss or owner?"

"I have. He wants me to come in Friday evening, 6:00 p.m. He wants to see how I do. I was there last weekend."

"You were almost on time to pour me a drink." Vandorn glanced at his watch. "Time for me to be hitting the road. My poison man won't make it now. But we've had a productive emergency session. If you could keep it inside your gigantic brain. . ."

Vandorn was standing up. Dennington followed suit. "Let's talk Saturday morning," Vandorn added.

As the conspirator pair parted outside the coffee shop Vandorn felt more than he formulated in thought what strategy he would adopt.

He would have Gus bring him, Vandorn, two types of poison. One, a simple emetic, would be for Eldy Dennington. He would ingest some of that, take the after-effects as if he had drunk molten glass, and disappear to the nearest hospital while. . .

Drinking strychnine in a glass of kir, Gennett would go howling. His pains would be unendurable. Without immediate help effecting removal of every swallowed drop, he would be mortally sick.

Two simultaneous cases of hideous stomach distress would lead to the inevitable conclusion that there were two victims. But one, Dennington, would survive easily. There had to be a third man for the police to pursue.

Gennett? Recognizing the message spelling mortal danger, he would leave Franklin, decline further Pregnant Man activity, or succumb to the poison.

Later. . .

Ensconced behind his office phone, Vandorn tried all three numbers that he had for Gus Gustafson. The third time was the charm. Gus could supply the needed stuff.

52

His friends called John Gennett a "natural-born salesman." In first-ever encounters it was his custom to try to leave a positive impression. Arriving at the Madsen Clinic, Gennett also consciously enjoyed the VIP feeling he had as the switchboard operator directed him to where he and Adamson could wait in comfort.

They had been seated no more than a few minutes when Brand appeared, welcomed them, shook hands. Moments later, Madsen entered and greeted them similarly. Brand did the introductions and Madsen said, "I feel honored here--meeting an outrider in the epic of human reproduction."

"Not I but you gentlemen," Gennett said. "I'm just the unsuspecting but eager instrument." Amid light laughter he added: "I hope you don't mind, but I've brought my bodyguard."

"I'm glad," Madsen said. "We're counting on him too if circumstances change. Shall we go look at some of our facilities?"

With all four men gathered in the "Operating Theater," Madsen said, "I believe Em has briefed you both on what to expect. But I'd like to ask whether you still have questions. Or have thought of any new ones."

"I'll be absorbing female hormones and other nostrums," Gennett said. "I'm still wondering about female bodily changes."

"We can't really be very specific," Brand said. "You could grow rudimentary breasts. Your voice might change. But we're facing beginners' guesswork."

"I can live with that. We'll all learn something."

Adamson had drawn a small notebook from a trousers pocket. "Okay to make notes?" Gennett asked. "You gentlemen are making history, as I said. And Mart and I believe anything this revolutionary should be recorded, at least in summary form."

"No problem at all," Madsen said. "We may just ask for copies once we carry this project off."

"You're both on the mailing list," Adamson said. "In fact you *are* the list."

"One thing we need before we can really set a date to start is your health report," Brand said. "That's about the only thing lacking. Your man Quarles got your signatures on the releases and other documents."

"He did." Gennett added, "I felt as if I was signing my civil rights away." He smiled. "And then in the end it was only logical legal stuff."

"I have copies." From a faux leather briefcase Adamson drew some papers that had been stapled together. "These are all you need," he said. "Or so I was told."

Brand accepted the documents, scanned them quickly. "Any questions on these?" he said to Gennett.

"No. I do have some on what I can expect in terms of weight gains and appetite increases or decreases, things like that. We talked about this pretty superficially some weeks ago--," he was looking at Brand,-- "but if you have other thoughts I'd appreciate hearing them."

Brand said he would make notes. For the most part, he said, the changes would not be grotesque, with the exception of the steadily growing bulge in front. "It might be embarrassing to appear in public," Brand said. "That would be normal until we've done this a couple of thousand times."

"I have women patients who carry a little horn," Madsen said. "It serves them well when they're in crowds. They toot."

There was general laughter. "That reminds me," Gennett said. "Can you deliver a patient's preferred sex?"

"Boy or girl? When we are able to do that," Brand said, "we'll dress in primitive shaman robes. With a buffalo skull for a hat."

Again there was laughter. "I'm semi-serious," Gennett said. "I don't think I'd know how to raise a girl child."

"Either way, boy or girl, it would be pretty much the same challenge. I haven't been in the role, so I'm going on experience through others' eyes." Madsen spoke softly, seriously. To Brand, he was trying to soften the mood.

"None of us can change the gender-preference equation. That's a job for nature," Brand said shortly. "I think what we should do is determine whether we want to go ahead on the present basis and settle on a convenient date for an initial implant."

"I agree totally." Martin Adamson spoke with let's-move-on firmness. "And in fact we've really made up our minds. For us, a good first date would be a week or 10 days from today."

"Settled," Madsen said. "Ten days it is. A Friday evening at 7:00 p.m. okay with you gentlemen?"

To Brand's relief, the conversation shifted into a discussion of details. Adamson and Gennett left amid pleasantries. Brand resolved to send a reminder note to Gennett and Adamson. He wanted no mixups while Madsen was effectively donating his time and skills to this landmark first-ever effort.

He would search for more data for Gennett. He would find something in his baboon notes.

53

Brand had in mind a personal/private conversation with Madsen. Deep down, he was finding, Laura's proposal had struck a macho chord. In his own balanced sense of propriety and systemic integrity he had never felt or heard anything similar. He needed a sounding board.

He broached it to Madsen directly, after everyone had left. Almost shyly, he first alluded to Mrs. Phillips's suggestion as going beyond consideration. Madsen answered in all seriousness. "It may be something you should consider for both psych and practical reasons," Madsen began. "Practical--we've had no success with her cryogenic sperm, so perhaps it's a time for a change anyway. Psych--your mojo may have some immanent or ingrained efficacy that no other might have. Between us, I'm a generic disbeliever in the operations of government. But I'm a great adherent of the Shakespeare dictum--'There are more things between Heaven and Earth than are dreamed of in your philosophy, Horatio'."

"I'm thinking of the negatives. The professional model. The need to maintain a separation--independence--between doctor and patient in all personal or intimate ways."

Madsen held up the tubular device that Brand had created for the process of implanting embryos. "Look at this. Don't you think this is pretty personal in its own right?"

"Yes, in a different way. It's not as personal as bodily fluid--the essence itself, not even considering its critical role in the formation of new life."

"It's a difference of degree and function. But you're drawn to Mrs. Phillips' suggestion or you wouldn't be bringing up the question."

"You're so right."

"Remember that she needn't ever know."

"I've thought of that too. If I really thought--." He let the sentence hang.

"If you really thought she'd never know?"

"Exactly. And that's part of this dilemma. I'd want her to know and wouldn't want her to know. The secret would burn a hole in my conscience. Or my memory bank."

"If I read you right--and it's the way I've read you since the first day we met--you'll be able to live with it. You may even develop a kind of detached pride. You will, if she becomes pregnant, have gone a long step toward helping her--*again*. Since you've done it once, by bringing her to me, I think you could do it again and actually sleep better at night."

Brand smiled thoughtfully. "You should have been a lawyer, or maybe a politician. You could talk the sap out of a baobab tree."

"I'm just trying to put this whole thing in perspective. In what for me seems to be a normal perspective. And I think you need to know one other thing. If you donate the sperm for the next series of tries with Mrs. Phillips, I'll simply tell her it came from a sperm bank--and I selected it to save her the trouble. The donor wants, for a lot of usual reasons, to remain unnamed. Completely anonymous."

"There would be no way to trace it?"

"No way. I'll arrange the handling here. It will be in a capsule from a sperm bank. So have no fears. It'll be your secret and mine."

"I've decided. I'll come in Saturday morning if that's a good time. I'll do the Petri dish routine. When we have an embryo--or several of them--we can alert Laur--. We can alert Mrs. Phillips that we're ready to implant again. Sound possible?"

"Perfect. You'll only want to have the male element here before Saturday, and delivered to me. You'll want to have a likely sounding company name on it."

"I'll bring it in personally."

54

The summons to Dr. Schofield's office had teeth in it this time. No more "We would appreciate. . ."

He had brought the hand-written message home to show to Jennifer. As Vandorn expected, she performed perfectly in the role of the ever-solicitous helpmeet. "They've got to have something to do," she said. She read the note as a speed-reader would: running her eye down the sheet. "Otherwise they wouldn't earn those billions."

She had little or no faith in the group her husband had joined, now called CAMP, just as she had no empathy with or understanding of the group's cleanup mission. But if Jim saw purpose and merit in this kind of moral crusade, it was okay with her. Maybe the town did need some purging.

One thing stuck in her mental throat. Why did they have to lower a meaningless righteous boom on Franklin's best theater? So it ran some raunchy flicks now and then. The theater remained dark, didn't it? The ads for the movies were, to her way of thinking, pretty unspectacular, even modest. She knew because she attended the "better" movies from time to time. She hadn't wanted to lose that outlet, always enjoyed with her friend Rosie.

"Are you going to see them?" Jennifer continued unnecessarily, "See what they have to say?"

"I know what they'll have to say. They'll tell me the University doesn't want its sacred name dragged into free-for-alls like we had at the council session. As if I had anything to do with that. They should be hollering at Brand. He's the one spreading slander--he and that so-called gynecologist, with his wild imaginings."

"Can't you just tell them it's all a lie? Or a whole pile of lies?"

"It would just keep the pot boiling. I'll keep it as private as I can and let it blow over. Anyway, it's only a bunch of blarney; my helper did the community a favor by getting rid of that animal before it chewed somebody's arm off. The rest, about my ordination, is hearsay."

Vandorn glanced at his watch. "I should be heading out," he said. "The boss wanted me there by 2:00 p.m. and I'll make it by a quarter of. That'll impress them."

They exchanged cursory kisses and Jennifer said, "Give them a few shots."

"That's my plan."

"Dr. Levenson was going to join us." Dr. Schofield's voice was ice-cold. "But he's been delayed. I can state our case."

He shuffled some papers that lay before him on the desk. Vandorn could see newspaper clippings among them. "I'm sure you know dam well what has gotten under our collars."

"Something about the City Council hearing would be my guess." Vandorn had made up his mind: face up to it, be firm but not obsequious. Blame others when possible.

"Correct of course. First we've been reading that your ordination as a Catholic priest never took place. That you were asked to leave the seminary before you reached that stage in your studies. If true, that doesn't jibe with your personnel file. In those documents there's sworn testimony, statement after statement, sworn documents indicating that you served as a priest until you voluntarily gave up your vocation."

"There's a long story there." Vandorn leaned forward, concentrating. He had determined to sort through what he remembered; he would put his own cast on it. "I was so close to ordination, as I realize in my unclouded moments, that it actually seems that I made it to and through the ceremonies. Sounds strange, I know, but--."

"But?"

"That's about as close as I can come to an explanation. I know it's not much, but it really does feel like I made it. We went through ordination dry-runs."

Dr. Levenson appeared, walking noiselessly on the carpeted floor. Vandorn moved as if he wanted to stand, but Levenson held up a beefy restraining hand. "No need for formality," he said. Vandorn leaned back, relaxed.

"I've been on the verge of telling Dr. Vandorn that he's on probation here," Schofield said. "We talked about this earlier."

"We did," Levenson said heartily. "You're thinking of the false information in Dr. Vandorn's personnel file."

"Yes, I am. In any case there's an almost-reasonable excuse that Dr. Vandorn and I have been talking about. And I'm willing to stay with probation if that's satisfactory from your perspective."

"I mentioned before that such a decision would be acceptable to me. Why, we've got errors and exaggerations in three-quarters of those files. That's true in the faculty group at least."

"I'm sure," Schofield said quickly, dropping the subject. "We should also talk briefly about the dead baboon--the animal that everyone is calling a monkey."

"That was a total misunderstanding," Vandorn said. "Some kid wanted to see that animal--and even feed him. It sounds nutty, but I was trying to help. I came away with a bite for my pains."

He held up his left hand. His injured finger still bore the latest and smallest of the bandages it was receiving at Franklin General.

"Who was the kid?" Schofield said. His eyes were focused on Vandorn's face. Improvising, Vandorn developed an explanation he had devised for such occasions as he was now experiencing.

"He was a friend of a friend. I think he was a student somewhere, probably high school level, but maybe college. It seemed that he had some research interest in baboons."

"A med student?" Levenson sounded doubtful. "Wouldn't someone like that know where to view baboons close up--in fact, wouldn't a med or pre-med know about our Zoo?"

"I don't know. It does sound odd. I just got this sort of thrown into my lap. I can guarantee it won't ever happen again."

Both administrators sat silent. Vandorn hoped one of them would signal that the cross-examination was over. But neither spoke. For his part, Schofield toyed with a letter-opener. Levenson seemed to have exhausted his questions.

It was Levenson who turned the session toward a harmless ending that would give relief to Vandorn. "As I've said before, we've gotten just about every imaginable crisis that had the earmarks of the crime of the century--and turned out to be a handful of dust," Levenson said. "Some fiasco that wasn't worth pursuing. That's where we are here, as I see it."

He moved as if he were rising, but then settled into his chair again.

Playing the humble petitioner, Vandorn dropped his eyes and waited to see whether he would survive with the probationary penalty that Schofield had mentioned earlier.

It ended quickly. Schofield stood, and Levenson followed suit.

55

They had dinner early. For Laura at least, five-thirty was an early dinner-time. It seemed to matter very little to Tim, who could eat the late-day meal at any time.

He would be eating again by 9:00 or 9:30 in any case. That was the time for a top-off snack that often consisted of more than the regular dinner.

With dinner at five-thirty, she could eat her usual light repast, finish the dishes, and have the evening for a visit with her parents or an appointment with Dr. Madsen and Dr. Brand.

Those appointments--she thought of them as meetings--trysts--because Dr. Brand was regularly part of them--had become integral to her life in just a couple of months. In a kind of reverse effect, she almost feared the date on which the doctors would tell her she was carrying a child.

Even that, she told herself, would not terminate the opportunities to see Dr. Brand. She would need periodic examinations, consultations, possibly injections. She would, she believed, be able to continue the evening meetings.

Tim had become so indifferent to her maternal ambitions that she had told him she was continuing to receive embryos unsuccessfully. In six or seven weeks her visits had become like stops at a church to light votive candles. Tim seemed to see it as a kind of hobby that could go on for months or years. He had read somewhere that cloning Dolly the world-famous sheep had taken "ages."

How many "ages" he never inquired.

Finishing the dishes, Laura said she had to run. Tim lowered his newspaper. "Dad or doc?" he asked.

"Doc."

"They getting any closer?"

"I don't think it's a matter of getting closer. I think it's a matter of succeeding or failing."

"You running into Van-, Van-, what's his name these days? Or did they can him after that City Council brouhaha?"

"Everyone says he's still teaching. But he's been silenced by the University, I think."

"Just so he stays away from here." He began to read again.

Driving to Madsen's clinic, she felt a rush of anticipation. She would be starting on a new regimen--or a new combination of egg and sperm. She had seen no sense in explaining that to Tim; and she found it inspirational that a new "father" was emerging from some frozen darkness to help her. While she would have chosen Brand as the "supplier," at least she could depend on Madsen to provide high-grade sperm.

Arriving at the clinic, she joined the usual mood of reunion/celebration. Following standard procedure, she donned her loose hospital-style draped clothing--rendered "decent" by a light garment of her own.

She was feeling the incisions more than on previous occasions. From her supine position on the adjustable bed she said, "I think I'll need new skin down there."

"You're feeling the curette?" Madsen said. "Sorry about that. We are making quite a few cuts." He had paused in his work. "Do you think we should wait two-three weeks, or more, before we try again?"

"Oh no. I'm fine. I was just a making small talk."

"Think of the woman who had 12 caesareans."

Laura laughed. "If I get to one, I'll be the happiest mother on earth. And that reminds me. I hope you'll have some time to give me just a little information about the near-genius who supplied the male element this time."

Madsen, concentrating on the stomach area in which he was about to implant an embryo, paused again, briefly. "It's pretty skimpy information, but I'll go over it again if you want. The people who preserve these samples promise total secrecy to their donors."

"I can understand why. And please bear with me. I can understand how sensitive all this is. You could have lawsuits filling every courtroom in the land if they did it otherwise."

Laura relaxed visibly. Brand, holding the implantation device, said, "This is ready when you are, Doctor Al." He held up the device in his rubber-gloved hand. "It's also sterile."

"I'll need it in seconds."

Madsen was stitching up the tiny incision in the skin of her stomach when Laura spoke again. "I have the feeling that it will work this time," she said, sounding to herself as if she had been mysteriously offered the thought.

"Two great minds," Brand said. "I had the same idea." He stopped to watch Madsen placing a small bandage over the incision.

"That bandage will fall off or wash off, as usual," Madsen said. "And you're free to dress and go. We should set a date for another try unless you'd prefer to let your skin heal for a while."

"Let's pick another date. Another try." She had sat up with Brand's help. "I'll be okay in another week or so."

"Take one more half-minute and I'll tell you what they had to say about our new male element donor," Madsen said. "First, highly intellectual, near the top of the top quartile. Also inventive. Has what some claim are talents that go together: he's gifted in both music and math. Finally, he's a family man; that means normal instincts."

"I approve of normal instincts." Laura laughed, a tinkling sound, and held out her hand to let Brand help her to the floor. As she stepped down in her flimsy clinic clothes, he recognized the hyacinth scent that she favored.

56

Seeing Gus Gustafson enter the university's Union Hall, his reddish moustache as bushy as ever, Vandorn had to wonder. Toby Rhodes, his tablemate, was as dissimilar from Gus as a sparrow was from an emu, at least to Vandorn's critical eye. But he hadn't brought the two of them here to compare faces, body builds, gene pools. He had only incidentally noticed that both had moustaches.

He had brought them together to broach a new plan, one that Toby was pushing. Vandorn would let Toby explain it, make sure Gus could supply the lethal or less-than-lethal fluids, set a date. Having heard what it involved, Eldy Dennington had declared himself ineligible. That meant, to Vandorn, that LeBaron had gotten to him.

Greetings went the rounds. Vandorn set the scene for talk as he had planned. "Gus," he said, "I'm going to let Toby explain our needs the way he's figured them out. We'll need your help, as planned all along."

Toby looked around. No nearby tables were occupied. "It's pretty simple," Toby said, modulating his voice. "We're figuring on sweetening a fancy drink. The sweetener would be one of your mixtures--enough to make a pretty strong poison out of a taste or two of a wine-sized drink. In fact it's kir, mostly wine. The potion could be fatal, but wouldn't be if the target gets medical attention right away."

"That sounds definite enough," Gus said. "I take it you'd need more; a second 'potion'?"

"We would," Toby answered with animation. "I'm figuring it this way. We get one guy sick, they're gonna find the poison left in his drink. They're off on a hunt for a poisoner. One person. But they'd start with the bartender. That's gonna be me starting Saturday."

"Listen to the rest, Gus." Vandorn said while hunching closer to the table.

"If you can give us something blander, weaker," Toby said. "It'll work this way. First I send his glass over to the Pregnant Man as they're calling him. Then I drink another, weaker mixture. Some pretty harmless emetic--that's what they call the stuff that makes you puke?"

"It is." Gustafson was listening closely, his eyes on Toby.

"And I go off howling, vomiting, hollering for a cab to the hospital." That turns out to be a second case of poisoning. But I'm not in danger, the other guy could be."

"And the investigation, if any, goes tearing off in search of a third man, the poisoner of two people," Vandorn commented.

"Right," Toby answered. "I would have dumped any stuff left in the containers--which are little bottles, I hope."

"Ingenious," Gustafson said. "They would be. It'd be an easy order also. Two identical bottles, both marked with some code name that you'd know. Color coded if you want. Glass, I'd suggest, because they're smashable. Plastic might survive."

"All right on."

Gustafson looked at Vandorn. "What's your timeline?"

"I'll have to call you next Sunday. Toby here will be doing a dry run this coming weekend."

"Sounds like you've found a way to put the fear of God in somebody."

"I'm--we're hoping it works out that way. Hoping they decide to give up on this stupid project."

"What they're calling Pregnant Man?"

"Exactly." Vandorn glanced at Toby. In his voice there was a kind of pride mingled with relief as he said, "Thanks to Toby here, I think we've got a great chance to scare the poop out of some people."

"While staying out of the limelight."

"Right. I'm saving my act for the mastermind of all this jungle uproar."

"Don't tell me, I know who. If his name begins with B-R."

Their three chairs scraped on the parquet floor as the men stood to leave.

57

Dressed as if for supervisory work out of doors, John Gennett walked into the Madsen Clinic waiting room. Martin Adamson was close on his heels. Both were seated when the girl in the glassed-in reception cubicle saw them. She had been on the telephone.

She had just told a friend that the doctor was going to launch a big experiment in the next hour. She wasn't supposed to talk about it, so she would tell him the details when they met later.

She asked Mr. Gennett if he was Mr. Genate. When he said yes, correcting her pronunciation, the girl alerted Dr. Madsen who was washing up for a scheduled job of minor surgery. The doctor suggested that the girl show Mr. Gennett to the change room. She could also notify Dr. Brand that the gentlemen were on hand.

As an afterthought, the doctor asked the girl to tell Mr. Gennett to put on a hospital gown over his underclothes. He could wear the gown frontwards, not backwards as would be usual.

Dr. Brand was prepping also. Told that both Gennett and Adamson had arrived, Brand walked the few yards to the dressing room, also called the change room. He welcomed the two men. He also repeated Dr. Madsen's instructions. He went back to the refrigerator to check once more on his newly hatched embryo.

Brand did not mention that they were half an hour late. He would do that later. He, Brand, was due at home half an hour ago, an uncomfortable thought. Michelle was losing patience with his late hours.

Gennett finished pulling on the hospital gown--with the opening in front. At that moment Brand reappeared. "I'm a little nervous," Gennett said. "But I suppose that's normal."

"For a first try in a first-ever project, I'd say it would be expected," Brand said. "If you're ready here, we can move to the Operating room-- just down the hall."

Dr. Madsen was waiting for them.

Working with Laura Phillips, Madsen had become accustomed to soft surface tissue. But as he probed gently to make sure he was locating correctly, he found Gennett's belly just below the button to be almost the same as Laura's. He would have preferred firmer flesh, but was fully accustomed to working with what the patient brought.

"I think I've got it," Madsen said to Brand after a while. "Would you open the incision just a fraction and take a look?"

"Yes, of course."

Using tiny clamps, Brand pulled the lips of the opening apart gradually. Gennett drew a quick breath, almost inaudibly. "It's a little painful," Brand said. He was thinking of his similar work with baboons. "This will take just a second--isn't that what they all say?"

"It's nothing I won't live through." Gennett had relaxed somewhat.

"I'd say you're on target," Brand said to Madsen while holding open the incision. Without hesitating, Madsen picked up the "superlap," as Brand called it, and inserted the expulsion end into the opening. A movement of the plunger and the fluid in the laparoscope flowed out. It was the work of seconds, and almost at once Madsen with-drew the lap.

"Closing time," Madsen said. He was bathing the lap in a transparent liquid. Quickly, Brand took the three or four stitches that would close the opening. He covered the wound with a bandage.

They talked briefly afterward. Having dressed, Gennett accompanied by Adamson went back to the Operating room. Madsen and Brand were programming their next appointments with Laura Phillips and Gennett.

"Am I pregnant?" Gennett said, smiling as he entered the room. Adamson was also smiling.

"Not likely," Brand said. "It could take a long time. It's not exactly as hard as winning a lottery, but it comes close."

Madsen spoke. "You remember Dolly the sheep? They tried I believe 277 times before they made that effort work. I've been telling everyone that. But it's true, we've got better equipment and we're working toward omentum impregnation. But that may mean our task is either easier or more difficult--we just don't know in advance."

"We do know it's totally possible," Brand said. "The procedure has worked on primates--with no serious problems after the embryonation."

Gennett had become serious. "I don't think I'd last through 277 sessions," he said. "I'll be burning a joss stick for a quick jackpot."

"We'll do the same," Madsen said. "And we'll see you in a week."

58

Tim Phillips had exhausted his patience. It was high time, he thought, for Laura to give up her crazy fixation on motherhood, having a baby, call it what you want. As far as he was concerned, it simply made no sense to continue down a road that obviously led either nowhere or into baby-bondage.

He said as much at dinner a couple of nights after her most recent bout with the two oddball doctors, Brand and Madsen. For Tim's money Brand was the crazier of the two, what with his literally "monkeying" around, his entertaining an ape in his garage, his nutty ideas about human reproduction.

Brand should be put away, Tim believed. Then things would quiet down. Madsen would--could--go on with his regular obie-gyne practice and all would be well in the community. The other madman-in-residence, Vandorn, would have a clear field. Or he could share a padded cell with Brand.

"Why don't you just give it up?" he said as he finished the meatloaf and mashed potatoes. Because the meatloaf-mashed combination was one of his favorites, it gave rise to expansive moods. He was experiencing one now.

"I won't ask what you're talking about," Laura said after a pause to finish chewing. She had wiped her mouth carefully before speaking. "I know without asking. And no, I have no urge right now to sign up for a class in tatting or Conversational Italian."

"I never suggested either of those or anything like them."

"It doesn't matter. They all sound like time-fillers, and that's your intention." Thanks to whatever alchemy, Laura felt different this evening, and she wished Tim were capable of sharing the sensation. She could imagine no hope more forlorn: with that thought prominent in her awareness, she began to busy herself with the cleanup and the dishes. This evening the chores irritated her.

She culled her memory. The collected lore that she had heard and read--"The guesswork in Off-trail Reproductive Medicine," "Planning the Wanted Child," "Transgender Problems and the Law," even "The New Assisted-Reproduction Technologies"--all of it seemed futile: efforts to pierce to the core rationale behind this revolution. Whether they took stands pro or con, all the theories, all the chatter, all the tinkling cymbals of moralists or conservatives, all of it, ethical and religious preachments included, rang as empty as a marble in a dried gourd. They missed motherhood, personhood projected, love incarnated.

What counted lay in the woman's heart. The means of achieving fertilization were multiplying, with *in vitro* competing and perhaps overwhelming Nature itself--but also opening doors for those with special needs. Like herself.

Out of the welter of respectable theory or exposition and the matching mountain of balderdash and bunk, she saw what kept her tied to a paternal neuter, a perennially, voluntarily childless mate. If that characterization was sprouting as an ungainly growth in their marriage, he had watered it; it had taken root and was there, and in the exact time absorbed by that process she had been traveling in the opposite direction.

Neither of them could change. That was what kept them in the same house and the same relationship, at arm's length: her hope of maternity. The child would need two parents; would need the perks of a decent life-style.

That thought was becoming hateful. But bargains with life were unavoidable. Everyone on earth faced them at one or another time. She would accept the bargain and survive--and hope that Tim would find space in his slide-rule world for the newcomer she would one day bear.

Her hand moved, impelled by the urge to call Dr. Brand. If that were possible, she could talk away her present grey mood. He seemed to have the right words in every situation.

Letting her thoughts run along that line while scrubbing at the evening-meal dishes, she made a decision. She would walk the two blocks to the drugstore and call from there. She would have made an escape from this work and this eccentric atmosphere. She could invent an excuse for calling Brand and take it from there.

Tim had moved to the living room. He was sitting wrapped in his *Wall Street Journal*, apparently oblivious to whatever she might be doing.

"Going out to the drugstore while it's still light," she said to Tim's newspaper. He grunted. "Do you need anything?" she added, and this time received no response at all.

She was out and starting the walk when she realized that she felt different. She had eaten lightly, as usual, and despite that she felt as if she had the most trifling extra weight in her stomach. Meatloaf had never been so weighty or hard to digest or so lumpy as this. She was entering the drugstore when a thought broke over here like a wave.

It had only been a matter of days--three? Four?-- since she had been at Madsen's clinic. But she felt with an access of instinct that she was with child.

"It's not likely, but we'll certainly do the necessary testing," Brand said. "In the meantime, I'd advise you to take the precautions you'd take in a normal pregnancy, only more so. All that adds up as common sense. There are no hard and fast rules. If there's one generic rule, it's probably this: Take it easy."

"I feel more at ease, just talking about it. Do you realize, we just started the new male element the other day."

"I'm very aware of that," Brand said in a voice that seemed to fade. "And if it has really happened--if you have a growing embryo--it's both miraculous, probably a first, but truly history-making. We've been figuring it would take 25 to 50 implants to achieve pregnancy." Brand paused to clear his throat. "And here you are, or may be."

"All evening I've been wondering why I felt different. I don't even know how to explain it. At moments it feels like an added weight. At others, I have only the vaguest sensation that something new is taking place."

"And it started this evening?"

"I don't even know. I'm sorry if that sounds silly. Do women with normal pregnancies have these whatevers, intimations?"

"In my experience, yes. And usually they're right. They are pregnant. The strangest part is that they may have no clue at all if they are abdominally pregnant. In the normal course of events that type of pregnancy is very rare. There was such a case earlier this year."

"A nine-month gestation?"

"Yes, I believe so. During that whole stretch the mother-to-be had to practically live with her doctor."

Without thinking, Laura said, "I'd like that." Hearing a short, appreciative laugh, Laura tried to backtrack. "Excuse me, Em," she said, "I didn't mean that the way it sounds."

"No apologies needed. What we have to do right now to be safe is make an appointment for you at Madsen's. I'll meet you there and run some tests. Partly, that means take some fluids, have them analyzed. Maybe tomorrow."

"Exciting!" It was almost a cry, and Laura half-turned to look around. A man stood behind her. He was reading a paper that he had folded so that a single column showed and could be read.

Laura held up a finger to indicate that she was almost finished with the phone. "Lady!" the man began, and stopped, seeing her face at an angle. "I'm okay," he ended lamely.

Brand was waiting at his end. At Laura's suggestion they agreed again that Brand would try immediately to establish a time and date for some lab tests. He would call her back at the drugstore: she would wait for the call. If they missed one another, Brand would call her in the morning.

The man with the newspaper moved to the phone as soon as Laura stepped away from it. She waited ten minutes, twenty. Standing closely behind him, she maintained her "place" in case a line should form.

Standing became tiring. Her earlier intoxication with the thought of instant pregnancy waned, subsided. She felt tired--and suddenly the phone was free. She moved close, hand poised to snatch the receiver. When it rang after a few seconds, she seized it, almost dropping it but catching it by the cord.

It was Em. He had set an appointment for the coming Friday evening. It was the best Dr. Madsen could do. It was two days away.

"I'll be a nervous wreck by then," she said, invoking one of her favorite cliches.

It was the best they could do, Brand repeated, and elicited a promise that she would "navigate at three miles an hour." It was his gently euphemistic way of telling her to slow down, Laura realized.

"I'll remember," she said. "For both of our sakes--the newcomer's if there is one, and mine."

"Include your doctor," Brand said. "I'm going to mentor you through this, after all."

"How true. You're included. And I'll see you Friday."

"Keep me posted daily at my office, just to ease my mind."

"Will do." Hanging up the phone, Laura pursed her lips and made a kissing motion, intending it as a tender farewell to Brand.

A woman who had been standing behind Laura, waiting for the phone, saw the gesture and smiled.

59

Any bar that had been functional for a couple of years or more had an air--a scent--about it that betrayed the kind of clientele it attracted. So maintained Toby Rhodes, onetime professional bartender and occasional bouncer. For the latter avocation he had for years taken lessons in various martial arts.

He had gone clean at his wife's insistence, giving up the bartending and forgetting much of what he had learned about martial arts. But he found he couldn't work for anyone else in a superior-subordinate relationship. He had ended up borrowing enough funds to start running his own ice cream parlor. To his own amusement, the term *"parlor"* implied a degree of magnificence, or at least size, that the 12-by-20-foot store hardly merited.

Even more ironic, he found that he could only make a buck if he stayed open evenings. His wife again became accustomed to dining alone and making his life miserable. He decided to take a job driving a taxicab. Driving during the daylight hours, he found again, hardly yielded a living wage.

After talking with Vandorn and Gustafson, he was more than ever determined to try working evenings at the Kitkat Club--if they would hire him.

He would pilot a hack by day, wear an apron and toss together drinks by night. He knew the job would be temporary.

It would work perfectly, he figured, because the cab had to end the day in a garage located only a long block from the Kitkat.

Applying at the Kitkat, Rhodes could see after five minutes that he had won the job but had to listen to twenty more minutes of eulogies from the owner-manager. Part of the presentation dealt with the sometimes "demanding" regular customers, who made up in "sensitivity" and "discrimination" what they might lack in "gregariousness."

"I've dealt with picky people off and on for years," Rhodes said. "I've always gotten along with 'em. The trick is to just listen."

"A good method if you give them what they want," the manager said. After a moment's thought he added the word "promptly." The qualifier came at the moment when Rhodes was about to ask about his hours and days.

"Before I forget," the manager said, "we'd need you weekends-- Fridays, Saturdays, and Sundays. You up to that?"

"Well, I was thinking of more days, but for starters that's fine." He was thinking, *I won't be here very long anyway.*

"Then we've got a deal," whereupon he started talking money.

While the manager did some figuring on the bar Toby Rhodes went over the behind-the-bar layout. It seemed to have everything a well appointed bar might need. Or what a neighborhood night-haunt might need.

He was examining the impressive ranks of bottles on shelves behind the bar when he found the kir. He had a hand almost poised to reach for it when a thought hit him: *don't show any special interest.* And he moved on.

At home, telling his wife that he would be starting in three days, he expected another hurricane. But his wife, Marilyn, took a deep breath and said, "Well it could be five days a week, I guess. Three sounds better."

"And I won't be there more than a month or two."

"I guess we can stand that."

Arriving fifteen minutes early for work on Friday afternoon, Rhodes found, to his gratification, that the Kitkat was jumping. In his bartender decalogue of preferences nothing made for monotony like empty tables. As his eyes became adjusted to the subdued light he could see that the booths were nearly all occupied, as were several tables.

He allowed the day bartender to instruct him on things that he knew or could see. To prove that he was an eager learner he asked a few questions. For example, he asked whether it looked like the usual Friday night crowd.

"It is that," the incumbent said in a mild brogue. "Just about the same as the last Friday and the one before that. And I'm Sean Kiley."

"They all know each other--Mr. Kiley?"

"To a certain extent. Most commonly, from my observation, they fall into a pecking order. A few are quite well known and some or all of the others come to see those best-known patrons."

"They must come to drown a thirst and forget the week too if my memory is still working."

"Most certainly it is the norm. But we have one or two regulars who have gained some unusual fame very recently. I'm not fully certain what the game is. What I hear is that it has to do with a medical breakthrough."

Acting mildly interested, Rhodes said, "No rumors about the kind of breakthrough?"

"Rumors that I can't believe. And that brings us to *my* memory, they all involve Mr. Gennett. You won't want to look now, but he's sitting squarely across from us. And if you don't mind, I see some empty glasses. If you'll excuse me."

Rhodes washed used glasses, keeping busy. Bartender-waiter Kiley was returning to the bar when a young woman entered and followed almost on his heels to the bar. To Rhodes Kiley said, "Did Brummell tell you--we have a waitress to help out after 5:00 o'clock on weekend nights?" Kiley was carrying a tray of glasses that he set on the bar.

"And that's my closing bell," Kiley said, "When Margie here arrives." With a reflex motion he untied the backside knot that secured the flaps of his apron. Stepping around the bar, he threw the apron into a large green plastic bag.

With a jaunty wave, he was gone. Crossing the broad floor, he waved to several tables and groups in booths.

Like a private club, Rhodes thought. Plus a new element, someone to talk to. Margie had come behind the bar herself and was gracefully pulling on a light apron. As she finished, she held out her hand. Rhodes' right hand was wet; he dried it hurriedly and took the proffered shake. "I'm Marge," she said unnecessarily. Rhodes introduced himself as Toby.

Suddenly the Kitkat Club seemed to darken. As the light dimmed-- for Rhodes, the available illumination was being quenched slowly--it became more difficult to identify the bottles that were so neatly lined up on the shelves behind him. He had just located the kir bottle, with its Creme de Casis label when Margie appeared next to him.

"They're monkeying with the lights," she said. "They get it real dark and then start playing their sex games."

"How do we get light back?"

"They'll turn 'em on. They know I'll just hide back here until the lights go on--and before that they don't get nothin' to drink."

Rhodes relaxed. "How do they control the lights?"

"I don't know. Nobody's been able to find out."

"Spooky." Changing the subject, speaking to the pale whitish specter that Margie had become. Rhodes asked whether many of the "weekend crowd" had specialty drinks, exotic drinks, unheard of drinks.

"Some do, yeah," Marge said. "Mr. Gennett's one. He likes that liqueur stuff."

"And nothing else?"

"Nothin' else that I know about." Her voice became softer. "I think I'd know if he ordered anything else."

"Mr. Kiley mentioned him. He's sort of famous, I hear."

"I don't know whether you'd call it famous. Sounds crazy as a bedbug, you ask me."

"How crazy?"

"If I'm understandin' it, he's gonna be a guinea pig on some medical project. His friend--he's there now, on the other side of the table-- you just can't see 'im just now--his friend's goin' for the same nutty experiment, what I hear."

"They tell everybody this?"

"They don't tell, they just talk about it. They sort of make a big thing out of it. Our boss says what's said here stays here."

"You don't know what they're talking about?"

"I don't, no. They say he's tryin' to get pregnant. To me he don't seem to have the right tools for that. But maybe there's a way I never heard about. Anyway, a girl is pretty safe around here."

The lights were coming back up. "We're back in business," Rhodes said. "Got any orders there for me?"

"Sure have." Like someone making a bank deposit, Marge laid three order forms on the bar. She immediately separated one of the three. "This one's for Mr. Gennett," she said. "It's for that oddball premixed stuff, kir."

60

The sheet had Emlyn Brand's name on it as the authorizing doctor. Set up in two columns, it provided little boxes next to a list of about 70 items. Some items were spelled out, others abbreviated.

Dr. Brand had placed X's in five boxes, all identified by initials. The X's meant he wanted lab results on those items.

Not that it mattered, but she was curious; Laura Philips trusted Dr. Brand as she had never trusted her husband. *In this instance "trust" had nothing to do with fidelity. Rather, it had to do with that most capricious and even cryptic of all qualities: reliability.* Brand needed the lab's verdicts as the keys to her probable status--pregnant or not. She was leafing disinterestedly through a magazine called *Bride* and thinking of Brand when the woman at the lab window called her name: "Laura?"

She followed the woman, went through the lab routine: weight, blood pressure, push up a sleeve for blood extraction. The aide was very efficient, very considerate. To Laura's private amusement, she made positive clucking sounds as she checked and noted her findings.

Finished, the aide told Laura that "The doctor will be in contact with you."

Stop at his office? It would be an easy walk, a few minutes, less than a hundred and fifty yards in lovely fall weather.

Brand's office door was open. He was examining papers in an open filing cabinet drawer. He turned when she mentioned his name, smiled when he saw her. "You've been to the lab already," he guessed. "Have a seat?"

"Only a minute. I know you're busy." For a moment her memory went on autopilot. She could remember, envision, recreate the first time she had been inside this office. The memory came unattached to a date, but she knew it had been a morning, much like now.

"Still got the sensation that you're gestating?" Brand said.

"I do. Is that crazy? I don't really feel that I'm going to change in any way, but unless it's in my imagination I feel different, as I told you. Can it be my impatience?"

"Possibly. It could also be real. And we would want to check your condition anyway. I use *condition* in a medical sense."

"I understood. The other part of this is that I have hundreds of questions. Then when I want to ask them, like now, I forget them."

Brand had taken a seat. "Ask away now if you think of any."

"One that I meant to ask even before my implant appointment had to do with the male element. Is there such thing as a profile of the man who supplied the male element--to use our usual euphemism?"

"There must be. I'll ask Dr. Madsen. From what he tells me, very few people do that work. I find that amazing in view of the fact that we're in the midst of a reproduction revolution--as everyone says. I don't doubt it since I'm actually part of it."

"A life-saving part. And I already asked Dr. Madsen. When all this is over I'm going to see if someone will write it up."

Brand hesitated, examined the papers he had drawn from his files. With fingers stiffly gripping the papers, he quelled a manual urge to tremble.

Laura rose to her feet. For Brand, she might have been uncoiling. "I've taken enough of your time," she said, and stopped at the doorway. Speaking in subdued tones, she said, "There is one more question that occurs to me: If or when I'm pregnant, will I be reporting to you primarily or Dr. Madsen?" She waited at the door expectantly.

"We will be sharing the duties--if I can call them duties. At times you may have a choice."

"You know what I'm thinking?"

"No, but I'd like to know."

"You said once that a woman who's pregnant abdominally has to practically live with her gynecologist." She smiled. "Remember?"

"I do remember. Now I'm trapped?"

They laughed together. Then she was gone.

The sound of Laura's shoes in the hall grew fainter, quickly went silent. Brand closed his office door and immediately placed a call to Dr. Madsen. The doctor was busy, but the girl took a message. Dr. Madsen would call back.

61

Rhodes called Saturday morning, making Vandorn's day. The message was succinct.

"The place is up for grabs over Gennett's big adventure," Rhodes said, a little breathlessly. "If they were trying to keep it hush-hush, they've dropped the ball. Gennett and his asshole buddy are practically spending the millions they're going to pick up."

"That means you got the job."

"Yeah, no problem. It was like they were waiting for me. The waitress tells me they've had two or three tenders quit. I can't say I blame 'em. The place gets a little rowdy after a few rounds."

Vandorn could hear Jennifer as she opened and closed drawers. She was preparing to leave for her occasional weekend job as "house mother" to a dozen or more pre-schoolers. She loved the work. As Vandorn appraised the job, it fulfilled in a harmless way her maternal instincts.

So far, it hadn't disturbed their long-standing agreement to put off having kids.

On the phone Rhodes coughed.

"It sounds like you've got an ideal situation for what we're planning," Vandorn said. "Busy place, lot of noise, booze flowing, Gennett half blotto."

"You've got the picture. I could do it next week. I can do it and still cover my tracks."

"Hold there if you would. We should ponder this face to face. How about my office in an hour?"

"Sounds fine."

Toby Rhodes hadn't shaved, and his cheeks were heavily shadowed. *Like some of my students*, thought Vandorn as the two men shook hands.

"I didn't get out of there until after midnight," Rhodes said. "Midnight's supposed to be closing time, but the joint was still half full when I left."

"Everything we've heard about Gennett is true? He has one favorite drink--what's the name again?"

"Kir. There's about a bottle and a half on the shelf still."

"And that's it?"

"They might have more stashed somewhere."

"You mentioned on the phone that you could leave the stuff but not leave tracks. I've been trying to figure out how that could be possible."

"It's simple. I serve him out of one bottle, making sure we empty it in one evening. That means pour some down the sink if there's some left when we close."

"I get it. The other bottle has the potion. You leave it for the next day."

Rhodes smiled. "Right. and I'm sick the next day. I don't show up. Act as if I have the same thing Gennett has." A smile continued to play around Rhodes' mouth.

"I see what you're saying. But how do you make sure that it gets done if you're not there on the second night--if you don't take the light stuff and go into a mild funk? That's the part that's going to have the cops looking for some outside poisoner."

"I've been wondering about that. I had decided that would be a little dangerous. If I drink the strong stuff, I'm the one that goes to the morgue, not our PG Man."

"It's too chancey if you're not there to make sure Gennett drinks the right stuff; we may be laying a trap for ourselves--or you, as the last man to have access to the kir bottle."

"Maybe." Rhodes scratched the back of his neck. "Let me noodle this again. You may be right."

"I don't want to order this juice unless you'll be there to make sure Gennett drinks his share." Vandorn got slowly to his feet.

Rhodes frowned "Okay, okay. It's a done deal. Let's try to get it over with next weekend."

"My feeling totally. I'll call you when I have the juice. The price for you remains the same if we do the job the way we've just agreed."

"Great. Consider it done. Now I've got to meet my old lady."

"So do I. We'll probably meet in the supermarket."

Leaving, Vandorn dawdled. He was thinking *close call. First Eldy, now Rhodes.*

62

She could lift the house she shared with Tim. She could leave the ground and cleave the air like a swallow. No longer a mere woman, she had acquired, by some alchemy, transcendent attributes.

And it all derived from the feeling she had, the sensation that she was *with child*. She found it hard to sit still, to wait for Dr. Brand to call her with the verdict. "A miracle," he had said, "if it has really happened." He was being pragmatic, going by the laws of averages, taking the realistic--to him--view. Trying to protect her from possibly severe disappointment.

The phone rang. Answering, knowing already who would be calling, she heard a strange voice. Her premonition had been correct.

"I'm Kathy Edwards, the female voice said factually, "free-lance writer. Have I dialed the right number?"

"You have." Laura thought quickly. "I have a rather sensitive situation here, and I'm wondering whether we might talk, compare notes, see if we can work out some arrangement."

"We should try. It's the way I'd like to go."

"Can you stop by here?"

"Of course, if you're in Franklin--and your phone number would indicate that."

"Is now a good time?"

"Sure. It's ideal for me."

Seated at the dining-room table across from Kathy Edwards, Laura realized that her earlier sense of buoyancy had waned. Her mind now lay open to a prosaic description of what she felt as her need. She could proceed on that basis.

"I'm what my doctor calls a historic case," she began. Continuing, she told the woman across from her about Brand's work in general and in particular with reference to her. She had begun treatments, she said, correcting herself at once to use the term "procedures."

Kathy sat attentively.

A tall, somewhat thin woman of perhaps thirty, Kathy made notes from time to time: a word, a phrase. She had a tape recorder running only a foot or two from Laura's knees.

Kathy spoke during a pause. Her choice of words, or questions, suggested to Laura that her visitor might be able to provide what was wanted. That seemed true even though Laura had no concrete picture of what end-product would satisfy her.

Kathy's first question touched on the core problem. "Do you have any firm or clear idea of what you'd like to see as a record of your experience?"

"It's very vague. I know I want to have a narrative of everything in case my luck becomes the model for other women in similar or identical situations."

"You'll want names, dates, places, descriptions of techniques? It could get complicated if that's the case. Not that *complicated* means it can't be done. It only means more research, probably a longer narrative, as you call it."

The simple but thorough account in newspaper style that Laura had been picturing was growing; she could sense it. Yet, she thought, why not? Would the achievement of birthing deserve less than a full account, a thorough treatment?

"I'm trying to imagine what the final document might look like," she said. "Whether it would be even readable if it went into too much detail. Or, whether the detail is necessary to make it worth doing."

"Could you sketch in a few words what you're project is--what your role is--since that seems to be the principal factor?"

"That's possible if not very easy." Making an effort, Laura let her recollections frame the early, pleasant period when she and Tim were discussing kids, a kid: what she was imagining as a stage of wifely fulfillment. There was pain in the memory in view of his recent changes of mood and involvement.

"I can say that my husband and I decided that we'd complete our family if I were to achieve motherhood. Does that sound strange? I was, and remain, unable to become pregnant and bear the normal way because of sicknesses and operations performed years ago."

"Your husband was favorable?"

"He was, at least initially." Laura felt the bitter aura of the recent derangements and differences between her and Tim. "I guess here is where the rub is. I heard of--found--a doctor who could promise me a way to become pregnant, bear a child. He could do that even though I have no uterus."

"Is there a simple answer to the inevitable question--How is that possible?"

"You've heard of abdominal pregnancy?" Kathy was nodding. "The doctor's method is somewhat similar, but it takes place intentionally, not accidentally. The doctor has tested his method on monkeys--he calls them baboons."

"If I may inject a personal note, I can think of three friends who might seek out your miracle doctor."

"I can give you a reference if he'll sit still for it. He's a wizard."

"Are you pregnant now, may I ask? And is that accomplished by implanting an embryo? That would seem--."

Laura interrupted gently. "Yes, it's done that way. I've so far had only one implant, and the doctors tell me it could take dozens of tries."

"And you're ready for that?"

"Absolutely. With the pencil she was holding Laura quickly sketched a smiling stickface. "But you know, I feel as if it has succeeded. I really feel pregnant."

The conversation had become a talk between women with common interests. "I add my best wishes to your own high hopes," Kathy said. "I can see why you want to see this story in print somewhere."

"I'm at the point where I think it would have to be published far from here. In a newspaper maybe."

"Are there local problems?"

"There's one local problem. You live here, so you've probably heard of it. It's a local organization that's trying to purify the community. That's what they claim."

"This professor what's-his-name?"

"You've got it. He teaches something--ethics, I think--at the university."

Kathy set her pencil on the table and turned off the tape recorder. "I can write your article," she said. "I can do it with any slant you want--or just as straight news. You know, 'Franklin woman bears test-tube baby'--something like that. But I'm afraid if that mad monk is still making headlines I'd have to have my name deleted from the final product."

"You're thinking of possible violence."

"I am. Wasn't this professor--is his name Vandorn?--the one who killed an animal not long ago? An animal that was in someone's garage?"

"He's the one. That professor recently joined this community-morals group. They got the City Council into their case a few weeks ago."

"I was there. That man is terrifying." Kathy cleared her throat. "I hope you can understand my concern." Abruptly she added: "Your doctor must be Doctor Brant."

"He is, yes. Brand, with a d. A different type altogether. A gentleman and I have to say, a dedicated man."

"I think the friends I mentioned earlier tried to get appointments with him. He was too busy."

"I think he works day and night. That's almost no exaggeration."

"I can believe it." Moving her purse from the table to her lap, Kathy continued: "Can we still do business? I know I'd find your story fascinating--and challenging from a research angle."

"We can do business. I'll figure out what to do with your report when we get to that point."

Kathy set her purse back on the table and picked up her pencil. "I may as well start collecting evidence--research," she said. "Would you have any documents or papers on Dr. Brand's work? Would you have the wrappings your semen came in, also the name of the female donor?"

"I'll start looking and asking."

63

"It looks to us like you're pregnant--and that alone will make history! Congratulations!"

Dr. Brand couldn't have sounded more elated if he had won the lottery. Hearing the news, trying to absorb its deeper implications, Laura had qualms; she sensed apprehension. With a living human being inside her, a new responsibility loomed. She saw it as an enveloping blessing that came accompanied by a dark shadow.

She sat back in the big chair that she used when talkative women friends called. *There,* she thought, *that's better.* "This is embarrassing," she said. "Just what I've been praying for, and even expecting, and I'm speechless. Deep down though, Em, I have never felt more ecstatic, more fulfilled even while I'm almost trembling at the thought of the responsibility. Is that what happens when a woman becomes pregnant as she nears the age of forty?"

"I would say everyone would react differently. You've been through so much to get here, and it comes as a surprise even though you've been convinced that it had happened."

"It'll take me the rest of the day and all of tomorrow to get used to the reality--the unbelievable reality. You know, I was convinced that you would find a way to make the implant work this last time--and I still feel it was my confidence in you that did it. And in Dr. Madsen too, of course. I can't say it often enough--there's nothing like trusting your doctor."

"We try to do things according to rules and techniques, and sometimes it works. That's my feeling."

64

Why in the living hell it should have taken so long to get some simple stuff lay beyond Vandorn's power to figure. A day, two days would have sufficed. But *five* days? He suspected that Gus was trying to jack up the price.

No matter. He would deliver to Rhodes, get fate's wheels turning.

Conserving every drop, he had added some of the stronger potion to the vial containing the emetic. Good old Gus had placed two skull-and-crossbones symbols on the lethal fluid. One such symbol identified the weaker nostrum.

Rhodes was waiting in his car when Vandorn drove up in front of the North End drugstore. The exchange took seconds. As Vandorn handed over the carefully re-wrapped box containing the vials, Rhodes said, "I'll be laying the trap this Friday and he should be stepping into it Saturday night. We've got just enough fluid in the kir bottles."

"Great. You're sticking with our program?"

"I am. I'll be sick Saturday night, play-sick."

"Sounds great. Let's talk Sunday. There should be some other news by then."

Toby Rhodes took from his right-thigh pocket the vial that he had inserted there. Once again he checked--insurance against mistakes: as expected, he saw a single skull-and-crossbones symbol.

Certain that he would be able to find the milder potion, he restored the vial to the same pocket. He had already tested the child-proof cap; it had come free without difficulty.

The niggling suspicion that Vandorn was walling him in dangerously with his "two-victim" plan wouldn't die. It wouldn't even diminish. For Rhodes' taste, the plan certainly made it certain that the primary target would receive--and drink--the hot stuff. But in doing so it put Rhodes right in the trench with the bomb-squad.

He patted his right-hand thigh picket. There it was: the "two-symbol" vial.

The Kitkat seemed abnormally quiet. On the far wall, in what seemed to be their favorite booth, Rhodes could see the four of them, Gennett and Martin Adamson and their two weekend cronies. From time to time their exchanges became noisy but not rowdy. A couple of times Rhodes had also caught the word "quarrels" or "Quarles;" it meant nothing special to him and he forgot the word.

Unlike the past weekend and Rhodes' generalized experience, the talk throughout the room seemed to be putting brakes on the drinking. Margie had time to josh with certain patrons. A lazy thought skipped through Rhodes' brain: did Margie feel *safer* in a crowd of male homosexuals--or had she a natural talent for mingling with anyone of either sex?

The thought faded. She was coming toward the bar with her Orders book in her left hand.

Rhodes set the order sheet in front of him on a dry shelf-like surface below the level of the bar. The order was safe there--from prying eyes if there were any or from drafts that might waft away Margie's scribbling.

Setting up the new orders, Rhodes tried to estimate how soon sandwich orders would start to arrive. He knew from experience that "bartime" had its own symmetry and rate of progression. It obeyed its own chronometry, especially in a mostly male clientele.

He had under any circumstances to follow the imperatives that customers imposed. But he liked to anticipate things. This evening in particular, he wanted to ride atop events: to control them.

Margie moved like her sharp-eyed, live-wire self. Kept busy, she navigated from booths to bar and back through the relative dusk. A deft sense of obstacles guided her through tables, chairs, and customers. Another sense enabled her to evade the occasional reaching hand and its proffered gentle pat or friendly swat.

"Ya reachin' fer the moon?" she said once within Rhodes' hearing. Or again: "Keep yer claws to yerself, my dear."

Each time she smiled.

The evening wore on. Someone turned the music up. Rhodes had no ear for much of it, and found it easy to ignore. Sandwiches began to appear on Margie's tray, procured from the special window that connected with the kitchen. Gennett had another glass of kir, his third. He was not "showing his booze," as Margie would have put it, but the conversation at his table had grown louder.

The clock on the shelf behind the bar was closing on 10:15 when Rhodes began his preparations. Margie was taking and dealing repartee at a corner table. As a functional part of her charade-like participation, she was waiting for a one of the drinkers to finish his beer and give her the empty. *If you didn't take the empties back fast, one or more would surely end up in shards on the floor.*

By Rhodes' calculations Gennett was almost due for another kir.

One of the kir bottles was a little less than half full. First, Rhodes retrieved from his pocket the vial he had examined earlier. A glance told him it bore a single skull-and-crossbones. As instructed by Vandorn, he quickly poured what he estimated to be half the contents into the bottle.

He set up two glasses, a cocktail size for Gennett, a wine glass for himself. From the partly-filled bottle, already laced with the dynamite, he poured a full glass for Gennett. He added to his glass only a dollop from the "innocent" vial.

Margie was breaking free, walking toward the bar. At the same time John Gennett was waving his empty kir glass to attract the waitress's attention.

Everything broke loose. Margie placed her order sheet on the bar and Rhodes started filling it. Margie turned, saw Gennett, and went to take his order. Half-way to the Gennett booth Margie realized that it was an "all-four" order. She had not brought her tray and went back to get it.

Rhodes had the earlier order ready and on the tray. While Margie wove her way back to the waiting table, Rhodes completed the order for Gennett's table. He had set up the two beers and one kir, and one wineglass of Merlot for Adamson. A fifth glass was for Merlot for himself--a draft for the moments after Gennett had drunk his poisoned kir.

He would share and exaggerate whatever sickness might afflict Gennett. He, Rhodes, would plead illness, leave in what he foresaw as partly a feigned attack of the heaves. Play-acting, he would be gripping his stomach. He would swear that he would return for the Sunday night shift.

His sickness would be real but mild.

The stomach pains began to rack him violently before two minutes elapsed. He straightened up with a supreme effort, tried to walk. With Margie suddenly at his side, propelled by another set of hands, he struggled toward the exit. This was real, not feigned.

Leaving his station behind the bar, he had enough mind-presence left to sweep his wine-glass to the floor. There it smashed.

Approaching the door, people surrounded him. Many sets of hands were supporting him, not quite carrying him.

He groaned so uncontrollably that he felt idiotic. He had, however, no way to stop. The vomiting began as he neared the exit. He had just started to pass through the entrance when he heard an unearthly scream from the Kitkat's interior--a scream so piercing, so filled with pain and terror that it might have come from a dozen victims under torture.

His escorts were shouting. In response a taxicab pulled up to the curb. Struggling into the vehicle with Margie's help, Rhodes heard her call for his home address. At that moment his bowels went out of control.

The pain increased. He could smell the load that filled his trousers, seeping and surging like lava.

His voice sounded detached, ululant at first, a shriek that nonetheless formed words. "The hospital!" he shouted. "Emergency!"

The taxi shot ahead, turned at the next corner.

Doubled over, alone in the back seat, Rhodes remembered the vials of poison. Reaching for his pocket, missing it, and reaching again, he found one vial. He tried to hold it up, thought he saw two death's-head symbols, and hurled the small container out the cab's window.

The window was open. His good luck, he thought.

When Rhodes awakened he was lying in a clean hospital bed. The fire and brimstone that had tormented him had dissipated. But his entire stomach region burned as if it had been passed through fire and retained some coals.

There were tubes in his throat. A garment that felt like a diaper bound his middle and his crotch. Turning his head with an effort, he became aware that a woman in hospital whites was studying a machine next to his bed.

"Good morning," the woman said. "How is our patient this morning?"

"Our patient is hungry. What happened to me?"

"You ingested something horrible. Something almost lethal. You're lucky to be alive. Whatever it was you had, and we're still trying find that out, it was deadly. You got here just in time."

"What's here?" His voice felt and sounded hoarse.

"Franklin Memorial Hospital."

Rhodes lay back. The few words of conversation had wearied him. For a moment he was outside time. He realized he had dozed. But he could sense that the nurse was still there, still at the machine.

"Is that machine sucking me dry?" he said.

"Not dry, just clean we hope. That toxin you drank had to go--all of it."

"What I remember--," he began, and stopped. What he was not remembering belonged to silence. As he pondered that, sorting, it struck him forcefully that he had tried to sicken someone; had fed him a toxin, as the nurse called it. Suddenly his curiosity ballooned as his determination to remain silent also intensified. What had he drunk?

He had to maintain silence. But had he gotten rid of both vials? Were there only two? Had he seen one with three of those prophetic symbols? He remembered throwing one from the window of the cab. Two?

He would forget it, try to sleep. His stomach was a slowly relaxing inferno. Without opening his eyes he said, "Am I allowed to have water?"

"You will be in about half an hour," the nurse said. "I'll keep the time."

65

Rending the interior vapor as the bartender was exiting, Gennett's screams had instant effect. A pall of expectant horror settled over the Kitkat crowd. For several long moments the shrieks rose and fell. Each conveyed more agony than its predecessor.

Those who could see the activity in the Gennett booth were instantly transfixed. The vomiting began then, continuing as it seemed for minutes. Partly digested food scraps were intermingled with streams of stomach fluid. Much of the fluid consisted of the dark-hued kir.

The need for rescue action galvanized both the other three in the booth and others at surrounding tables. They reached Gennett in a wave. Like Rhodes, Gennett had difficulty straightening up. He had even greater difficulty walking. He had hardly started toward the door when the helping hands were literally carrying him.

Frightened but not confused or incapacitated, Adamson felt with one hand for the keys to Gennett's car. The single key that he always carried for emergencies was there, one of a set of six. First making sure that Gennett had adequate assistance, Adamson hurried on ahead. He reached the exit door in time to hold it open for Gennett and his escorts.

Shouting that he was "getting John's car," Adamson ran the few yards to the parking lot. The car started. In moments Adamson was skidding to a stop in front of the Kitkat building. Three men were supporting Gennett under the half-dome that gave cachet to the entrance. Seeing the car, Gennett made a tortured signal with his right hand. His screams had become heavy groans.

While Adamson stretched painfully to reach both passenger-side doors, Gennett's rescuers half-carried him across the sidewalk. Lifting and pushing him they placed him on the back seat, gentle hands using main force.

"I'll need help," Adamson shouted. "All of you!" He waited the few seconds until all three had found room in the car and slammed the doors.

The car tires shrieked again as Adamson stepped on the accelerator. Arriving in uncounted minutes at the apartment shared by Gennett and Adamson, once again they found ways to lift/carry Gennett into the building and up to the second floor. Adamson took sole charge as they transported Gennett to a bed and laid him on it. In an instant he had doubled up. His groans grew louder.

They had been in the apartment less than an hour when, by agreement, they had done all they could. Gennett seemed half-asleep, but his groans continued in softer tones.

They discussed next steps quietly in the living room. "What are we overlooking?" Adamson asked his three assistants in desperation. "Before I let you guys go."

Consensus formed without further conversation. With mournful groans as a backdrop, they agreed that Gennett would need the care that a hospital could provide.

"Now or in the morning?" Adamson said. "Morning," came the answer.

Alone with his lover, Adamson tried to read. He had hardly begun when Gennett's groans took on a frenzied quality. Leaving the easy chair that for him was as comfortable as a bed, Adamson went to check on Gennett. Nothing seemed different, but the note of mortal torment persisted.

He had to do something. *Soothe*, he thought. Wetting a towel with cold water, he swabbed Gennett gently: the face, the hands. As he rested, watching and listening, the groaning resumed.

Was he imagining things? Did the groans sound less tortured?

Adamson moved a straight-backed chair next to the bed. For what seemed like a long time he studied Gennett's face, listened to his breathing, stroked the back of his right hand. That hand lay free but was clenched tightly.

The clock on the dresser gave the time as 3:45. He had been home now for more than three hours, by Adamson's reckoning. For a terrible moment he watched as Gennett struggled with something that was racking his whole being. Were those drops of perspiration on his-- Gennett's--forehead?

With the damp cloth that he still held, Adamson wiped Gennett's face. He did it so tenderly that the rag hardly made contact.

Now Gennett's forehead looked dry.

Thinking of their more than eight years together, Adamson closed his eyes tightly. He didn't know why. Could that keep you from crying? Could you banish negative thoughts by squeezing your eyes shut?

The groaning continued, and Adamson suddenly had an obsessive urge to do something, take action. HELP! But what? He couldn't move Gennett without help. He had cleaned him up on first reaching home. He had made *the patient* as comfortable as humanly possible.

What? He walked to the telephone, located in the traditional place, the front hall.

He dialed the Franklin General Hospital number. A sepulchral, detached voice answered: a voice perfectly suited to Adamson's sense of the terror of the hour. He heard himself say, "I've got a very sick man here. Is it possible to get an ambulance to bring him to the hospital?"

"Ohhh? I don't know. It's a weekend morning and Emergency is very busy. Our ambulance is out on a run." There was a pause. "Can you bring him here?"

"No way. He weighs more than 170 pounds. It took three--no, four of us to get him home."

"I can take your name and address and phone number. Once we have help we can call and say we are on the way. But it can take maybe an hour."

"I don't care. I think we need help. Fast. You'll need a stretcher."

"We'll do our best. Let me have your address first."

The telephone awakened Adamson; the ringing invaded and terminated a troubled dream that immediately dissipated. As he lifted the receiver, Adamson realized with weary anxiety that silence pervaded the apartment. The absence of sound struck him as a violation of nature.

The same hospital employee was calling back. The ambulance had returned, he said. "Do you still need assistance with your patient?"

"Yes, of course." He had hardly spoken when the stillness seemed to revive. "Could you hold for ten seconds?" he added.

"Our crew is waiting for orders--." He was finishing when Adamson set the phone down noiselessly. In the bedroom what he saw would stay with him forever.

Gennett lay twisted on the bed, his upper body half over the edge, arms dragging close to the floor. Moving quickly, Adamson turned Gennett's head so that he could see the face.

He would have described the expression as a look of beatific peace.

Gennett was beyond any need for a hospital. The employee on the phone told Adamson that he would have to call a mortuary. "They have people who pick up bodies."

66

A change. A no-work Saturday evening for Dr. Brand. With wife Michelle he would shed the yoke, at last deliver the concert they had been picturing conversationally for days. Following the performance by the Franklin Symphony, they would dine at Luigi's, once a favored haunt and still ranked high locally. For Brand the restaurant's Tiffany lamps and Persian rugs whispered softly of long-planned trysts.

Brand as usual finished dressing first. Waiting for Michelle to put the final touches on her simple-but-chic dress and her night-out makeup, Brand played with the girls. It had become commonplace that when he had time for them these days they seemed unfamiliar. They talked almost like adults. Each had grown beyond any expectations that he could have entertained. Moke, the older, even *walked* with what Brand diagnosed as a new awareness of budding female maturity.

Playing Monopoly, younger sister Joanie always won. For Brand, inheritor of a long-nursed belief that more women should pursue scientific or accounting careers, there was comfort in that realization.

There was also pride. And the element of pride was growing.

He was thinking he would have to spend more time with the girls. As if timed, at once the phone rang. It was Laura. Michelle was already descending the stairs from the upper floor.

Brand heard Laura saying "Em, I had to talk to you."

"Glad you did. But we're on the way out--."

"Do you have one second?"

"A second I can always spare." With Michelle listening in the background, Brand felt uncomfortable. He could turn slightly and observe as Michelle paused, waited. She would be listening to him.

"I'm geared to my appointment next week," Laura said. "But that's not why I'm calling. You've heard about the murder and what looks like an attempted murder?"

"I have. In fact, I'm already involved. Mr. Gennett was our volunteer for the pregnant man project. So it's a terrible loss even though we hadn't yet achieved impregnation."

"What do you do now?"

Time was passing. They would be late, would stumble to their seats in the dark concert hall.

"John Gennett's friend, Adamson, has already volunteered to take Gennett's place. But I see my passengers waiting for their chauffeur--me."

"I'm sorry," Laura said with sincere contrition. "But you--could we talk tomorrow--I'm wondering about possible crazies going after other patients of Dr. Madsen. She paused, and Brand thought she must have set the receiver down; but it still buzzed; they had a connection. Laura said then: "I'll call in the afternoon, if that's okay."

"It's fine. We can settle everything. In the meantime, you shouldn't worry."

"Thank you. I'll try not to."

Michelle was tapping one foot at the coffee table, where the Monopoly game was lying spread out. "Okay, my dears," Brand said. "We're off--you to grandma's and we to feed some monkeys."

"They're baboons, and you're going to a concert," Moke said.

"Now who could have told you that?" Brand asked, joking.

Like a flying pesky insect the phone call from Laura flitted unseen and unmentioned throughout the evening. Superficially, with Brand taking the role of determined escort, they enjoyed it all. But the concert's closing selection, a concerto by Buxtehude, left both Michelle and Brand unsatisfied. The choice seemed to both of them a poor one. That appeared to be particularly the case because an earlier sequence had been excerpts from Mozart, all of them entrancing.

At Luigi's they ran into neighbors with whom they had nothing in common--and were invited to join their table. Michelle responded with panache that they were celebrating a personal anniversary. With

Brand in her wake they walked to a table at some distance from the neighbors'.

"Well done," Brand said.

Michelle didn't smile. "Someone's always jumping into our communal life," she said. "Just once we have to put a foot down."

."It was still well done. I'll have to remember that line. It even discourages conversations."

"That's the point. You lose if you have to explain." She studied the menu. Without looking up she continued: "How *does* the murder affect your projects? Dr. Madsen's name is already in the papers as the specialist treating Mr. Gennett. Will your name also start hitting the headlines?"

"I would hope not. I may lie low for a while. Especially if they tie it to the one madman who's probably the master mind anyway."

"Vandorn?"

"The very one. He hasn't been named, but I wouldn't be surprised if they found him complicit. Or if they found that he had engineered the whole thing. The bartender and poor Gennett."

"I'd like to hear you say you're going to give the whole project a wide berth. At least for a while."

He lowered the menu he had been studying. At the moment it represented his trump, his means of disengagement. "I've got to consider that, I know. But I also have to consider the people I'm working with-- four, five, more of them. Like Madsen, Adamson, Quarles, Archer, and Phillips."

"Some I never heard of."

"They're trying to figure out whether there will be a bonanza flowing out of all this work."

"Still? After all this poisoning, one man dead, another very sick--."

Michelle had ended her sentence suddenly. For a brief interval they remained silent. Their attention remained focused on the food choices.

"I'm going to skip the famous pasta tonight," Brand said. "And go for something really poisonous." Realizing what he had said, "Sorry about that," he added. "I meant that I'm going to violate all my good dietary resolutions."

"And order what?"

Eyes focused on her menu, Michelle remained silent. Brand let his mind and eye wander. If he ever went into the restaurant business, he would model its spaces, its comfortable cushioned chairs, and its thoughtfully placed tables after what he saw here. Just as here, he would have soft "civilized" music--the kind that respected cogitation and *sotto voce* conversation.

Michelle folded her menu, indicating that she had decided. "I'm going to commit alimentary sin, same as you," she said. "If the waiters haven't gone home, we can order."

Brand looked around. As if he had been waiting for such a head movement, a waiter appeared next to their table. Michelle gave her order--an Italian beef sandwich on a hoagie roll.

She settled back in her chair while Brand ordered. "Can we talk now?" she said. When he nodded she made a statement that sounded accusatory. "Whatever she said on the phone, I'm in full agreement about the danger. I heard Vandorn's name, and that's all I have to hear."

"I can't help the police this time. He got off last time even though I offered all kinds of evidence."

"But that was an animal. And even with your evidence--the handkerchief for instance--they didn't want to bring a professor into court. Franklin lives on its University, its University Hospital, its sports teams; well, you know all this. But this time it's one accomplished murder and another that went awry for some reason."

"The second guy, Rhodes, went to the hospital. The papers are suggesting that that's why he's alive. Stomach pump."

"Doesn't it look to you like whoever dreamed this up was trying to kill two people, not just your pregnant man?"

Before Brand could fashion an answer, the waiter arrived. Very formally, he waited while a younger man set up a little folding table. Placing the trays he was carrying on the side table, the waiter moved them to the larger table occupied by Brand and Michelle.

As he left he said, "Enjoy!"

"I think we should concentrate on this kingly repast," Brand said. "I can't answer your questions anyway. But I can think about them."

67

The Friends of John Gennett had reached deep, to judge by the massed drifts of flowers that nearly buried the gracefully contoured urn. That altar display answered the question that had been occupying Brand since Saturday, three days past. No longer would he have to act dumb when asked, earth burial or cremation?

Standing in the open door to the chapel, he watched the mourners as they took seats toward the front, or altar, area. A steady hum of voices suggested that those arriving early, as Brand had, were acquainted with one another as well as with the deceased. As the pews filled up, one by one in orderly fashion, it seemed to Brand that an organized, integrated community was gathering. Heightening the impression, two or three front pews on both sides of the center aisle accommodated women only.

While the men wore dark, somber clothing--sweaters and slacks for the most part--the women were uniformly dressed in peacock colors and innovative couturier styles.

Where to sit? Deciding that a rear pew would fit his needs and enable a graceful exit if necessary, Brand waited while four young men passed on their way toward the forward pews. Brand was moving to take a rear seat when a hand plucked at his sleeve. Before he could respond, Laura's scent communicated her presence. She was smiling when he turned to greet her. As if timed for that moment the solemn strains of funeral music flowed through the chapel. The sacred song served to mask Brand's question.

"What brings you here?"

"A shared revolution," Laura said readily, "if I can call it that. I might say a sense of communion with the deceased."

"I had just decided to sit in the rear and take my chances. Join me?"

"That's also why I came. I'm supposed to stay in close contact with my specialist, remember?"

"Touché," Brand said as he followed Laura into the last pew on the left side of the chapel. "But don't we have an appointment at Madsen's tomorrow night?"

"We do. I'll be there." As a kind of postscript, she continued, "Hoping to see you."

"It's in my datebook."

The music had modulated. A resonant voice was praying in conjunction with the softer strains in low harmony. "The Lord giveth, and the Lord taketh away," the voice intoned. A pause followed, then another brief prayer:

"Be it remembered that in striving to achieve our worldly aims, be they ever so altruistic, we may come to the empty city. Even when keeping to our chosen course without a single misstep, danger lurks."

The voice faded away. The music soared to heights familiar from medieval symphonics. As that mood settled into the crude and mundane, the voice returned. . .

"As the Oracle has said, 'The marsh drains into the deep. The superior man will make the supreme sacrifice in the pursuit of his purpose.' So spoke the Oracle."

Again the voice went silent. Brand felt Laura shifting on the pew next to him. Leaning toward her, "You okay?" he said, whispering.

"I'm fine," she answered, "maybe a little turned off by the superior man and his fate."

The music rose again to an uncomfortable crescendo, and lingered there, drowning conversation.

As quickly as it had risen to new orchestral heights, the music dwindled again almost to total silence. Hardly had the sound reached a new, steady, thoughtful level when a handsome, grey-haired man wearing dark clothes and a clerical collar appeared on the platform supporting the altar. In words carrying traces of an accent that Brand could not place, the new speaker called on the "many Friends of John Gennett" to step to the altar and say a few words of praise in love and friendship."

A heavy-set man, age perhaps 30, stood at once and walked to the lectern. "I wrote some thoughts in tribute to John," he began. "If the deep sadness of this occasion and this day seem to fill me with inner tears, bear with me. Like most of you, my capacity for tolerating violent visitations of the kind exemplified here is extremely limited.

"But we need not linger on bitter thoughts. We should, rather, examine this murder--for murder it was--to extract, if possible, the obvious lessons. For me, these lessons cry to the heavens--if not for vengeance, then for eradication, equalization, call it by any name meaning recognition that our lifestyle deserves an objective review. No longer should we have to live, work, and recreate in a kind of political oblivion. No longer should we walk the streets as second-class citizens, or encounter daily discrimination in housing, in some forms of worship, and in our choices of gathering-places."

The speaker shifted, leaning indifferently against the lectern. His voice became a freight train gathering speed and shedding steel-on-steel thunder.

"It's criminal that in a supposedly free country we should see members of our community taken from us by stealth, in the most cowardly manner imaginable. Consider it," he nearly shouted. "John was with friends. Minding his own business. Yes, he was engaged in an experiment that would put the nation over a border, suddenly in uncharted territory insofar as childbearing and childbirth are concerned.

"He volunteered to act the guinea pig in that experiment. He was prepared, with his special friend Martin Adamson, to care for and raise his issue.

"Friends, fellow members of our community, John's death was not an accident. Those who see subversion in anything different found a way to terminate his experiment--and his life. I would like to ask that anyone with any knowledge or suspicion of any one person or any group that could or might have designed John's death--I would like to ask that friend to speak out, talk to the police. We simply cannot brush this episode aside--forget it.

"With diligence and imagination we can solve the ugly mystery of John's death."

The speaker stepped off the dais and went to his seat. He had hardly made himself comfortable on the cushioned pew when a second speaker stood. Walking quickly to the lectern, he began without preamble.

"I'm not up here to harangue you," he said in a high voice. "I'm here to ask your most extravagant welcome for one we all should know. He's the man who was working with John to revolutionize the ages-old roles of the sexes.

"I want to give you Dr. Emlyn Brand, embryologist without peer. Cheers may be unseemly in church--but clapping is not." As the speaker started to applaud, the crowd in the pews did the same. The men stood, smiling while continuing to clap. Many turned to find where Brand was sitting.

Over the din the speaker said as loudly as he could without screaming: "Dr. Brand, would you do us the honor of a few words?"

Brand stood slowly. Now all the faces had turned; he was the focal point of this concentric scrutiny. While his mind raced, exploring for a theme, a subject for brief disquisition, his senses seemed to shut down. He could hardly hear--or had the crowd gone silent watching him? Some of the faces appeared darker than others. He decided they were black.

Only his aural sense seemed functional. It, in fact, brought him both Laura's familiar scent and the fumelike exhalation of burning incense.

The colliding scents were confusing. "Thank you," Brand said in what had become a taut silence. "Thank you, but I'm not the one we--anyone--should be lionizing. John Gennett should be our avatar, our object of honor, of esteem, even of veneration."

He let the silence creep back. Now he had a theme. He could linger with it for a while.

"Even in a professional relationship it's possible to take the measure of a man," Brand continued. "There are moments when the clock and the medical system work in tandem to effect a pause. In such circumstances, even in the few times we were able to carry through my still experimental procedure, we had time to talk.

"I learned to admire--no, treasure--Mr. Gennett. I realized what I couldn't know when he and I first talked. I came to realize that he wanted to *parent*. He wanted to create new life in the most responsible way. We hadn't talked twice when I ceased to wonder what would happen to his issue--to any new life that his physical self might bear." The faces remained immobile. Leaning with his hands against the back of the pew ahead of him, Brand had settled into an explanatory mood, a professorial stance. He would continue a little longer.

"Many of you know that we utilize baboons as experimental animals. We do that out of respect for the sanctity of the human body-- of the right of each of us to know that we as human beings are not merely laboratory dummies.

"We had done that before trying to embryonate Mr. Gennett. We showed him the evidence. We let him know that one of our key experiments was aborted by the murder of one of our animals. We thought he should know all that, and he thanked us.

"We've explained this as well to Mr. Adamson. We see no overt threat, but we--my medical colleague and I--believe caution is appropriate."

A voice sounded, deep and apparently angry, while Brand took a breathing spell. "We both know about the community ethics prof," the speaker said. "Isn't he the one who murdered the baboon, Dr. Brand?"

Caution! Had he said too much? Brand lifted his hands off the back of the pew in front of him and waved them slowly, palms out, forward: a calming gesture. "There was evidence indicating that," he said quietly. "But he was never charged. And the animal, of course, was the property of University Hospital and Research Center. But he was in my care."

"Isn't the prof the one we should focus on in John's case? He was in the papers again not long ago--calling for a community-wide purge or something like that."

A rumbling began among the men. From silent, relaxed listeners, they appeared to be coming alive with an electric surface perturbation.

"We can't make too much of 'prof,' as you call him," Brand said to the new speaker. "The culprit in Mr. Gennett's death could have been any one of several people." "The finger points to the prof, though." The answer had come instantly. "I think my colleagues here would back me on this--that John was almost universally loved and respected. He was a leader of our community in all kinds of ways."

"I'm sure--," Brand began. The voice cut him off again.

"And the more I think of this completely unjust death, the more I'm convinced that some of us should call on the prof. What is his name again, Dr. Brand? Van-something?"

"Vandorn. One word."

Mention of Vandorn's name touched off more turmoil. A few of the men who had stood earlier rose again to obtain better views of the speakers. Some of the women were also standing, mouths open as if ready to cheer.

No cheer came. The murmur and babble of voices had become general among the men. Now and then a voice rose above the spreading unrest to call for action--a committee, a community police force, a vigilante company, a street patrol in a particular neighborhood.

In the hubbub the rites and observances for the dead seemed lost, forgotten.

Largely overlooked now, Brand felt strongly that the time for extrication from the chapel had arrived. It was perhaps overdue. He turned and helped Laura to her feet--Laura who it seemed had weathered the flourishes of oratory and temper without a word or gesture. She stood at Brand's shoulder, mouth slightly open, and continued to gaze sympathetically toward the babble of male voices. Over them all at this moment, the deep voice that had been speaking called out above the din.

"Thank you. Dr. Brand, for taking part in our somewhat unusual obsequies. We'll be keeping track of your work with Martin--and wishing you a universe of success." As the farewell continued, Brand noticed that Adamson was detaching himself from the scene close to the altar, approaching Brand and Laura down the central aisle.

"I want to say thanks as well," he said. "To both of you for taking part today." He shook hands gently with Laura and then more firmly with Brand.

"Everybody here thinks John's murder was directed at all of us," Adamson said. "That's why they've been so riled up."

"I can understand why they think that way. They're probably right."

Adamson frowned, then smiled. "May I call you early next week?" he said to Brand. "I'm anxious to get started--really to carry on with John's beginning. I'm dependent on you for that."

"We'll try to get you launched next week. You can call me at my office."

"Will do. In the meantime I'm going to try to tamp down the tempers that we've got boiling here today."

"I'd say we don't need any more violence. I wish you luck."

"Thanks."

As unobtrusively as possible Brand exited the pew and waited while Laura followed him into the aisle. "Did you see what was just going on in the front of the church?" Laura asked.

"No. I was busy with Mr. A."

"They're forming a committee of some kind. Signing people up."

68

The day that had begun with brilliant orange-red streaks across the eastern sky was dying in grey haze. Inside the chapel, silence ruled where there had been lively conversation only an hour or two earlier. Except for the three men who had lingered to conspire, the mourners had left.

Nothing else had changed. The urn and the flowers that almost concealed it were still in place. Vigil lights still flickered. Pleasingly, the last wisps of incense smoke mingled, for anyone interested in funerary fragrances, or a funerary poignancy, an olfactory proclamation of death.

Chris Flowers, who had first engaged Dr. Brand in long-range conversation, sat comfortably sideways on one of the front pews. He could simply not let go of the ugly fact of John Gennett's passing. His frustration had twin, or even triple, footings. There was the fact that Gennett was gay, as they all were. That made murder *per se* insulting in a society that supposedly welcomed all peaceful lifeways.

There was the fact that John Gennett had been a personal friend, a man who would loan you money if you needed it--and take an unreadable I.O.U. in return. And of course there was the reality that Gennett had volunteered for a very challenging ordeal--the impregnation and gestation project. In the course of that effort Gennett would have sacrificed weeks of his active life in what Chris saw at least as a contribution to equality between the sexes.

The "wake," as they termed it, had left them on beds of nails. All three of them--Chris, Evan Ratigan, and Merton Slater--had during the long afternoon traversed the rough ground between passive acceptance of the death to a restlessness that touched the soul more than any other constituent element.

Their three-man rear-guard was puzzling mightily to find a course of action. To do *something* that would alleviate the pain of loss. Perhaps they could avenge the death and thus lift the weight of this global profanity.

"I've got to say it again," Evan Ratigan maintained. "We've got to start somewhere. Rhodes is the obvious place. And he was still in the hospital yesterday." Evan, the other two knew, always spoke softly while delivering firm, thought-out assessments.

Chris shifted on the pew to find a more comfortable position. As the undeclared, unanointed leader of the group of three, he felt a special responsibility. In an informal, back-bench way he helped keep the homosexual community legally unobtrusive.

"You're right about one thing, " he said to Ratigan, "we do have to start somewhere. I find it a little hard to believe that he will prove to be anything but another victim of the usual poisoner, but let's at least try to tap his brain-box. What's our best pitch?"

Slater spoke after a brief pause. "Treat him like a victim. We don't at this stage know that he's anything but that. Sure he started bartending at Kitkat only a week or two before this murder. But let's give him the velvet glove at least at first. See what happens."

A librarian, Ratigan had another thought. "Can we take another day?" he said in a thinking-out-loud manner. "I'd like to check on some things I think I'm remembering about Rhodes."

"That is?" Chris asked.

"That he was at the recent City Council dust-up with members of that community vigilante bunch. What did they call themselves? CAP? CARP? Something like that? Any way, the hubbub was pretty thoroughly reported. I'd like to see what they said."

"Where would that take us?" Slater was clearly asking out of developing interest.

"I have the feeling there will be a connection to Professor X, their big-mouth spokesman. Also I believe Rhodes is a member of the vigilante group."

Flowers clapped his hands together. "Evan, you're a latter-day Sherlock. Can you do what you want to do tomorrow? We'd be best off to get to Rhodes before he goes home--catch him while he's in the hospital's clutches. We could just say we're friends and want to say hello."

"I can finish the research in an hour or two--and look like I'm working," Ratigan said with a shy smile.

By agreement they met in the hospital lobby at 6:00 p.m. Evan Ratigan insisted that they first take a few minutes to absorb what he, Ratigan, had learned. They found seats in a corner of the hospital lobby.

"As I suspected, or remembered, Rhodes was a member of CAMP-- which stood for Community Against Moral Pollution," he said. And Professor James Vandorn is the group's head, or leader. The president, I think. They had gone before the City Council to ask the Council to put an end to Dr. Brand's experiments. Not his regular lab work in the hospital, but his experiments with baboons and now humans."

Ratigan took a breath. "There were actually two bursts of publicity for this cabal. One hit the papers, including *Gay Pride* after a debate in our local TV station. In that case viewers got to meet only Vandorn, no other members of CAMP. It was a call-in show. Near the end Vandorn lost his temper and overturned the table that separated three of them-- the announcer, Vandorn and Brand."

"I seem to recall that that created quite a stir," Flowers said. "There was a rumor that the university would can Vandorn as a troublemaker."

"And he's still there, a professor of Ethics, if you can believe that."

69

"Can you take a few more minutes?"

Emerging from the chapel and its voices and sorrows, Laura stopped in the deep light of early afternoon. She stood on the top step of the five that led down to the walkway and to the parking area in the rear.

"For a special patient, of course," Brand said. He was still semi-consciously processing all that he had heard and seen inside, still adjusting from the mood of empathetic mourning. He had, he reflected, learned to like John Gennett as a person. The task of replacing him with Adamson would grate a little. But Adamson had become the surrogate, the vehicle to realization of Brand's own Grand Plan.

Perverse thought: *If Adamson lives.*

"I came here to see you more than anything," Laura said. She stared ahead, across the chapel lawn, across the quiet residential street that echoed the scene's undercurrent of benediction. "I needed to talk about my home situation just a little."

"Let's sit in my car. We can talk privately."

She nodded, started down, running a supportive hand along the brass railing that divided the steps in the middle.

In the car they sat as driver and passenger. "Could a husband be jealous of a gestating embryo?" she began. "And can the jealousy turn the husband into a mean-spirited he-devil?"

"That's what you're facing?"

"I'm afraid so. I've been kidding myself into thinking he'd come around, start welcoming my little package." She patted the slacks covering her stomach area. "It's gotten steadily worse--or I'm going steadily crazy." And it's been only a few days, or weeks, since I made my announcement. *Our* announcement. It's funny, but I've come to see you, the agent, the doctor, as the father."

Brand felt a shiver run through his upper torso, a cold wind of involuntary agitation.

"I know you're busy, and you have your own problems," she said. "But it always helps me to talk to you."

"I have an ear made for listening. All doctors do. It's even taught in some med schools now."

"In you it's nature. And I know a lot of women go through this. I wonder how they cope--or survive."

"If I were to guess, I'd have to say that it depends on the two people. Both probably have to give a little, or a lot in some cases."

"I've thought of that. And believe me, I've tried. But whatever happened, he's unreachable. Our friend Vandorn had something to do with it, that's my feeling. And Tim thinks Vandorn is a complete charlatan. A fake."

"And you inherit the effect."

"Yes. I guess I really have one key question: What would you do? I have to admit, I think my mommy project is part of it."

"First, if possible you should try to ride with it. These changes may seem to be basic and permanent. They often fade away without a trace."

"What if they get worse?"

"Hard to say. Let's take a couple of minutes when you come to Al's for your next checkup. I'll be pondering in the meantime. After all your prepping and now nurturing, I think you've got to give your next generation every chance. Speaking of that, if you decide you want to know the sex of your passenger, we'll be able to tell in a few weeks."

"The way I feel now, I'm tending toward secrecy. Leave everything as quiet as possible. As unknown as possible, or as unobtrusive as possible."

"Probably the best way to go."

As Brand spoke, five or six of the crowd that had been attending the Gennett memorial passed Brand's car enroute to their own cars. "Time for us to wend our homeward ways," he said.

Laura had her hand on the passenger-side door handle. Turning back as if she had forgotten something, she leaned back toward Brand

and with both of her own hands pulled his head down. Their lips met, separated. Immediately afterward the car-door opened and she was stepping down to the macadam surface. "See you at Dr. Madsen's on Thursday evening?" she said. Her door slammed as he nodded yes.

70

By agreement Chris Flowers would act as their formal leader and spokesperson. As Ratigan and Slater knew, Flowers could employ his deep voice to order, curse, plead, blaspheme, denounce, praise, or ingratiate himself. They expected him to do the latter while in Toby Rhodes' hospital room.

By good fortune Rhodes was alone. Several plates of variant sizes sat on the tray that lay on a wheeled table next to his bed.

The door of room 425a stood open. The room inside seemed unlighted. Flowers rapped with his knuckles. From the interior the three heard what sounded like a groan. Flowers entered quietly, waiting then for the other two to follow him.

Rhodes was rubbing his eyes when they stopped on both sides of the single bed. The patient's eyes flicked back and forth, from Flowers on his left to the others on the right. So softly as almost to be inaudible, Flowers said, "We're a delegation, Mr. Rhodes, from our church. They wanted someone to stop and see how you're doing."

Rhodes seemed to settle deeper in the bed. An almost imperceptible movement of his mouth could have been interpreted as an evanescent smile. "Thank you," he said. His eyes rolled slowly, spreading the thanks around.

"Are you able to eat?" Flowers continued. "Someone told us that was a problem, and you had to stick with soft foods, things like the milk-toast we had as kids."

Nothing that bad," Rhodes said. The smile flickered again, "But everyone does tell me I should be glad to be alive. It was just because I came here and they could--." A cough began, interrupting his speech.

As the cough settled and went silent, he resumed his low muttering: "--pump me out."

"Someone was watching over you," Flowers commented. "And praying. And that's what we've been doing today, a lot of it. We were also wafting up a few prayers for the dead--for Mr. Gennett, poor guy."

"Poor guy," Rhodes echoed.

"But we were told to ask you if you needed anything," Flowers went on. "Bring you something to read? Some favorite food to eat--food you're allowed to take?" He paused, waiting for a comment or request; nothing came. "Also someone suggested that we should ask if you needed to have anyone called or notified. Relatives? Siblings?"

"Thanks, but I think it's all been done. My wife was in yesterday and today. She was going to call anyone important." He spoke slowly; but a faint bloom had returned to his voice. "I have two sisters. She was going to call both of them. I told her to make it sound like nothin' at all."

The guests remained silent for half a minute. "But it's not 'nothin' at all'," Flowers said. "It's serious business. One dead, you here. That reminds me, have you had any visitors? Sometimes they can make the time go faster. People like some of the ones in your pollution group? You must have friends there."

"I did. Not any more. That's the way I look at it."

"I hate to hear it. We all need friends, people with common interests."

Rhodes opened his mouth to speak; and closed it. "That's over," he said. "No common interest. One's wrecking it for all of us."

"That's terrible. No way to get rid of her?"

"Him. It's a him. And he hasn't even been up here to say hello."

"Sounds like a fair-weather friend."

"Worse. No friend at all. Thinks he's boss of the ranch. At meetings he--." Rhodes' sentence trailed off.

Flowers' voice oozed commiseration. "But that's terrible. Can't this boss of the range be fired, given the heave-ho? He sounds like the death of the party."

"He is."

"That reminds me. Have you talked to Professor Vandorn recently? Wasn't he active in your group?"

"He's the guy I'm talking about. I haven't seen him at all. Not since--. Not at all. I hope I can keep it that way."

Flowers shifted, the signal that it was time to go. In seconds Ratigan and Slater were also moving, saying their goodbyes as if they had been full participants in the conversation.

Rhodes was yawning as they left.

71

From the kitchen window Michelle could see the back yard all the way down to where the shrubbery backed up against the fence. The fence plus vegetation made a pleasant screen, especially when everything was in midsummer leaf.

Michelle could have watched for hours as Em and the girls played-- or until they stopped kicking their soccer ball. The girls' played the game with sound effects; their cries that heralded a good shot reached the kitchen as little screams.

Em could entertain them as she, Michelle, had never learned to do. Not that it mattered. She felt with certainty that they loved and respected her. That thought led to another: that she would be their gentle mentor in the serious female avenues of life. She was in fact accruing early proof. Her older daughter, Moke, was already bringing her "playground" questions. The most difficult had to do with the differences between boys and girls.

Her rule: answer factually but in politely euphemistic terms, not vulgarities. Such answers were possible in all cases she had encountered so far.

She and Em talked about it from time to time. He agreed fully with her strategy--which in effect, for her, was no strategy but honesty. It made her more secure about her policy because Em approved, but that was in part due to her memories of her own "facts of life" education.

Her mother, acclaimed by everyone as a "most loving person," became irretrievably tongue-tied when sex surfaced in any guise, even the most elementary. The result had been for Michelle--as she reconstructed it--a slow, embarrassed maturation. Tossed on the turbulent rapids of need and unanswered curiosity, she free-lanced. Never an off-color word, phrase, or sentence broke the random conversation of the playground but she heard it and filed it.

At night she would wonder. How did other girls of nine, eleven, thirteen understand what was happening to their bodies unless they talked to their mothers?

How did her mother manage to become pregnant twice?

None of what she collected on her own ever codified for her the one most important element of a male-female life of loving sex: the deeply personal communion that takes place between a man and a woman once the spirit of total giving is achieved.

Em had taught her that never-written truth. Five to seven years of marriage were behind her before she could couch that reality in words. As a necessary coordinate to the basic truth she wrapped herself in the determination to hold Em whatever the cost. And there she tripped on another absurd simplicity: to keep him and their marriage she had to harness her tongue.

Here, these weeks, it became especially like slavery, or thralldom, when he had to keep evening appointments at Dr. Madsen's.

She had a dish towel in her hand and a smile on her face as the soccer game ended in bumping and excited voices in the entryway. "Grass stays outside," she heard as Em performed his final coaching chore and the girls shed their grassed and perhaps muddied all-purpose shoes.

Dinner passed too quickly, beginning and ending almost as an afterthought. As happened two-three evenings a week, Em had to shower and run. As always he left with comforting words. "Be back as soon as I can break free. But we've got both Phillips and Adamson tonight."

Michelle told herself she was crazy to feel slighted. With an effort of the will, she set herself to ride herd on the girls during homework time. "No TV until homework's done."

She felt cruel as she dispensed the orders. But every year seemed to pass as the last one had. With her enforcing rules.

Roused by the sound of the doorbell, Michelle listened first for the other noises that would place the girls in the kitchen. The comforting laughter that came next settled Michelle's mind quickly--and awakened her. Had she actually heard the doorbell?

It rang again, this time impatiently.

Her book had fallen while she dozed. Picking it up, she carried it with her to the front door. A switch activated the light on the front steps, and she opened the door.

A man stood there. Because the light fell mostly behind him, his face lay largely in shadow. The figure seemed familiar, but from where?

"Is your husband at home, Mrs. Brand?" The voice had a timbre that Michelle associated with unpleasant events. She remained silent, digging at her memory. As the name came to her, she stepped back.

"He can't talk to you, Dr. Vandorn. He's--he's busy."

"Not home, is it? Well, will you tell him I came to talk agreement. An arrangement that will help both of us. A concordat. And you don't have to back away. I'm here in peace."

Michelle said, "I'll tell him." Stepping forward, she closed the front door part way. At the same time she silently thanked Em's thoroughness. He had made sure the storm door could be locked. Even the flimsy screen that filled the upper half of the door seemed to offer security.

With a sudden movement Vandorn turned. "I'm leaving a message for him," Vandorn said. "It'll be in your mailbox."

She closed the inside door and turned the bolt. It was now double-locked. She would leave it that way.

She turned to go to the kitchen to find that the girls were watching from the kitchen doorway.

72

The clock on the wall of the "Prep Room" in Dr. Madsen's clinic gave the time as 7:02. Laura noticed that, marked the circular voyage of the second hand, and heard the door from the waiting room close.

She had changed already, had pulled on the light flowing garments that she wore during Dr. Brand's examination. She was checking the time to be able to tax him good-naturedly on his two minutes of tardiness. She had even been re-reading her notes to make sure she had not forgotten anything that might be significant.

The new life in her had become, quite naturally, her taskmaster. By her own free dictate. And Em had approved. "Keep notes?" he had said. "Why not? I'd advise it."

It was almost as if he had a personal interest in the embryo that was gestating in there.

She was gathering the notes when he knocked firmly on the Prep Room door. "Come in," she called. As he poked his head in, she smiled. Seeing him, no matter how often that occurred, she always felt that a smile was appropriate. "How's our *werdende Mutter* this evening?" he said.

"What kind of *Mutter*?" she said, holding the smile. "I warn you, it better be nice."

"Oh it is. It's what you see in public conveyances in Germany--*mothers-to-be*. You're supposed to surrender your seat to pregnant women. A practical idea."

"A thoughtful one."

"That too. But are you ready to give me some blood?"

"I'm ready to give you anything." Briefly, she put a hand in front of her face, feigning embarrassment. "Well, almost anything."

"Indian-giver! As we used to say a few hundred years ago." He followed her into the OP Room. In quick succession he weighed her, took her pulse, gripping her left wrist; and measured her blood pressure. "All routinely normal," he said. "Not that any of these things are unimportant. They're all critical--indicative of one thing or another. Now for the blood. We got the lab results."

"Do they answer all your questions about me?"

"Most of them. You recall, we talked about this, I believe?" The likelihood is pretty strong that you've got the requisite hormones in the right quantity, but we have to make sure for the sake of your passenger."

"I remember major and minor hormones."

"How right you are. The major ones are GCG, Prolactin, estrogen, and so on. The minor ones are pituitary and growth elements. My intention is to check on both categories. We'll try to stay current on both types for one reason only."

"And that is?"

"We're in uncharted territory. Somebody may have tried this before, but we have no report on what he or she did. What precautions were taken, what injections were given and when. I'll be trying to develop a complete guide to wombless motherhood. You'll own all rights."

"I don't want any rights. I just hope to hear that other women tried the same method and made it work. But all the credit should go to you. Before we met and talked, I had really given up."

"I'm glad you decided to try this. But remember, this is a long grind and a tough one. And you're just starting the journey. Now can you read or translate your notes?"

Laura picked up her notes and shuffled them. "This is such mundane stuff," she said. "It'll probably put you to sleep. But here goes. . ." There was a pause, and she began again. "Physical exertion, low level. House cleaning, like vacuuming, picking up things off the floor. Standing too long--is half an hour, doing dishes, too much? Steps to the second floor--limit ups and downs? Stairs to the basement, very steep--ignore them? Had to reach to re-hang a picture, and pic weighed nearly two pounds. Okay to hang?"

She waved her hand in front of her face, as if fanning herself, then went on reading.

"Medium level (of work): We've been cutting our own lawn and trimming a local hedge for years. But Tim has no time, wants me to push the mower around. I'm afraid. The mower runs too hard for me."

Brand broke into Laura's monologue. "Obey your instinct on that one," he said. "That could be heavy work, especially if the lawn has dips or little hills in it."

"It does. Whole areas are at a slant."

"I'd hire someone for all your outdoor chores. No use chopping wood, cutting the lawn, or rebuilding the shed if you have one." He was smiling, enjoying the reading and watching Laura. In imagination Brand could envision Laura as the Great Earth Mother, a fulfilled matron with six or seven abdominal pregnancies on her resume (and long since divorced from Tim).

But married again?

Brand heard voices in the Waiting Room and remembered that Martin Adamson had an appointment for his initial physical and introduction to pregnancy.

When Brand explained to Laura that he had other responsibilities, and what they were, she "forgave" him but sounded disappointed. "Just so you have room for me next week," she said. "And remember, you owe me two minutes."

He waited until she had donned her street clothes, then saw her to the door to the Clinic. The door opened on a hallway that led to elevators to the ground floor.

Looking down the deserted hallway, Laura started walking toward the elevators with slow steps. "I wish you could go with me," she said without turning.

73

Vandorn saw the men approaching across the open part of the fieldhouse. He had been warming up in the corner reserved for fencing and thought nothing further of them.

He and the fencing master, Herr Stromberg, had let their schedule fall by the wayside. *My fault*, Vandorn thought. He hated to make resolutions, or to promise changes. But this time he would be justified if he established a schedule, cleared it with Herr Stromberg, and kept to it.

On Tuesdays he had nearly two full hours between morning classes; the answer was to devote that open time to fencing practice. Make it a Tuesday regimen. Then with equally reinforced determination, set another time. Two workouts a week would, he felt, be completely adequate. Filling the gap between morning classes would be especially advantageous because it would give him an ironclad excuse for not going home to find that Jennifer wanted him to go with her to run errands.

The errands always turned out to be impossibly time-prodigal.

The men were only 30 or 40 feet from the fencing area. Their determined appearance, their dress, and their air of cold purposefulness was distracting. With a finger-signal to Herr Stromberg, Vandorn called a temporary halt, putting an end to their warmup exercises. *"Pausezeit,"* he called in the simple German he was trying to learn from the fencing master.

The visitors were only a few feet distant. One, the apparent leader, spoke directly to Vandorn. His epee dangling in his hand, Vandorn faced the visitors. "We'd like to have a few words with you alone," the man said in a deep voice. He had the chest development of a weight-lifter. His companions looked somewhat older, but shared the physical attributes and general look of athletes.

Speaking English to avoid misunderstandings, Vandorn stepped to where Herr Stromberg was shaking his head. "Give me five minutes while I get rid of these characters," Vandorn said. As the fencing master walked away, Vandorn turned to face the newcomers. He had seen newspaper pictures of the Gennett vigil. His intuitive guess would have associated the visitors with that event.

"What can I do for you?" he said indifferently.

"You can tell us what you know about John Gennett's death," Mr. Deep-Voice said.

"Who are you anyway? The local vigilantes?"

"That's your role. We've learned that much. We only need the rest of the story. Where you got the poison. What you're paying Rhodes. All the gory details."

"I don't think there's any use in continuing this," Vandorn said. "You're talking riddles," he added with a shrug. He had his epee by the handle. In a kind of silent reference to the fencer's weapon, he examined the point.

"We've visited Toby Rhodes," Deep-Voice said. "He thinks he's a victim, same as Gennett. You'd be interested in knowing what else he told us. Anyway, you can ask him that yourself. What we're telling you is this: You've got two weeks to get out of this town and don't come back. Next week this time, if you're still here, we're going to the police. If you disappear, we're going to wait a couple, THEN go to the police."

"This is the phoniest fucking thing I've ever encountered." Vandorn sounded defiant in his own hearing. But a thin small needlepoint of doubt, a dot as diaphanous as a soap bubble, had formed in his head. He would trade venom for poison.

In the brief silence he said, "Now will you get the living hell out of here? I've got stuff to do. And I'm behind in my practice."

Mr. Deep-Voice let the silence continue. A fraction of a minute passed. "Okay," he said. "We've told you what's going to happen. When they lock you up for murder, you can ponder your remaining options. They won't be good."

Deep-Voice glanced at his companions. "And just so you'll know, this gentleman on my right is Mr. Quarles. He's a lawyer. And this man to my left is Orville Hamilton. He was a close friend of John's."

"If you'll excuse me--," Vandorn began. Mr. Deep-Voice cut him off.

"And I'm Lincoln Elliott. I worked with John Gennett." If you want a final-final word, it's this: We're going to get rid of you, get you out of here, in jail, or worse."

Vandorn watched as the three turned and started off. None of them gave a backward look.

For Vandorn, the soap bubble had acquired a measure of additional mass. The three visitors represented three Furies in male garb. The depth and breadth of their will to vengeance stood out in every line of their attitudes.

In his momentary irresolution he had forgotten their names.

74

Kathy Edwards, researcher, adjusted herself carefully on the living-room couch. Wearing an expression that combined determination and frustration, she folded her hands in her lap. She had set her briefcase on the floor between her feet.

Laura appeared with a small tray bearing two small cups of tea. She saw them as party cups, not demitasse, though she had both. For her, the demitasse size was impracticably tiny. She had stored the half-dozen that she had accumulated or received as gifts; the perfect place for them was on hooks in a breakfront cabinet. She stored hers--beloved miniatures!--that way.

"I'm afraid I've struck a wall," Kathy said. She had taken one sip and set the cup down quickly. "And it's not even a long story."

Smiling, reminding herself that this had been a shot in the dark, Laura said the polite thing that happened also to be true. "We're both taking a huge chance that anyone could do what we--I--wanted done. That's identify the man who contributed the--we've been calling it the *male element*. And I'm happy to continue with that terminology. From what you've told me, that's our missing link."

"I'm disappointed," Kathy hastened to assert. "But the problem you run into is that there are only a few organizations, and they call them, vulgarly enough, sperm banks. I found four in the United States. There are supposed to be a few in foreign countries. But I thought I'd better check with you before going that far afield. It would enormously increase my expenses. And doing it by mail--well, I had to concoct a whole system of lies even for the stateside firms."

"We knew from the start that it wouldn't be easy." Laura remained studiously empathetic. *The woman was doing her best on a difficult task.*

"It seems almost inevitable--I guess you could call it the geography of the situation. It seems almost unavoidable that the source of such a--product would be local. As she finished her thought, Kathy's thin face turned pink verging on red.

"That would be my thinking, though I never really thought very deeply about it. Now I'm trying to do that, and I'm finding that, yes, the source might be local."

Kathy had obviously pondered what she said next: "That means in the most typical case, or preponderant case, that the male element would have come from someone you know." Her face turned a deeper red as she added: "Pardon me, with topics of this nature it seems that *double entendres*--double meanings--are unavoidable."

"No need to apologize. It's a difficult thing to discuss and we can only do our best."

"It is. I guess the core question is whether you want me to continue. To do it, I believe I would need some help from you."

"Help from me? Whatever kind?" *Whatever*, Laura thought immediately, was an unnecessary word; it suggested subtly some kind of error or miscalculation on Kathy's part. She remained silent, however.

"I'm thinking of a friend who works in a police laboratory. A crime laboratory. He says you can use DNA, I think it is, to identify someone. For example, if you have some fluid or some hair from a person, and can find some other part of him--or her--you can see if they match. If they do, you may have the answer."

"So you're saying we might have one part and would need to find another part. Then see if they match. . ."

"Exactly. But you would need to find the different parts."

"Where would we start? I couldn't just take two separate fingernail clippings from my husband, for example and see if they match. We know they would."

"I'm not certain of this, but I would guess that your doctors would have kept some of the male element that you got. And that you would somehow 'borrow' a drop or two."

In the sudden silence Laura thought she heard, far off, hyena laughter. She drained the last few drops from her teacup and found them cold. "Can I call you in a week?" she said, making a move to stand and thus terminate the interview. Whatever happens, you've already told me you have about all you need to write up my personal part of the story."

"I do."

Both women stood.

75

Every maze has an exit.

With that energizing motto as his guide and theme Vandorn had made up his mind. He would thwart the "three thugs," as he mentally sketched them.

Leave Franklin? He would wear a plastic bag as a head-covering first. And before any new action measures he would case the landscape, make certain that Rhodes had ratted, soft talk Georgia into unlocking some clout, find out whether his name was being bandied about with reference to John Gennett's demise. He would forget any concordat with Brand--on the assumption that his unanswered overture had been in vain.

Vandorn wanted to leave it at that. He had deliberately refrained from visiting Rhodes in the hospital. Why awaken somnolent dogs? Better to pursue his professorial routine, go back to his exercise program. And prove the thugs were phonies. Thwart them legally.

He pulled up along the curb in front of Georgia LeBaron's posh homestead. Everything here bespoke old money. Pressing the doorbell, Vandorn could hear chimes inside the ornate door. Fully half a minute elapsed before the door opened. Face to face with Georgia, "I was passing," Vandorn said. "Thought I'd stop and see where we stand on CAMP. He took a step forward, the way door-knocker salesmen do.

Gratifyingly, she opened the door a little wider. "I look like a *Putzfrau*," Georgia said. "But when you arrive unannounced, that's the risk you run." She gently closed the door behind Vandorn. "Let's sit in here. It's comfy."

She guided Vandorn into a tiny parlor that offered just enough space for three antique chairs and an old-fashioned writing desk. "I do my letter-writing in here," Georgia said. "In total privacy."

"A rare achievement." Vandorn shifted, hearing the chair creak as he did. He was breathing a faint musty scent.

Leaning forward in her chair, Georgia seemed to be expecting a short conversation. "What brings you to my modest quarters?" she said. "What can we settle without holding a meeting?"

"There are three homosexual thugs out there. They're blaming us-- CAMP--for John Gennett's death. Making threats."

Against whom?"

A thought occurred, and Vandorn added, "Probably the whole CAMP leadership."

"What kinds of threats?"

"Suggestions of bodily harm. They talk about going to the police. I believe they're considering legal action if all else fails. They seem to be very serious. Their community is up in arms apparently."

Georgia pulled gently at her left ear. "Bodily harm is serious. But people go to the police every day of the year. They bring in lawyers at the drop of a hat. If they do either of those things, we could get lawyers who could tie it up for years."

"The bodily harm card seemed to be the one they're most serious about. We're all involved--the CAMP officers, leaders, whoever. I'm thinking we all need writs, you know, prohibiting contact of any kind, harassment, stalking. They've started with me."

"Have they," she said primly, "any information that we don't have? There are all kinds of rumors floating around. About how Gennett died. About Toby and how he got poisoned too. About the police investigation and where the poison came from. Both poisons. I think we need some clarification. Toby's spreading rumors about you."

"I know for a fact that the thugs are out there, making threats. They interrupted my fencing session. They're throwing wild charges around about CAMP. So maybe we're reaching somebody, but in the wrong way, or at the wrong time."

"Toby--you must have heard--has dropped out of our group. Totally. He says he was used, a victim, didn't know what was going to happen--either that Mr. Gennett would die or that he, Toby, would get seriously sick. And without him, what can we learn? The police are looking for some third party. Maybe someone who goes to that club. What do they call it? Kitkat?"

"I think it's Kitkat." Vandorn spelled the club name. As he did so, he was arranging what he was hearing. Georgia appeared to be moving away from obtaining legal help or protection. But those were Vandorn's primary needs or best hope, in particular the writ. "These friends of Mr. Gennett," he continued, seemed pretty bloodthirsty. My feeling is that we should have the legal protection, then meet as a group and see if there's any further course of action."

"We'd have to know more," Georgia said. She reached to her writing desk and picked up a small notebook. "What if we figure on meeting in a week? We could meet here. This place is like a bank vault. I can hardly open the front door. We should get only our governing body together. But first we should also find out whether Dr. Brand is still endangering that woman's life."

"Mrs. Phillips. I'll see what I can find out."

"I'm in favor of that for one reason: With a larger group we might fall into a morass of rumors, none of them true."

"Something to be avoided like a plague of ants."

"One thing," Georgia said in a voice ripe with admonitory emphasis. "Toby's been saying to some people that you wanted to see Mr. Gennett 'put away'--that's the phrase I've heard. You should maybe clear that up before we meet or do anything else."

"My God. With Toby out there spreading lies?"

"We should have that straight. To get legal protection, my lawyer contacts would want to know the background--and the names of the people we're avoiding. Your thugs."

"That might be difficult. The three of them sort of ran in and ran out while I was at my fencing lesson. But I'm going to find a way if I have to put an ad in the queer newspaper." Vandorn smiled. *Clever line.* But Georgia was building too many roadblocks. "I'll start today," he said. "I think this is important because they're talking about our group, our program. That's what they're really trying to do--shoot us down."

He was standing, preparing to leave. Georgia didn't insist that he stay. She only said as she led him to the door, "Let me know what would be a good date for our officers' meeting?"

"Will do." He was descending Georgia's front steps as her door closed. With that symbolic closure, he thought, he was left with the violence card. He couldn't wait a month. Maybe not a week.

76

The incubus of his deadline suddenly bore on Vandorn like a five-ton anchor. It disgusted him. He rationalized that he was getting old, or that some infection was eating away at him. He refused to believe that the three thugs, with their idiotic doomsday deadline, could rattle his concentration, keep him awake at night, or make him shop around for an alternative place to live.

Eight days had passed since the thugs had given him their deadline in the fieldhouse. Eight days before he decided to call on Toby Rhodes. Eight days that left six, that shrank his time to the point where each individual Ethics class felt like a time-trap.

Rhodes lived in a condominium. His was one of six units, a converted six-flat in a block of such buildings. Vandorn rang the bell, then heard nothing until a barely audible voice piped from the wall: "Who is it?"

"Jim Vandorn! Calling to see how you're doing."

The door began to buzz; Rhodes was releasing the front-door lock. Opening it, Vandorn marched in; *marching* was how he pictured it.

The hall door giving access to the Rhodes unit was standing open. Once inside, Vandorn experienced a quick access of near-nausea. The air was foul with a smell like that of a hospital room for nausea sufferers.

Toby Rhodes sat wrapped in blankets despite the room's warm temperature. Positioned among pillows on a couch, he waved Vandorn to a chair. "Make yourself comfortable," he said, and slid down so that he was deeper in the pillow cradle.

"You still sick?" Vandorn said. "I thought you'd be running a marathon by now."

"The docs want me to rest for a few more weeks. That stuff you found almost did me in." Hearing the wispy voice, Vandorn felt anger rising. Impatience was diffusing into anger. He tried to remember what he had come for.

It came back clearly. "What are you telling the cops?" He said loudly. Instantly Rhodes was shsshing him with a finger to his lips.

"Nothin'. Someone tried to get me and that other guy. But you got the wrong stuff." The irritation in Rhodes' voice fed Vandorn's rage. As he realized that he would neither establish nor learn anything here, he wanted some kind of retribution.

This fool will play sick until he comes out the king of the pity circle. While I'm harassed, threatened, insulted.

With a sudden, clean movement he rolled the blankets surrounding Rhodes and threw them on the floor. "Now get up?" he commanded. "Move! You've faked long enough." He flung the door open and pointed out. "Let's see you walk up and down that hallway--once! Go!"

"I'm not supposed--." Rhodes whimpered. He stood free of the couch.

"Go before I kick you out!"

In his stocking feet Rhodes went, uncertainly, navigating the empty hall with his hands running along one wall to steady his progress. Reaching the end of the hall, he turned and came back, still supporting himself by touching the wall. Back at the doorway he brushed past Vandorn and, reaching the couch, fell on it.

Vandorn lifted the blankets and threw them on Rhodes' prostrate form.

"You don't really know me," Vandorn said. "Anyone asks, you met me once. You had no business with me. Got nothing from me. Got it?"

"Uh-huh." The answer came in a whisper.

Vandorn stormed out, slamming the door.

77

"Dr. Brand?"

"Yes, this is Dr. Brand."

"This is Jim Vandorn calling. I'm wondering whether we could meet. I think our differences have gone on long enough. I'd like to see if we can't work out a peace treaty of some kind."

"Give me a hint. What are you thinking? Who gives up what in the interest of community peace?"

"Nobody. We talk, probe the possibilities."

"I'm very busy. If you can tell me what your premise is, what kind of agreement is possible, I'll listen now. I wouldn't have time to meet."

"Well, of course you're working with Mrs. Phillips. Also Mr. X, who took Mr. Gennett's place. That's quite heroic of him."

"You know a lot. But I really do have work to do. Unless--."

Vandorn, interrupting Brand, said, "You know our group wouldn't mind if Mrs. Phillips succeeded." Talking faster, he added, "It's Mr. X, the pregnant man, he's the one we'd like to talk about. For example, there's adoption--."

It was Brand's turn to interrupt. "I've got a laboratory call here. If you don't have anything else to say, let's talk some other time."

"Soon? In two days?"

"I'm busy!" Brand said with asperity. "Please get off the line."

"You could give me the names of those three thugs, friends of Gennett who are running around like a bunch of assassins."

A secretary passing in the hall outside Brand's office heard the crash of the telephone receiver in Brand's office. She peeked in to see if anything was amiss. Brand was smiling behind his desk. He had his hand on the phone.

"That was a salesman who wouldn't say no, Alison. But thanks for looking in."

Brand waited for a long minute, thoughtfully doodling. Making up his mind, he reached for the Franklin phone book. Finding the phone number for the Police Headquarters, he dialed the number and asked for the Chief of Detectives. He and Chief Callahan were well acquainted, and had been since Brand had helped Callahan's wife through a "preemie" scare, a premature birth.

Brand asked if he could talk with the detective they had on the Gennett murder case. "I may have a few clues to contribute," Brand said.

78

Cudgeling his memory, Brand reconstructed those work- and rage-filled days of Baboon Terry's sojourn in the Brand garage. Framed distinctly in recollection, his discovery of the animal's body returned in full horror, a monument to nameless brutality. His private-eye work had borne some fruit, Brand thought with satisfaction. His subsequent loss of interest seemed cause for regret.

He could finger Vandorn in that death. Had he done so while the murder was still fresh, might he have saved Gennett's life?

He ran a caseworker's eye down his list of the clues he had found: the clues he would now turn over to Detective-Sergeant Thad Dorian. Among others, he had listed the monogrammed handkerchief, the fragments of bone, some traces of Baboon Terry's fur.

A polite knock on the door of his office roused him to the present. On his invitation, the door opened and the detective entered. A broad-shouldered man in street clothes, the detective ranged above Brand by four or five inches.

"This is fortuitous," Dorian said. "You were next on my list. You beat me to it."

"I was working with Mr. Gennett, as you know," Brand said. "We had this ground-breaking experiment going. He had volunteered for it."

"I've gotten feedback on it, and would really appreciate some details."

"Details I've got. Have a seat?" With Dorian seated, Brand described his pregnant man project. He started with the animal trials and their uniform record of success. He added basic information on the search for a volunteer, the instant acceptance and rapid response in the gay community, Gennett's total cooperation.

"Now you want to know why I called you," he said. "Without knowing how far you've progressed, I believe there may be a connection between some earlier events and Mr. Gennett's death." Again touching on highlights, Brand told of Terry's murder, his own subsequent research. He admitted to a belief that Vandorn had killed the baboon.

"This Vandorn," Brand said, "poisoned another of our experimental animals--another baboon. He likes to work through others, it seems to me. He also likes to use poison. Or so it seems. Would you look at this collection?"

Dorian stood, then leaned over to examine Brand's "clues," gathered after Terry's death.

"This hanky," Brand said, "was wrapped around Vandorn's finger when he reported to Franklin Hospital ER the night of Baboon Terry's death. They told me that. In this little capsule I've got some fragments of bone. I believe they were bitten off the killer's finger by my baboon just before he died. I found them in the animal's mouth."

"Marvelous evidence. May I take it with me? And do you have a few more minutes?"

"For this, no time is too much."

Comparing notes Brand and Dorian discovered common suspicions. Primarily, both believed that more persons were involved in Gennett's murder than one--Rhodes; and how he was involved no one could fathom. Rhodes was clinging doggedly to his contention that he was the second poisoning victim.

Brand believed with equal doggedness that Vandorn's signature lay over the entire Kitkat scenario.

"If we could find the source of the poison, we might be halfway home," Dorian said. The stuff they used isn't available at any old drugstore."

"My God, you just reminded me. There's a locked cabinet in the university's Chemistry Department. It's loaded with all kinds of lethal oddities, all carefully catalogued."

"You may have just saved my job." Dorian was smiling. "Who would I call to get a look at this treasure?"

"The chemistry prof is named Gustafson. He's in the university phonebook. He would have access to the cabinet."

Dorian wrapped Brand's evidence carefully, then took it with him when he left.

79

"Why don't you give it up? Let CAMP go straight to hell!"

Vandorn injected the near-maximum of rebuke into his response. "Because LeBaron called and asked me if I'd make it tonight. She said if I weren't going to be there, she'd call it off. 'No use meeting.' Those were her words."

He speared a cherry tomato and moved it to his plate. Then he took two more. This was the way he liked tomatoes. Jennifer got them especially for him.

"Isn't your deadline--the *meaningless deadline*, as you call it-- running out?"

"It's got a few days to go. And when I called it meaningless I meant it." He popped another tomato and talked through it. "The real reason for going tonight is I'm hoping Georgia has good news for me. A way to get those thugs out of my life."

"And if not?"

"I may spend a weekend out of town. Make 'em think I flew the coop. Come back in time for Monday classes."

"I told you. If you're going to be staying with your Uncle Mort, I'm going to spend some time with Lola. I'm not going to stay here alone."

Vandorn pushed his empty plate away and stood up. "Just so I know where you are."

"So you're really going?"

"Absolutely. I won't be long. There won't be more than four or five people there." Vandorn picked up the copy of the *Franklin Advocate* that he had picked up on the way home. The front-page headline read, "MURDER PROBE REPORTS NEW CLUES!"

The note on the LeBaron front door was an invitation. "Door not locked. Come in," it read.

Vandorn pushed the door open and stepped inside. At once he could hear voices engaged in subdued conversation. Following the voices he found Georgia and Eldy Dennington seated on opposite sides of a walnut dining-room table. There were greetings. Vandorn took a seat and laid on the table the file he had brought: his notes on CAMP's various meetings and planned or completed projects.

Georgia spoke, asking Vandorn whether he would like a liquid refreshment. When he answered politely in the negative, Georgia said, "I checked with Eldy. We decided I should invite Toby to join us. He said he'd make it if he was up to it."

"He's still recouping from whatever he drank," Eldy said. "And it's getting to him."

Idiocy, Vandorn thought. Why hadn't he listened to Jennifer? In an effort to set a soft, plausible tone, he mentioned his visit to Toby Rhodes. "I tried to get him moving," he said. "I don't think he appreciated it."

"He says you were beating up on him," Eldy said. "I wasn't there, so I don't know--but he was pretty much crushed, right, Georgia?"

"He was. I told him you were probably trying to help him."

"I most definitely was," Vandorn said gratefully. "I'm really sorry if he--."

The door-chimes sounded. "That could be Toby," Georgia said. "He forgot to read my note. Or he can't see it. She left the room to greet the new arrival, returning in half a minute. Rhodes followed her. He was wearing what appeared to be pajamas under a light, hip-length jacket. His face had developed hollows at the cheeks, and his eyes seemed to have sunk deep into his head.

He might have been wearing a horror mask, Vandorn thought. But in Rhodes' case the disheveled hair and the unshaven jaws matched other features to create an effect of ghastly repulsiveness. To look was to feel shock.

After a minute or so of making himself comfortable, Rhodes lifted his eyes and fixed them on Vandorn. His breathing came in shortening cycles. At some point, it seemed, he would have to relax and take longer drafts. Instead, he began to shout.

"He's the one," he began, screaming the words. "He's the one who hurled me out of bed, made me walk, run--when I was alone. He's the one that tried to kill me in that club! He changed the poison." Rhodes' voice changed, went into a pseudo-intimate register, and he said, obviously imitating Vandorn: "All you have to do is take a little of this other one, the mild medicine. You'll look like a victim."

Rhodes' voice cracked. As suddenly as his outburst had begun, he went silent. "Now I don't know," he whispered. "He's the killer."

Suddenly Rhodes was standing. Taking two wobbly steps. From some remembered self-defense lesson he shot his right fist forward, catching Vandorn on the side of his head. The sound was like a hammer hitting wood. Vandorn spun, toppled, taking the chair with him. Rhodes backed into his own chair. He began to sob.

Folder in hand, Vandorn pulled the papers together, gathering them from where they had scattered on the floor. Standing, he nodded to Georgia and left, closing the front door quietly. In front of the house a car waited. A woman sat in the driver's seat, a book resting on the steering wheel.

There was just enough light, Vandorn estimated, for Toby's wife to read. He went to his own car, felt the knot on his head, and drove away.

Even the idiots were arrayed against him.

80

This was the document that would ensure his legacy. In layman's terms, it would make the case that the early years of the next century would see this entire American comity collapse in chaos. Moral chaos as distinguished from, but related to, economic chaos.

He reached, and there he found his draft, exactly where he had left it. One comforting thing about Jennifer. She left his things alone. She had reason, she said once; the stuff repelled her. Meaning: she didn't understand it.

He had planned it as a contribution to the *Ethical Record*. Rereading part of it, he liked it. He would take it with him when he left Franklin.

You are not only tinkering with the genetic structure and moral scaffolding on which the race grows and by which it is preserved and increased; you are violating the covenant that men and women have since the Creation been keeping with their Deity. Under that covenant, according to a premise as binding as any ever envisioned by Katkov in his Untersuchungen, *humans procreate in a preordained way. They act in pursuance of that premise as a given; they cannot depart from it, or manifestly violate it, or restructure it in any way without invading forbidden territory.*

Women bear children after insemination by a male; it was that simple. Discoveries of byroads to the same result only hurl defiance at the base principle, or indulge sinful divergencies from the laws as enunciated in the lessons of Sodom and Gomorrah.

The ethics of a premise that places all humans in a mutually fiduciary, personal relationship with God have echoes in the realm of genetics. Here, natural law rules. Just as good should be rendered for good, evil will be rendered for evil, for defiance or disobedience. Invade or disturb the natural order and Man will be compensated in kind. From in vitro creation of life Man will inevitably move to control of all genetic factors, to competition with God in cloning, to Frankel's vision in eugenics, to taboos broken, temples sharded; to entrance into forbidden regions where Man has no right to trespass.

Ultimately or immediately, ethics must adopt whatever viable strategy exists and comes to mind to combat the proliferating crimes against the human of the future. Biomedicine must not be allowed to overturn the edifice of centuries, to replace established tradition and moral development with reproductive gadgetry and artifice. The ethically immoral that becomes the scientifically feasible poses a double threat--complacency in error and renunciation of the traditional--moving Man toward the abyss called Ethical Impiety. . .

The phone rang, causing Vandorn to twitch with surprise. So thorough was his immersion in theory. Hearing Jennifer's voice, he relaxed. She at least remained unaffected by his flights of conscience through inquiry.

Jennifer was calling for no reason, or to ascertain whether he was home, or to leave a recorded message that she was at Lola's: all acceptable, reasonable. Let them watch the boob-tube. Lola the Airhead consorting with Jennifer who needed the company of an Airhead.

"I'll see you when you get here," he said. "I'm deep in de--, in trying to figure out some postulates." That was his word, *postulates*, when he wanted to turn away questions. And a moment later he could hang up.

One thing emerged with limpid clarity. Brand stood out as the master violator, the prime conspirator. Deal with Brand and the wildfire of the new reproductive paganism would likely disappear from Franklin's quiet middle-class public ways and medical laboratories.

Weeks ago Vandorn had noted down the name, address, and phone number of Brand's co-conspirator. They made a pair. Where Brand was the embryologist, Madsen filled the role of obie-gyne. A term from Hell. Madsen, according to rumor, too old to wreak havoc on his own; Brand too dedicated to his diabolic reproductive schemes.

Vandorn picked up the phone. Moments later he could hear a phone ringing in Madsen's office. As planned, a girl answered.

"Is Dr. Brand there? This is an emergency."

"No, he won't be here until Thursday evening."

"Thank you. I'll try the University lab."

Hang up. Step to the bedroom and his dresser. Riffle down through the clean, rolled-up socks, Jennifer's work. *She was good for something.*

The knife lay buried, right where he had hidden it.

He tossed it, encased in its leather scabbard, into the traveling bag that he was packing for his trip to Uncle Mort's. Back at the phone on its little table, he drew from his wallet the notes he was making. Most of the items had been checked off. Two sets of initials remained unmarked: EB and LP.

Thursday was three days off. It was time to spend some sightseeing at his uncle's--the country place he called "Mort's Motel." Three days to Brand's end.

He was reaching for the phone when it rang. He waited the four rings until his own recorded voice broke in, requesting the caller to leave a message. At once Gus Gustafson spoke, sounding subdued. Vandorn picked up.

"Gus. Great to hear your voice. I'm just sifting my calls."

"Smart. The cops will be looking for you--tomorrow if not tonight. They were here most of the afternoon. Two of them--. They knew about our cache of skull-and-crossbones fluids. Don't ask me how."

"It had to be Brand. He's the only one who knows about it."

"Maybe," Gus said. "Anyway I had to show them everything, all of it. They called in a special unit to come here and clean us out."

"Did they mention my name?"

"They found my checklist--recipients. Yours was at the bottom."

"God-damn!"

"I had no idea they were coming or I would have stashed the notes. As it was, I was afraid they'd toss me in the clink. That's all my old lady would need."

"What time did they leave?"

"Not half an hour ago. I'm telling you, it took most of the afternoon, with all the grilling."

"You say they might be here tonight?"

"I think so. They're bugged about Gennett. I got the idea that everybody's on their case. To at least find a suspect."

"Gus, I'm going underground for a few days. Back in three days or so. I'll call in sick for a few days. I might be checking with you from out of town."

"I'm going to be getting out of here early for a while. Go get a beer and go home."

"Wise move. If I have to call, I'll try your home number."

"Right. Have a good trip."

"I'll try. *Auf Wiedersehen*."

"*Viel Glueck*."

One to go. It took seconds to reach Jennifer and instruct her to stay at Lola's. "I'll be at Mort's for a few days," he said.

"They're really after you, aren't they?" She sounded like someone trying to conceal *Schadenfreude*.

Vandorn went through the condo he had shared with Jennifer for six years. In the bedroom he felt a twinge of regret; at certain times she had been great in bed. His rounds completed, he zipped up his traveling bag and left. As he was closing the front door, standing in the vacant hall, he heard the doorbell ring.

He went back into the unit, locking the front door behind him, and left by the back, or emergency, entrance. He was on the road, heading for the highway south, in less than ten minutes.

81

For Brand, the crowning virtue of the Madsen Clinic lay in its arrangement; its cabinets, plumbing and other fixtures, its patient-related furniture. To find what you needed, you usually had merely to look into the cabinet or drawer nearest the place where you would normally need the item.

Preparing for sequential visits by Adamson and Laura, he had begun to lay out the things he would need. They included primarily for Laura a syringe and the supplies that went with that instrument, items like cotton, gauze, medical tape. For Adamson he would need the special laparoscope that he himself had invented plus a curette and some sundries similar to those he was setting aside for Laura.

He was finishing his prep work when he heard Laura's silver-toned voice. Alerted, he thought he detected a new quality in her speech. He became sure of it as he listened further. Her successful embryonation must have wrought the change: given her, as it did him, a deep sense of achievement? Success? Self-worth? Fulfillment?

She greeted him warmly. They exchanged their now usual fraternal kiss. "Any changes?" he asked. He listened while she considered. "I can't stop eating," she said. "Even Tim has noticed. He thinks I'm going to outweigh him one of these days."

"I'll resign from your case when that day arrives."

"You'll have an argument if you try to resign. I've even given my passenger, as you call him-her, a name."

"Which is?"

"Emlyn. Your name. I think it's most--."

"You'll do me a big favor if you'll change it to Tim. Or Joseph. Or--what's your father's name?"

"Rodney. But I hate that name."

"Can you find another one? People will get the wrong idea if your neonate has my name."

Brand had been examining Laura's incision, now almost invisible. Laura's mention of her choice of a name had distracted him. He could feel his face flushing red.

Laura was watching him. "I'm sorry," she said. "I thought it would be fitting, that's all."

"It's hard to explain. And no harm's done--if you can find another name." He gestured toward the straight-backed chair. "If you'll step over here, I can take a blood sample."

Taking the blood, Brand pictured in imagination the effect his own name could have if actually given to her child. Tongues might cluck even absent such a name connection.

He would ride it out. Much could change in the seven or eight months until she could deliver. Madsen would do the delivery.

The baby would keep Laura busy at home. Daily tedium would rule.

He was making out the blood-test sheet, noting the elements that should be checked in the analyses. At that moment he heard a shout from the front of the office suite. It would have come from the reception area.

Brand stopped, listening. Laura watched him, fear and curiosity intermingled in her expression. She was staring at Brand. She had instinctively gathered her hospital gown more closely around her.

Another shout sounded, louder, followed by a heavy thud. In the next instant the door leading toward the back of the suite opened and Dr. Madsen entered. Almost simultaneously the other door that led into the hall and out to the reception area opened.

Vandorn stood in the opening, his clothing rumpled. In his right hand he held a Green Beret knife that slowly dripped blood.

"Your turn, Brand," Vandorn said. "I'm putting you out of business."

Laura screamed, a strident howl that touched a galvanic nerve in Brand. The impulse to fight intensified. Accustomed to consider every next stage in crises, he surrendered to instinct. He would not remember all that happened.

The scent of hard liquor filled the room. Keeping Vandorn in immediate sight Brand sent memory exploring the wall to his right. Next to the cabinet memory paused, gave answer, stopped at the little metal cylinder that Madsen provided in every single room.

Brand reached to his right and it was there, the office-model fire extinguisher. A wrench and it cooperatively came off the wall, sprang free of the laughable metal clamps that, untouched, held it ready for use. It became a substantial weight in his hand, a weapon. A thing to propel as Brand had once propelled basketballs while in college. Laura was screaming again; in Brand's brain it became Coach Wells' shout, "No lazy passes! Move it!"

Brand moved it while watching the knife-gripping hand as it approached, beginning a downward arc.

Coach Wells' drills, once practiced to the point of second nature, could still guide muscle movements. Brand could sense the sudden power. Aiming instinctively, he let fly. The cylindrical extinguisher struck Vandorn in the lower face. He was spitting teeth when Brand made another instinctive move: his left hand caught Vandorn's right arm at the wrist. Its progress stopped, the two men stood locked as Vandorn's arm flailed for release.

Moments passed while the knife danced inches from Brand's left shoulder and chest. At Brand's right, desperate to help, Laura was on her feet. She had picked up the extinguisher, and was trying to pound Vandorn with it. Distracted, Vandorn lowered his right arm. He lashed out with his left hand, pushing Laura off violently. Hurled backward, she struck the wall and dropped to the floor.

The distraction became opportunity. Brand began to twist his assailant's right hand and arm around to his back. Gradually gaining leverage on that arm, he bent it further back as Vandorn turned with it.

What Brand identified later as the X factor entered. With douts of blood smearing his face, and with his shirt streaked red, Adamson appeared in the doorway.

He deliberately stepped up behind Vandorn. Swinging a small weighted weapon, he struck Vandorn a vicious blow on the side of the head.

Suddenly unconscious, the ethicist slumped to the floor. The knife fell from his hand.

It has happened repeatedly over the centuries, Brand thought. Supposedly intelligent people have tried to divert the flow of history. Of progress. And have fallen victim to a makeshift weapon called a blackjack.

82

Summoned by Dr. Madsen, the police arrived in minutes. The scene of carnage in the Madsen Clinic spurred the two officers to emergency action. They began by calling for an ambulance and stretchers. Both Adamson and Vandorn were unconscious.

Explaining the sequence of events, Brand summarized. Vandorn had arrived uninvited and wielding a knife. The knife lay where it had fallen when Adamson had entered and probably saved Brand a serious wound or worse. The weapon that Adamson had used lay on the floor not far from the knife, a lethal appearing blackjack with flecks of blood on its business end.

Earlier, Brand continued, Adamson had apparently come under attack by Vandorn in the reception area. He had taken serious knife-wounds, had survived them and attacked Vandorn while the ethicist and Brand were wrestling for the knife.

Laura, wrapped comfortably in a blanket produced by Dr. Madsen, sat dazed in the room's single chair. She had placed one hand on her midsection, and sat with head bowed, awake but confused. She did not answer questions put to her by the police officers.

Brand had already examined her, finding no injuries that would require hospitalization or emergency treatment. She had, however, been driven against the wall when Vandorn pushed/struck her. Also, as Brand found, she had bled from the omentum scar. Her violent fall had reopened the incision in her stomach. Her embryo, nearing fetus status, may have lost its microscopic hold on life.

The thought gave Brand chills. How would he tell her?

Madsen had been checking Adamson's wounds. Vandorn's knife had left two long but superficial gashes in the candidate's upper body. Neither, Madsen believed, would be fatal. To the extent that he was able to clean and purge and bandage, Madsen covered the cuts, stopping the ooze of blood. He was finishing when the parameds rushed in with two stretchers.

They had brought their own leak-proof wrappings. Testing for life-signs in Vandorn, one of the paramedics left off the trial once, then tested again. A look at his partner, observed by Brand, telegraphed his conclusion clearly. It suggested that the blow to the right side of Vandorn's head would be or already was fatal. Finishing their wrapping and identification of the body, they removed it on a stretcher.

The parameds and the police were gone. The notes they had taken from Brand gave them enough for a preliminary report. They would return for more details as needed. They read the evidence as totally incriminating for Vandorn. Brand had described it bluntly; it was an attempt to commit two murders. Finding Adamson on the premises may have been unforeseen, but the evidence indicating an effort to commit homicide was clear and convincing. They had Madsen's medical description of Adamson's wounds.

Laura asked Brand to stand by while she changed into her street clothes. He was waiting outside the dressing room when he heard her barely audible call. She had opened her clothing and was pointing at the evidence of fresh, leaking blood. Hurrying, he bandaged again.

She was tight-lipped. "What do you think, Em?"

Her use of his name signaled hope. That mood paralleled Brand's own. "Don't know," he said. "I'll have to turn this one over to Al. It's out of my sphere right now."

She said what he feared. "Have I lost it?"

Their eyes met. She would know instantly if he lied to her. "I'm afraid: you may have."

"Is it my blood, or--?" She was letting him fill in the painful space.

"It would be yours." Changing the subject, he added: "I'll go find Al. Tell him what we think--and would like to do."

"What would you want to do?"

He could not lift his eyes from the floor. "Continue to take all possible precautions."

"Em!" It was almost a shriek. "Can we find out now? Promise that you'll tell Dr. Al? I have to know." Her supplicant hand reached toward him.

"If I can arrange it, I'll have it done in a couple of days. But Al has the final word." His left hand covered her right, stroking.

Madsen was talking on a telephone, making arrangements to have the clinic cleaned and repainted if necessary. The work would need to be done in the morning, beginning as early as possible.

With the call settled to Madsen's satisfaction, Brand asked if he, Madsen, would run the necessary tests, including X-ray, to ascertain whether Laura had indeed lost her implanted baby. If yes, would he perform the caesarean removal?

"I should have time tomorrow afternoon, " Madsen said. "Could you tell her I'll call her in the morning with a time. I'll want to do that in the hospital--Franklin Memorial. But first I'll confirm that she's not carrying life."

"She'll be indebted again. So will I. Would you remember to preserve the embryo for me? I'm going to conduct a simple burial."

Within 24 hours James Vandorn had been declared dead. The cause of death was a severe blow delivered to the side of his head by a hand-held weapon.

Following treatment and short-term hospitalization, Martin Adamson was released from the hospital. The knife wounds that he had suffered would leave scars, but not on normally visible surfaces of the body.

Following tests proving that her embryo/fetus had died, Laura Phillips underwent surgery with a local anesthetic to have the remains removed.

83

Braving a light, early fall rain, the two men followed a wide gravel path in Franklin's Queen of All Saints Cemetery. The shoes grinding in the gravel and the distant whiz and whir of automobile traffic were the only sounds intruding on the nearly palpable silence among the memorial stones.

The shorter man, wearing a black raincoat much like his companion's, walked a little ahead. Both wore appropriate headgear as protection against the rain. Reaching a place where a sign with an arrow pointed right, the two turned. The sign had just enough space for two words: "Heaven's Innocents."

The crunch of shoes on gravel continued. But the man in the lead was slowing down and glancing around. He produced from a raincoat pocket a small wooden box. "It's around here somewhere," he said. A moment later he sighed audibly. "There," and he pointed to a rock grotto that formed a protective shield over the small, marble figure of an infant in swaddling wraps.

Fifteen or so feet from the little grotto someone had dug a shallow hole in the ground. A low enclosure of fresh, reddish earth surrounded the hole on three sides. The fourth was open.

The shorter man handed the little box to Dr. Brand. "Want to do the honors while I say the Prayer for the Limbo Babies?"

Brand nodded. Both men removed their headgear. Crouching next to the hole, Brand set the box on the blade of a miniature shovel that lay alongside the hole. Suddenly, while the prayer began, a car horn sounded an abrupt accompaniment to the soft sibilance of the rain falling in the grass. "O Lord, master of earth and Heaven, O Lord who rules the seas and the stars, we offer this tiny seeker of life, helpless now in death, to the welcoming courts of Your dwelling. . ."

Letting the words soak in like the rain, Brand lowered the box with the toylike shovel until it slid off the blade and sat in the red earth. He withdrew the shovel and set it where he had found it. Standing, he watched the raindrops as they splashed on the tiny box. Head bent, he felt water running in barely perceptible rivulets down his cheeks.

The trickles were partly rain, partly tears.

Impatient because he had promised himself that he could accomplish this ritual alone, in matter-of-fact fashion, without histrionics, Brand concentrated, listening to the final words of the prayer. The undertaker put his hat on and Brand did the same.

The two shook hands. "It's always tough when they're preemies," the undertaker said. "Not even a chance at life."

"I couldn't agree more."

"You stayin' to say goodbye? Don't forget, they close here in half an hour."

"I won't forget."

As the undertaker trudged away, Brand picked up the shovel. He had time to fill the hole.

He was still at it when he heard again the crunch of shoes in gravel. It surprised him; he thought he had the cemetery to himself. When he turned, Laura was only yards away, approaching as if on a mission. Dropping the toy shovel, Brand stepped toward her. Wordless, the two met in a close embrace.

"They told me I'd find you here--and I should be mad," Laura said. "But I can't be, you stubborn man. May I look at your handiwork?"

"You may. I had just started filling up the hole."

Together they moved to the tamped-down grass at the edge of the tiny grave. The burial box was visible from where they stood. A thin sprinkling of the red earth lay over the box. "The container snaps shut," Brand said. "Carl, the undertaker who came out here with me, said it will provide almost the same protection as a casket."

"I'll dream of this." Turning away, Laura mopped at her eyes with a handkerchief. Trying to speak, she could only groan. Brand placed a comforting arm across her shoulders. Without resisting the arm, she wailed more loudly.

The access of grief and the body language of mourning continued for two or three minutes, rising first and then moderating. She began to sniffle.

"Don't mind me," she said. "I had such dreams. I'm also trying to get used to what I think I've figured out." Again she gave way to an agitated flurry of tears and sniffles. She seemed on the verge of keening or howling; instead, she choked back a sound that she barely, with great effort, controlled.

Feeling helpless, Brand placed a comforting hand on Laura's back. Her coat was wet, reminding him that they should finish and leave. "I have to finish this job," he said. "Filling up the hole."

As if galvanized, Laura took the shovel from Brand's hand. "Let me do just a little. I was to be the mother, after all."

He watched while she wielded the shovel. "Enough," he said, realizing that she was crying while shoveling. "Let me do the rest."

She gave him the shovel and he started again. This time he hurried. The remaining earth disappeared into the hole. While working he could hear Laura crying. Each new shovel-load precipitated an outburst of acute distress. In quieter intervals she made audible efforts to swallow her misery.

Finishing, he put the shovel back where he had found it. When he turned to face her, she was wiping her eyes and cheeks. "Sorry," she said. "Sorry to make a scene." With another step she closed the space between them.

They kissed, lingering; longing shared. Laura ended the brief communion. "Answer me one question," she said. "Swear to tell me the truth?"

He paused; nodded and looked away.

"The question is very straightforward. You would have been the father, wouldn't you?"

He nodded again. His eyes were glistening, inducing a feeling of embarrassment.

Her hand lay on his shoulder, as if she would not let him go. "You wouldn't let the death of a monkey stop your work, or derail it. I'm asking you to repeat this project, or engagement. Our project. Same conditions. Start over. Promise?"

Momentarily, his memory roved, ticking off the conditions that would make a new endeavor possible; none was lacking. Vandorn was dead, Adamson had also expressed his determination to try again (and again and again if necessary); and Madsen, wonderful Madsen, had promised continued collaboration.

"Promised," he said. "And now we'd better clear out of here before they close and lock us in.

Again the crunching underfoot, gravel providing an accompaniment Brand would forever associate with embryo death and light rain. The thought had hardly been registered in memory when the rain quickened. The drops became small globes that splashed on contact.

Holding Laura's arm, he picked up the pace. "We may have to run for it at this rate," he said.

84

The sexton was standing outside the entrance to the cemetery office. He wore a raincoat even though the building's overhang sheltered him. Hearing Brand and Laura, he turned. "I was about to come lookin' for you two," he said pleasantly. "The gentleman that just left, Mr. Pierce, reminded me you was still out there."

"We were afraid we'd be locked in," Brand said. "Thanks for watching."

"No thanks wanted. An' ye're welcome here any time."

"We'll be back."

"We'll have a marker out there in a coupla days. That's Baby Phillips, if I'm rememberin'."

"You're right. We'll talk to you tomorrow."

"I'm not goin' anywheres."

Walking on, still feeling the raindrops on his face, Brand took Laura's arm. The informal ceremony at the gravesite had exorcized his niggling sense of incompleteness. It had provided a kind of closure while sealing the record on a life that had hardly begun. To Laura he said, "Feel like a nightcap?"

"It would save my sanity." She paused, then said with an edge of humor: "Just not at the Kitcat Club."

"Follow me; driving. It's not five minutes from here."

She was smiling as she hung up the wet raincoat and took a seat in a corner booth. Brand slid in next to her. He could hear music, a sound so muted it was almost inaudible.

"I hoped we'd have a chance to talk before shutting down for the day," Laura said. "And do it out of range of a clock."

"It seems we've found the place. They also have liquid refreshments. If you've decided, I'm buying."

"I'll join you, but only if *I'm* buying."

"Sounds final. I surrender."

"I have to thank you for a lot, but right now for miraculously getting me, or us, through Vandorn's last stand. I suppose I shouldn't, but for some reason I feel sorry for him."

Seemingly out of nowhere, a waiter appeared. Each ordered a glass of wine, Laura white, Brand red.

Resuming, Brand said, "I'd like to feel some compassion for Vandorn, but when I think. . ."

"Of the people he could have killed?"

"Yes. I wasn't ready to see anyone of those people either killed or hurt badly."

"Put that way, I have to agree." Laura watched while Brand used two left-hand fingers to turn his wine-glass, touching only the stem. "And the fact that we came out of it whole and entire--that's a ticket to more of life. You and me, we've gone on for months now. What we were trying to do has ended in a wet muddy hole in the ground. And here I sit hoping the whole process continues. Or starts again. Hoping that nothing changes. That all the actors stay the same, that the goal remains the same."

"I can speak for myself. I'm applying for my old role."

She smiled. "You're the lead. But now will you tell me why this has become, for me, like true confessions? Something I have to dissect, distill? It's like growing up all in a week or a month. You watch part of you drop off, useless, your self-centered, self-indulgent segment. And you *feel* older; not old, just older. You even feel lighter."

"I think you've just described the process of maturation. We used to call it growing up. We sometimes reach it, they say, after a death, or survival in a violent confrontation, or a natural disaster. I personally believe we reach that phase piecemeal--in stages."

"We took the violent confrontation route."

"We did. Vandorn wasn't there to present us with an award."

"And here we are," she said. "Celebrating through tears." She held up her wineglass. "Let's offer one toast for your baboons, another for World Parenthood Day."

"That covers you and Martin."

Their glasses touched twice.